Springer
Berlin
Heidelberg
New York
Hong Kong
London
Milan
Paris
Tokyo

Contracts, Scenarios and Prototypes

Reinhold Plösch

Contracts, Scenarios and Prototypes

An Integrated Approach to High Quality Software

With 64 Figures

Springer

Dr. Reinhold Plösch
Johannes Kepler Universität
Institut für Wirtschaftsinformatik
Altenbergerstrasse 69
A-4040 Linz
e-mail: ploesch@swe.uni-linz.ac.at

Library of Congress Control Number: 2004103362

ACM Subject Classification (1998): D.2.1, D.2.2, K.6.3

ISBN 3-540-43486-0 Springer-Verlag Berlin Heidelberg New York

Springer-Verlag is a part of Springer Science+Business Media

springeronline.com

© Springer-Verlag Berlin Heidelberg 2004
Printed in Germany

Typesetting: Camera-ready by the author
Final layout: LE-TeX, Leipzig
Cover design: KünkelLopka, Heidelberg

Printed on acid-free paper   SPIN 10868426   45/3141/ba   5 4 3 2 1 0

To Michaela, Lukas and Julian

Contents

XII Contents

List of Figures

XII   **List of Figures**

Preface

What is this Book About?

At the beginning of the 21st century, computer systems—and especially software—play an important role in our society. Software is contained in virtually every technical device that we use in everyday life (e.g., cellular phones and cars). Furthermore, computers and their software are used for leisure purposes at home (the Internet and computer games), at the office (e.g., writing letters and order processing), and for more complicated tasks such as controlling steel plants or insuring flight safety. Therefore, the quality of software (e.g., its correctness, reliability, and efficiency) has become important not only in the context of critical systems (e.g., nuclear power plants) but also for our entire society, from business to leisure.

Software engineering is the practical application of scientific knowledge for the economical production and use of high-quality software [Pomberger96]. The discipline aims at developing methods, techniques, tools, and standards to fulfill these aims. The number of methods and tools available to the software engineer nowadays is overwhelming; nevertheless, many software projects fail—that is, do not meet their schedules, are over budget, do not meet the user needs, or simply have considerable quality defects. The numerous possible explanations for this situation include poor project management, unsuitable methods and tools used in the project, and poorly developed skills of the participating software engineers.

The challenge for researchers in this field is to provide methods and tools that can be applied by software engineers with average skill levels in average projects. Without defining precisely what "average" means in this context, it should be obvious that we do not mean a computer scientist verifying the correctness of the core real-time software of a safety-critical cardiac pacemaker.

A number of methods and techniques contribute to the quality of software specifications (e.g., Z [Spivey92] and state machines). Nevertheless, many of these techniques fail in the sense that they cannot be applied by average software engineers in average projects, as the mathematical skills needed are not available or the scope of the model is too narrow.

This book emphasizes methods, techniques, and tools that can be used by average software engineers in average projects for the early phases (analysis and design) of the software life cycle. Therefore, the important requirements for the methods and techniques are simplicity, preciseness, generality, and expressiveness.

Simplicity is perhaps the most important attribute. A complex method is unlikely to be applied throughout a project, as project members will always find reasonable-sounding excuses for not using them. On the other hand, simple approaches (with benefits that are transparent to the engineers) will be applied readily. Scenarios (use cases) are an example of a simple and yet powerful and widely applied technique.

A method or technique is *precise* if the product of this method or technique (e.g., a specification) is less ambiguous and error-prone than it would have been had the method not been used. A number of mathematically based approaches (algebraic techniques, higher-order logic) support the specification of software to a level of preciseness that facilitates automatic code generation. However, the challenge here is to develop methods and techniques that maintain a balance between preciseness and simplicity.

A method should be *general* in the sense that it is not only applicable in a specific domain but (in the best case) can be used productively for the three main classes of systems: information systems, embedded systems, and command and control systems.

Expressiveness has much to do with notational issues of a method or technique. We consider a method or technique to be expressive if it is reasonable to use it for documenting the results of analysis and design. This important requirement means that even those low-level techniques that might fulfill the above three requirements do not prove adequate at the abstract level of analysis and design.

The requirements discussed here are contradictory (e.g., simplicity versus preciseness) and the challenge is to develop methods and techniques that are balanced in the sense that all four requirements are fairly equally fulfilled.

This book deals with an approach that combines assertion and scenario techniques into a consistent methodology that can be used for analysis and design tasks. The technique developed can be combined with a prototyping-oriented software development approach.

Assertion techniques are theoretically well founded and are available in some programming languages. At the level of analysis and design, little work has yet been done [Waldén95]. Due to the popularity of the Unified Modeling Language (UML) [Fowler99], scenarios are widely used to document requirements or to express design ideas. A number of published reports [Broh82, Gomaa86, Gordon91] and the author's own experience [Plösch93, Plösch94, Plösch95] show that prototyping enhances the quality of software. Each of these techniques and methods (assertions, scenarios, and prototyping) fulfill the requirements stated above: this is discussed in depth throughout the book.

What is in this Book?

In the first part of this book (Chapters 1–4) we present the concepts of assertions and scenarios. In this part, assertions are dealt with in the tradition of Hoare triples [Hoare72] and their predecessors, without taking into consideration other interesting streams of research in the field of type theory or behavioral specifications (these are postponed until the third part). Nevertheless, this part builds a sound basis by providing the theoretic foundations and limitations of assertion techniques. Currently, assertion techniques are more widely used in late design and implementation phases, but hardly at all in analysis. We therefore present the role of assertion techniques in analysis. As the popular UML contains an assertion language called Object Constraint Language (OCL) [Warmer99], this language is presented and compared with other currently available assertion techniques. Best practices to be considered when applying assertion techniques throughout analysis and early design are discussed. Scenarios are introduced in a similar way, beginning with basic concepts, terminology, kinds of notation, and so on. As scenarios play an important role in UML too, we describe the scenario approach as defined by UML in the context of the general concepts and principles. The part about scenarios concludes with best practices for using scenarios in analysis.

The second part of this book (Chapters 5–7) focuses on a prototyping-oriented software development approach and presents general terminology, concepts, and success stories of prototyping-oriented software development. Assertion and scenario techniques are combined into a single methodological framework, and an approach model, as well as methodological issues, is presented. A case study shows the application of the approach. Because prototyping without adequate tool support is a difficult undertaking, we discuss general requirements for prototyping tools as well as prototyping tools that have been developed specifically for supporting the combined assertion/scenario approach. The toolkit that we present is suitable for prototyping tasks in the analysis and design phase, and its capabilities are presented by means of a case study. One important aspect of a prototyping-oriented approach is how the products of the prototyping process are used for design, implementation, or testing. The book presents a tool-centered approach that facilitates a smooth transformation of our prototyping results into implementation or test products.

The assertion techniques presented in the first part are basic. In the third part of this book (Chapters 8), details of assertion techniques are explored and related techniques are presented, all striving for enhanced interface or even behavioral specification of code blocks.

Who Should Read this Book?

The first two parts of this book are targeted at the software engineer in industry who is interested in modern techniques for enhancing software quality. In order to enhance the usability of the book, the approaches presented are always compared with popular techniques that are available in the realm of UML. This means that even when the techniques presented cannot be applied directly, these parts of the book should also show how the techniques that are available in UML could be better used.

On its own, the first part will interest practitioners and students who want to understand scenario concepts and OCL concepts of UML (i.e., their foundations) more deeply. This part is also suitable for students who are interested in assertion and scenario techniques, as it does not merely present a single method, but it relates general concepts found in the literature to popular concepts found in UML.

The third part the book is targeted at graduate students or scientists who want to gain a deeper understanding of assertion techniques and related approaches, or who are interested in assertion issues in the context of emerging component technologies.

Acknowledgements

Many people have supported in the one or in the other way the creation of this book. It is impossible to mention them all, but the following persons have particularly contributed to this work. Gustav Pomberger, my mentor supported and encouraged me throughout this project. I also want to thank my colleagues and former colleagues at the department of business informatics (software engineering group), who have always been a source of fruitful discussions: Josef Altmann, Dagmar Auer, Christoph Breitschopf, Joachim Fröhlich, Alice Ginzinger, Brigitte Grillmair, Michael Gütlbauer, Thomas Hilpold, Werner Kurschl, Josef Pichler, Wolfgang Pree, Hubert Rumerstorfer, Johannes Sametinger, Stefan Schiffer, and Alois Stritzinger. Some of them are good friends now. In particular I want to thank Rainer Weinreich (also from the software engineering group) for his friendship, for his encouragement, and for the excellent cooperation in our joint research projects. I also want to thank Springer-Verlag and especially Mr. Ralf Gerstner and his team for their patience and for their valuable input during the production phase of this book. Last but not least I want to thank the members of my family for their patience and love—I dedicate this book to them.

January 2004   Reinhold Plösch
Linz, Austria

1 Software Quality

Summary: The term "quality" is important in this book. This chapter presents quality attributes for software products and discusses their meaning in detail. In many cases, quality attributes are mutually contradictory; therefore, their relations are explored. The quality attributes defined in this chapter will be referred to in the remainder of the book in order to discuss the impact of the presented methods, techniques, and tools on these quality attributes.

Keywords: Software quality, Software quality models, FCM model

It is the ambitious goal of software engineers to develop "good" software. But what does "good" mean? Assessing a product (be it software or any consumer product)—that is, determining whether the product is "good"—has something to do with quality. The term "quality" may be seen from different viewpoints, which lead to different interpretations and definitions. According to Garvin [Garvin84], five different viewpoints—that is, approaches to the term "quality"—can be identified. The following definitions characterize the different viewpoints of the term "quality":

- *The transcendent approach:* "Quality is neither mind nor matter, but a third entity independent of the two ... even though Quality cannot be defined, you know what it is." [Pirsig74]
- *The product-based approach:* "Quality refers to the amounts of the unpriced attributes contained in each unit of the priced attributes." [Leffler82]
- *The user-based approach:* "Quality is the degree to which a specific product satisfies the wants of a specific consumer." [Gilmore74]
- *The manufacturing-based approach:* "Quality is the degree to which a specific product conforms to a design or specification." [Gilmore74]
- *The value-based approach:* "Quality is the degree of excellence at an acceptable price and the control of variability at an acceptable cost." [Broh82]

DIN ISO 9126 [DIN91], which follows the product-based and manufacturing-based approaches, defines the term "software quality" as follows:

"Software quality is the whole of the attributes and attribute values of a software product that refer to its suitability to fulfill defined or assumed requirements."[1]

This definition gives us an idea about software quality, but is still too vague. To be able to measure software quality, a systematic approach has to be used to derive metrics from the general properties of software. Quality models provide this in a systematic manner. A number of different quality models are known in the literature. One example of such a general model is the so-called factor–criteria–metrics model (the FCM model). Figure 1 illustrates the principal structure of the FCM model. According to this quality model, the quality of software is described by identifying quality attributes, often called "factors". In order to make each factor measurable, it is necessary to refine factors into quality criteria. Factors represent a more user-oriented view, while quality criteria reflect a more software-oriented view. The refinement process takes place until quality indicators—that is, measurable and assessable metrics—can be found for each quality criterion.

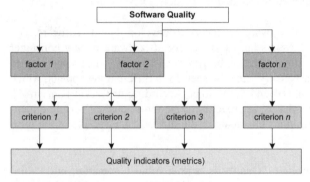

Fig. 1. The principal structure of FCM-Models

A number of specific quality models based on this general FCM approach exist; for example, the model defined by ISO 9126 [DIN91], the so-called FURPS model [Grady87], the model defined by McCall [McCall77], Barry Boehm's model [Boehm78], or the SATC model [Hyatt96]. Figure 2 gives an overview of the SATC model.

Figure 2 shows that a quality factor (e.g., product code quality) is defined by a number of criteria (in our case architecture, maintainability, reusability, internal documentation, and external documentation). Each of these criteria can be measured by using a specific metric—for example, *logic complexity* for the criterion *architecture*. The metrics given here can be found in the description of the SATC model, but should only be understood as starting points for further investigations on this issue.

---

[1] Translation from German by the author.

As we will refer to the criteria presented in Fig. 2 throughout this book, we give a brief explanation of the underlying meanings (for more details, see [Hyatt96]):

- *Ambiguity:* Requirements that may have multiple meanings, or those that leave to the developer the decision as to whether or not implementation should take place, are ambiguous.
- *Completeness:* A requirements document is complete if it contains all of the requirements specified in adequate detail to allow design and implementation to proceed.
- *Understandability:* Understandability relates to the ability of the developers to understand what is meant by the requirements document.
- *Volatility:* A volatile requirements document is one that is changed frequently. Additionally, the impact of changes to the requirements increases with the project time; that is, changes to the requirements document shortly before a software release have a higher impact and bear higher risks than changes in the early stages of the project.
- *Traceability:* Software requirements must be traceable to the system requirements (backward traceability), but must also be traceable to design documents and to source code files (forward traceability).

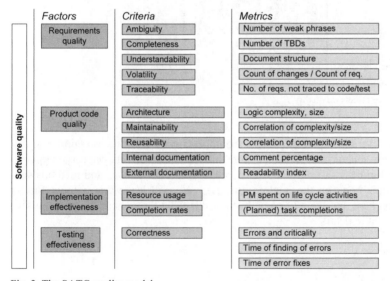

Fig. 2. The SATC quality model

- *Architecture:* This criterion deals with the evaluation of modules to identify possible error-prone modules and to indicate potential problems in reusability and maintainability.

- *Maintainability:* This is the suitability of the software for ease of locating and fixing a fault in the implementation.
- *Reusability:* This is the ability of the software to be reused in a different context or application.
- *Internal documentation:* This refers to the adequacy of the internal code documentation to enable and facilitate the maintenance of the software product.
- *External documentation:* This refers to the adequacy of the external documentation to enable and facilitate the usage and maintenance of the product (from the perspective of the system users).
- *Resource usage:* This is a process-related criterion that indicates whether the resource usage (i.e., personnel hours) correlates with the appropriate phase of the project.
- *Completion rates:* This is a process-related criterion that deals with the completion of deliverables—with respect to adherence to defined schedules.
- *Correctness:* This is the extent to which the product fulfills the underlying specifications.

	Ambiguity	Completeness	Understandability	Volatility	Traceability	Architecture	Maintainability	Reusability	Int. Documentation	Ext. Documentation	Resource Usage	Completion Rates	Correctness
Assertions	+	+					+	+	+	+			+
Scenarios		+	+		+		+						+
Contract- and Scenario-based Prototyping	+	+	+			+	+	+	+				+

Fig. 3. Positive effects on quality

The quality attributes presented here are important for us in the remainder of this book, as the techniques presented here have positive effects on certain quality attributes. Figure 3 shows the positive impact of the techniques and methods suggested in this book on the quality attributes. We will leave this without further explanation here, but we will come back to this table throughout the book and we will discuss it in detail.

2 Contracts

Summary: One of the most important notions to ensure correctness of software components is the concept of abstract data types (ADTs), introduced in the 1970s by Liskov and Zilles [Liskov74], and relying on foundation work done by Hoare [Hoare72] and Parnas [Parnas72a, Parnas72b]. Correctness formulas of the form P {Q} R (also called Hoare triples) are a mathematical notation and form the basis for assertions as understood in this book. On the basis of this notation, we introduce the concepts of "preconditions", "postconditions", and "invariants", to express the correctness properties of methods and classes. The idea of assertions naturally leads to the concept of a contract, which binds a method to its clients and thereby imposes obligations and grants rights for both of them. This concept, also called Design by Contract (DBC) and introduced by Meyer [Meyer97a], will be discussed in detail. Object-orientation is not only about information hiding and ADTs, but also about inheritance and associated concepts such as dynamic binding and polymorphism. Subcontracts guarantee the correctness of derived classes by insuring that assertions of superclasses are considered in all derived classes, and by insuring that preconditions may be weakened and postconditions may be strengthened in derived classes, if at all. The techniques presented are well suited to enhance the correctness of software components; nevertheless, a number of limitations are still present.

Keywords: Design by Contract, Preconditions, Postconditions, Invariants, iContract

2.1 Introduction and Overview

One major aim of software engineering methods, techniques, and tools is to enhance the quality of software. In this chapter, we deal with techniques that are suitable for enhancing the quality of specifications of interfaces to pieces of software. There are a number of different approaches to reaching this goal. One approach would be algebraic techniques or the use of higher-order logics. The focus in this chapter (as it is for the entire book) is on techniques and methods that fulfill the requirements *simplicity*, *preciseness*, *generality*, and *expressiveness*, as outlined in the preface of this book. We believe that in many cases pure and mathematical approaches do not fulfill the requirements *simplicity* and *expressiveness*, which are the most important ones in the general case. For specific application domains, simplicity and expressiveness are of minor importance, as any errors in the software may cause catastrophes. A more detailed discussion of this topic can be found in Finney [Finney96a] and Finney and Fedorec [Finney96b].

The approach in this chapter is to take a close look at the contract-based techniques that are available in some programming languages and systems. In many cases (e.g., Eiffel [Meyer92]), the concepts provided by a programming language or a programming system have a sound theoretic basis, but have an easier syntax, or omit problems that are important from a theoretic point of view but that are in most cases not relevant in a typical project. As far is necessary to understand the presented techniques, we provide the theoretic background.

From the point of view of design and implementation of software, clearly defined interfaces (classes, methods, functions, and procedures) play an important role.

Early programming languages that meet software engineering criteria—that is, that aim at enhancing software quality—are Simula [Dahl68], Algol [Naur63], Pascal [Wirth71], Ada [Ada95], and Modula-2 [Wirth83], or some lesser known programming languages such as CLU [Liskov76]. All of these programming languages have in common that they realize the idea of static typing. A type defines the set of possible values of the variables, parameters, or return values of operations. The type of the variables may change during execution (via assignment of values of a different type) or may be unchanging. A type that is unchanging is also called a static type. In a programming language with a static type system, the compiler can verify that clients use the functions or procedures properly; in other words, that they assign type-conformant values to variables or call functions or procedures with valid—that is, type-conformant—arguments. Static typing is also an inherent feature of modern programming languages such as C++ [Ellis96] and Java technology [Gosling96]. C++ and Java are typical representatives of the class of object-oriented programming languages, with their concepts of classes, inheritance, polymorphism, and dynamic binding [Meyer97a]. Here, for example, is the simple class (in Java syntax) BankAccount:

```java
public class BankAccount {
    void deposit(float amount) { ... }
    void withdraw(float amount) { ... }
    float getBalance() { ... }
}
```

In this example, the class BankAccount defines a number of methods (with the implementations intentionally left blank); for example, a method deposit, with a parameter amount of type float. The static type checking rules force the client to provide a parameter of type float to the methods deposit and withdraw.

This class therefore sets up a relationship between the user and the implementer of this interface. This relationship can be called a contract, and in its basic form it defines that the implementation of this interface will fulfill its specification as long as the client provides type-conformant arguments when using the interface. The client-side obligation is clearly defined here, whereas the implementation part of the contract is rather vague, as no description of the expected semantic of the interface—that is, of the individual methods, is given.

Therefore, besides the basic syntactical level roughly described above, other contract levels may be distinguished. Figure 4 (adapted from Beugnard et al. [Beugnard99]) illustrates four contract levels.

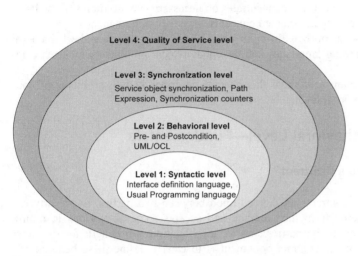

Fig. 4. Contract levels

According to Beugnard et al. [Beugnard99], the different levels shown in Fig. 4 can be roughly characterized as follows:

- The syntactic level is required simply to make the system work in a statically typed programming language.
- The behavioral level improves the degree of confidence in a sequential context.
- The synchronization level improves the degree of confidence in distributed or concurrency contexts.
- The quality-of-service level quantifies quality of service and is usually negotiable.

So far, we have dealt with the syntactical level on the basis of a specific programming language (in our example, Java). The specification of interfaces may also be independent of the programming language. Our BankAccount class specified as a CORBA object [OMG99], using CORBA's IDL, would look syntactically different but would have no semantic differences.

Types and type theory represent a major branch of software engineering research. Although type theory is an important basis, no more details will be provided here.

The focus of this chapter is on level 2 contracts; that is, on contracts at the behavioral level.

In Sect. 2.2 the fundaments for contracts are laid down. As far is necessary to understand the behavioral level, the theoretic background (type theory) will be given.

While Sect. 2.2 also is valid for imperative programming languages that are not object-oriented, Sect. 2.3 concentrates on necessary enhancements of the basic concepts to support object-oriented concepts, especially inheritance.

Section 2.4 categorizes different possibilities for supporting the behavioral level in programming languages and describes typical proponents for each category.

The concluding section of this chapter describes known problems of contracts at the behavioral level.

2.2   The Behavioral Level—Fundamentals

2.2.1   What is a Contract?

In everyday life, contracts are agreed upon between two parties. Each party expects some benefits from the contract, and accepts some obligations in return. Usually, what one of the parties sees as an obligation is a benefit for the other party. The aim of the contract document is to clearly define these benefits and obligations. Meyer [Meyer96] describes the contract between an airline and its customers. The benefits and obligations of the client and the airline are expressed in a tabular way, as shown in Fig. 5.

	Obligations	Benefits
Passenger	▪ Be at the Santa Barbara airport at least 15 minutes before the scheduled departure time. ▪ Bring only acceptable baggage. ▪ Pay the ticket price.	▪ Reach Chicago.
Airline	▪ Transport the customer to Chicago.	▪ No need to carry passengers who are late, ▪ who have unacceptable baggage, or ▪ who have not paid the ticket price.

Fig. 5. Passenger/airline contract

This idea of a contract—that is, the definition of obligations and benefits—is also applicable to software building blocks. Figure 6 shows the obligations and benefits for the method withdraw from our BankAccount example.

The implementation of the withdraw method therefore relies on the fact that the client accepts the obligations imposed upon him or her; that is, some restrictions concerning the value of the parameter amount. On the other hand, the implementation guarantees that the withdrawal of money will be carried out properly (see the specification of the obligation of the implementation in Fig. 6).

The client's obligations are called *preconditions*. From the point of view of implementation, the preconditions must be fulfilled by the client before the method is called. The obligations of the implementation are called *postconditions*. From the client's point of view, the postconditions must be true after execution of the method. The term *assertion* is used in this book as a synonym for individual preconditions or postconditions, whereas the term *contract* denotes the entire set of assertions for a program or a part thereof.

	Obligations	Benefits
Client	▪ The amount passed as the parameter must be greater than zero. ▪ The amount passed as the parameter must not exceed the credit limit for this account.	▪ The amount is correctly withdrawn from the account; that is, after the execution of this method, the new balance for this account equals the balance before the transaction minus the amount.
Implementation	▪ It must be ensured that that amount is correctly withdrawn; that is, after the execution of this method, the new balance for this account must equal the balance before the transaction minus the amount.	▪ There is no need to deal with amounts that are smaller than zero. ▪ There is no need to deal with amounts that exceed the credit limit.

Fig. 6. Withdraw money from bank account (contract)

This precondition/postcondition approach is one direction for the behavioral specification of software artifacts. As Parnas states (see [Hoffman01]), this specification technique is based on the work of Floyd [Floyd67], and on subsequent work by Hoare [Hoare69], Dijkstra [Dijkstra75], and Liskov [Liskov74].

2.2.2   A Glimpse into History

The general idea of a contract is to define how a piece of software carries out its intended function. As Hoare [Hoare69] points out, the intended function of a software artifact can be specified by making general assertions about the values that the relevant variables will take after execution. Furthermore, he states that the validity of results of a software artifact will depend on the values taken by the variables before that software artifact is executed. These preconditions can be specified by the same type of general assertion as is used to describe the results obtained on termination.

This relationship between preconditions, program, and result, often called the *Hoare triple*, may be expressed more formally as {P} Q {R}. The definition of this formula is as follows [Hoare69]:

"If the assertion P is true before initialization of a program Q, then the assertion R will be true on its completion."

In this context, the term "program" must be read as program, function, or procedure. If no precondition can be formulated for a program, the correctness formula is written as {true} Q {R}.

In the basis of this observation, Hoare formulates axioms and rules that may serve as a basis for proving the correctness of programs. We will not discuss this issue in further detail.

Parnas [Parnas72a] formulates a number of goals that should be fulfilled by a specification scheme for program elements:

- The specification must provide the user with all the information that he or she will need to use the program correctly, and nothing more.
- The specification must provide to the implementer all the information about the intended use that he or she needs to complete the program, and no additional information.
- The specification must be sufficiently formal that it can be machine tested for consistency, completeness, and other desirable properties of a specification.

The first two goals in particular resemble the precondition and postcondition idea as proposed by Hoare. The following code fragment from [Parnas72a] shows the specification of a push function and is used to illustrate the ideas proposed by Parnas:

```
Function Push(a)
    possible values: none
    integer: a
    effect: call ERR1 if a>p2 ∨ a<0 ∨ 'DEPTH'=p1 else [VAL= a; DEPTH= 'DEPTH'+1]
```

The idea that underlies this kind of specification is similar to the idea of Hoare's correctness triples:

- possible values: none just indicates that this function does not return any values. Functions that return values would state a type name here.
- integer: a can be viewed as a contract at the syntactical level (see above).
- call ERR1 if a>p2 ∨ a<0 ∨ 'DEPTH'=p1: This expression means that an error function should be called when the value of the parameter a is greater than some value p2 and when there is no space available in the stack. This effect can be seen as a typical precondition.
- [VAL= a; DEPTH= 'DEPTH'+1]: The value of the parameter a is equal to the value of a function VAL (not shown). VAL returns the top value of the stack without removing it from the stack. This effect can be seen as a typical postcondition.

Dijkstra [Dijkstra75] follows an approach that is similar to that of Hoare [Hoare69]; that is, he uses predicates as a tool for defining sets of initial or final states, for the definition of the semantics of programming language constructs.

The main difference is that Dijkstra proposes so-called "weakest" preconditions, that guarantee to produce the right result. Dijkstra uses the special notation wp(S, R), which means that activation of S (a statement list) is guaranteed to lead to a properly terminating activity leaving the system in a final state that satisfies the postcondition R. Such a wp can be called a "predicate transformer", because it associates a precondition with any postcondition R, which means that the precondition may be derived automatically. This is the major difference compared to the approach taken by Hoare, as Hoare's preconditions cannot be derived automatically but have to be stated by the programmer.

The discussion so far shows that the basic idea of preconditions and postconditions has a long tradition. In Sects. 2.2.3–2.2.5 the emphasis is on preconditions and postconditions for classes, without considering subtyping. The concept of behavioral subtyping [America91, Liskov94, Liskov99] and the associated problems are discussed in detail in Sect. 2.3.

2.2.3   The Formulation of Basic Contracts

In this section, we concentrate on technical issues; that is, what can be specified in an assertion in principle, and what is not allowed. There are no hints on how to use the technique properly. This question is postponed to Chap. 3. As shown in Fig. 6, the contracts have to be formalized to give us the opportunity to check the validity of assertions at run time or even at compile time. The descriptions of preconditions and postconditions are based on a syntax that is close to the OCL syntax [Warmer99]. A complete description of the syntax of our contract language SCL (Simple Contract Language) can be found in Appendix B. There are three major reasons, why we use our SCL language, and not directly OCL:

- We use SCL for a number of examples in our book, and we usually present contract examples in the context of specific Java classes, i.e., we use the Java programming language [Gosling96] to formulate classes, interfaces, and methods. It is not appropriate to use OCL here, as the OCL is tightly coupled with the UML and as it is not related to Java.
- SCL supports a subset of the OCL language; the subset is specified in a way that tool support for contract checking can be realized more easily. We used SCL as a basis to add contract checking support for the programming language Python and for the programming language C++ (see Chapter 7 for more details about our implementations).
- We want to emphasize that contracts are a general technique that are not only available by using the OCL language.
- We give a detailed introduction into OCL (accompanied by examples) in Chapter 3 anyway.

The contract for the BankAccount class (see Fig. 6) can be formulated as follows:

```
public class BankAccount {

    private float          _balance;
    private boolean        _blocked;
    ...
    public void withdraw(float: amount) { ... }
             pre: amount > 0 and amount <= getCreditLimit()
             pre: not isBlocked()
             post: _balance@pre - amount = _balance

    private float getCreditLimit() { ... }

    private boolean isBlocked() { ... }
    ...
}
```

Generally in our examples, preconditions and postconditions are written after the implementation body of the method. The number of preconditions and postconditions is unlimited. Assertions are Boolean expressions and therefore can either evaluate to true or false. Here some general remarks on semantics of assertions (explained by means of the above-given example):

- Any assertion has access to the value of the parameters (amount > 0).
- Any assertion has access to the instance variables of the class (amount = _balance). No assignment statement is possible in an assertion. It is therefore guaranteed that assertion does not change the state of the object directly. Note that the operation = in the expression amount = _balance is a relational operation that tests for equality.
- Any assertion may use methods (amount <= getCreditLimit()). This is a critical issue, as it must be guaranteed that a call to a method does not produce any side effects; that is, changes in the state of the object. In our contract language, we can assume that this property is fulfilled. In cases in which this is not supported by the underlying programming language, a contract verifier—or at least the contract run-time environment—must assure it. In our example with Java technology as the underlying programming language, this guarantee is difficult to achieve, as the Java language does not include the concept of a so-called const method; that is, a method that may not alter the state of the object (as available, for example, in the C++ programming language). A detailed and thorough discussion of this issue is postponed until Sect. 2.4.
- Any postcondition may access the value of an arbitrary expression (that is valid in the context of the method) at the start of the execution of the method. The expression _balance@pre is therefore the balance of the bank account before the withdrawal of the money. Of course, more complicated expressions can be used.

Additionally, method calls to other objects that can be reached via instance variables can be emitted and Boolean implications may also be used. To show this idea, we add a class Customer to our BankAccount example:

```
public class Customer {

    private String        _firstName;
    private String        _lastName;
    private float         _creditLimit;
    private List          _accounts;
    ...

    public boolean isGoodForAmount(float amount) { ... }

    public void addBankAccount(BankAccount account) { ... }
        pre: (_accounts->size() > 0) implies
                        _accounts->exists(a: BankAccount | not a.isBlocked())
    ...
}


public class BankAccount {

    private float         _balance;
    private boolean       _blocked;
    private Customer      _customer;
    private List          _transactions;
    ...
    public void withdraw(float amount) { ... }
        pre: _customer.isGoodForAmount(amount)
        pre: not isBlocked()
        post: _balance@pre - amount = _balance

    float getBalance() { ... }
        pre: not isBlocked()
        post: _balance@pre = _balance
        post: _transactions->forAll(t: Transaction | t@pre = t)

    private float getCreditLimit() { ... }

    private boolean isBlocked() { ... }

    private boolean hasTempOverdraft() { ... }
    ...
}
```

- An assertion has access to all methods that are available via other instance variables (e.g., amount < _customer.isGoodForAmount() means that the credit limit is also checked on a per-customer basis). The same problem as with method calls within the same class arises here; that is, it must not happen that a call of a method of a different class (in our case, the class Customer) has any side effect on the state of the system.
- (_accounts->size() > 0) implies _accounts->exists(a: BankAccount | not a.isBlocked()) is an example of a Boolean implication. If a customer already has an account, a new account may only be added when at least one account is available that is

not blocked. In general, a Boolean implication states that the result of the total expression is true if it is the case that, when the first Boolean operand is true, the second Boolean operand is also true. If the first Boolean operand is false, the whole implication always evaluates to true.

2.2.4   Contracts and Collections

Collections of objects play an important role in object-oriented systems. In our BankAccount example, for instance, every BankAccount manages a list of transactions (instance variable _transactions in class BankAccount) or a customer object manages a list of accounts (see instance variable _accounts in class Customer). Following the OCL language, SCL allows us to formulate assertions for collections. Three main types of collection are supported:

- A List is a collection of an arbitrary number of elements of arbitrary type. Objects contained in a list may be accessed in random or sequential order.
- A Set is a collection of an arbitrary number of elements of arbitrary type. Each object contained in a Set is unique. Objects in a Set are accessible via typical Set operations.
- A Map is a Set of pairs of objects. One element of the pair is used as key, and the other as value.

As already mentioned in Sect. 2.1, the emphasis is on contract-based techniques, as are available in common programming languages and systems, which in many cases do not support a functional programming style. Therefore, only a number of operations that are assumed to be side effect free by their nature are allowed in our SCL language[2]. To what extent the features available in SCL are supported by existing programming languages and systems is described in detail in Sect. 2.4. Fig. 7 lists all allowed operations on collections.

Collection	Operation	Description
Operations for all types of collection	boolean **contains**(o Object)	Returns true if this collection contains the specified element.
	boolean **containsAll** (c Collection)	Returns true if this collection contains all of the elements in the specified collection c.
	boolean **isEmpty**()	Returns true if this collection contains no elements.
	int **size**()	Returns the number of elements in this collection.

---

[2] Providing support for all kinds of operations on collections as proposed in the OCL is possible but it is expensive in terms of resource usage and performance, as it would be necessary to work with copies of collections, in order to omit side effects.

Additional operations for List	List **subList** (int formIndex, int toIndex)	Returns a view of the portion of this list between the specified fromIndex, inclusive, and toIndex, exclusive. (If fromIndex and toIndex are equal, the returned list is empty.).
	Object **get**(int index)	Returns the element at the specified position in this list.
Additional operations for Map	boolean **containsKey** (Object key)	Returns true if this map contains a mapping for the specified key.
	boolean **containsValue** (Object value)	Returns true if this map maps one or more keys to the specified value.
	Object **get**(Object obj)	Returns the value to which this map maps the specified key. Returns null if the map contains no mapping for this key. A return value of null does not necessarily indicate that the map contains no mapping for the key: it is also possible that the map explicitly maps the key to null.
	Collection **values**()	Returns a collection view of the values contained in this map.

Fig. 7. Allowed operations on collections

Besides these typical operations, the operators forAll and exists are supported for arbitrary collections:

- The forAll operator: This operator allows us to test an arbitrary Boolean expression for every element of the collection. The forAll operator only yields true if the expression evaluates to true for every element of the collection. One example is given as the postcondition of method getBalance of class BankAccount: _transactions->forAll(t: Transaction | t@pre = t), which means that after execution of the getBalance method all Transaction objects contained in the collection _transaction must be the same as before execution of the method; that is, they must not have been changed.
- The exists operator: This operator allows us to test an arbitrary Boolean expression for every element of the collection. The exists operator yields true if the expression evaluates to true for at least one element of the collection. One example is given as the precondition of method addBankAccount of class Customer: (_accounts->size() > 0) implies _accounts->exists(a: BankAccount | not a.isBlocked()), which means that a new BankAccount object can only be added for a customer when at least one BankAccount object exists that is not blocked (this only applies when the customer already has at least one account).

2.2.5   Invariants

Preconditions and postconditions form the basis for formulating correctness formulas. Additionally, invariants may be expressed at the class level. Every class can have an arbitrary number of invariants. Our BankAccount class with an invariant is as follows:

```
public class BankAccount {

    private float          _balance;
    private boolean        _blocked;
    private Customer       _customer;
    ...
    public void withdraw(float: amount) { ... }
        pre: amount > 0 and amount <= getCreditLimit()
        post: _balance@pre + amount = _balance

    private float getCreditLimit() { ... }

    private boolean isBlocked() { ... }
    ...
}
        inv: _customer != null
```

The invariant _customer != null means that before and after execution of any method of this class, this invariant must evaluate to true; that is, each BankAccount object must always be associated with a Customer object.

This simple approach for checking invariants causes problems in case of re-entrance as it occurs when using callbacks and object references. Most contract solutions currently available adhere to the simple checking technique mentioned above, which leads to problems in even simple situations:

- During the execution of a method it often occurs that a consistent state (which fulfills the constraints by invariants) is achieved by subsequent calls of methods of the same class which possibly violate the contracts, as they are called out of an inconsistent state.
- During the execution of a method it may occur that an installed callback function is invoked which leads to the execution of another method of the same class. This has the effect that the object possibly still is in an inconsistent state, as the originally called method is not yet finished and therefore could not establish a valid state.
- The same problem also occurs in classes that are tied together by means of notification mechanisms, i.e. by a set of classes that follow the observer pattern [Gamma95]. More generally this problem may occur in case of cyclic references exist between objects.

One pragmatic solution to this problem is to weaken the invariants and to state more strict versions as preconditions and postconditions for those methods where the problems discussed above cannot occur. Another solution would be to allow conditional weakening of invariants for the cases mentioned above; nevertheless this would require changes to the contract language. For a more detailed discussion see [Szyperski02].

2.2.6   The Correctness of a Class

Once we have a set of preconditions, postconditions, and invariants for a class, definitions can be given regarding the correctness of this class. Correctness is a relative notation, as no piece of software is correct *per se*. Correctness as defined by Pomberger [Pomberger96] means that the software system fulfills the specification that underlies its development. Preconditions, postconditions, and invariants form the specification of a class. According to Meyer [Meyer97a], the correctness of a class can be formulated as follows:

- For every public method r and any set of valid arguments x_y:

    { $pre_r (x_r)$ and INV } $Body_r$ { $post_r (x_r)$ and INV }

- For any valid set of arguments x_p to a constructor p:

    { $Default_c$ and $pre_p (x_p)$ } $Body_p$ { $post_p (x_p)$ and INV }

If a precondition or a postcondition is missing, the respective conditions (pre_r, pre_p, $post_r$, and $post_p$) are set to true. For constructors $Default_c$ expresses the fact that all instance variables of the class are properly initialized with the default values according to their type.

So far, this section has been about how to formulate contracts using preconditions, postconditions, and invariants. An important issue to be discussed has to do with when contracts are to be checked. In principle, two approaches are possible; that is, checking of contracts at compile time or checking at run time:

- *Checking at compile time:* This, of course, would be the preferred solution, since errors could be detected early in the development process. Unfortunately, this is not possible in the general case. According to Meyer [Meyer97a], it is not possible today to prove the correctness of realistic software systems written in full-fledged programming languages. If proof techniques were available, checking at compile time would not be sufficient for certain cases; for example, for hardware faults or errors in the proof software itself. Besides these technical problems we also want to point out that this is not the desirable path of development, as software engineers would have to be acquainted with formal methods in order to be able to verify the correctness of the software based on the specified contracts. This clearly violates one of our major goals for our proposed techniques. In the introduction to this book we stated, that *simplicity* is perhaps the most important quality attribute for a method or technique. A complex method or technique is unlikely to be applied throughout a project, as project members will always find reasonable-sounding excuses for not using them. Formal proofing techniques clearly violate this quality attribute.

- *Checking at run time:* This is the usual case. Most contract-checking tools throw exceptions (e.g., iContract [Kramer98]) or write log files (e.g., DBC for Python [Plösch97]). Checking assertions at run time possibly leads to performance losses. Therefore, systems that support checking at run time must provide reasonable strategies for selectively enabling and disabling assertion checking (see [Meyer97a] for a general discussion of this topic and [Plösch97] for an example of an environment that supports scalable run-time checking).

The above explanations show that it is possible to enhance the quality of software by defining the expected behavior by means of contracts. The problematic issue here is how to transform analysis results, which form the basis of any further design or implementation, into more formally specified contracts that may be checked automatically. This issue will be discussed in detail in Sect. 2.4.

2.3   The Behavioral Level—Object-Oriented Concepts

2.3.1   Contracts and Behavioral Subtyping

The emphasis of Sect. 2.2 was on fundamental assertion techniques; that is, preconditions and postconditions at a method level. Invariants (also explained in Sect. 2.2) are special forms of preconditions and postconditions that facilitate the formulation of correctness criteria at a class level.

In a fully object-oriented programming language, polymorphism, inheritance, and dynamic binding have to be taken into account. The most important issue here is that of polymorphism and inheritance and it's relation to behavioral subtyping. Typically, in object-oriented programming languages establishing an inheritance relationship between two classes establishes a subtyping relationship between these classes, too. This means, that an object of the newly derived class can be used instead of the original superclass. Additionally the rules for overriding methods, i.e., for changing the behavior of the class, are quite simple; the only requirement is that the overridden method must have the same signature as in the superclass[3]. There are not limitations concerning the semantics of the implementation. It is therefore possible to override a method in a subclass in a way that it is semantically inconsistent, i.e., does not adhere to the implicit specification imposed by the superclass. Nevertheless neither the compiler nor the run-time system has any possibility to systematically check whether a subclass really is a subtype in a behavioral sense[4]. Adding contracts to methods gives us the possibility to

---

[3] We do not discuss the implications implied by the availability of the concept of interfaces in Java or C#. Basically the rules are the same is described here.

[4] This meaning of behavioral subtyping for object-oriented systems was proposed by Barbara Liskov [Liskov94]. More details can be found later in this chapter.

state some requirements on the behavior of an overridden method. A class is a behavioral subtype if it also fulfills the contracts defined in the superclass. On the contract level this means that the implementation in a subclass must at least fulfill all contracts given by the superclass.

Pragmatically, we follow our BankAccount example and formulate a simple precondition for the deposit method (the example is intentionally kept simple to clearly show the problems associated with inheritance). A SavingsAccount is a special case of a BankAccount and has an additional precondition. The semantic background of the precondition in the SavingsAccount class (amount > 100) is that the minimum deposit on this special savings account is €100.00:

```
public class BankAccount {
    ...
    public void deposit(float amount) { ... }
        pre: amount > 0
    ...
}

public class SavingsAccount extends BankAccount {
    ...
    public void deposit(float amount) { ... }
        pre: amount > 100.00
    ...
}
```

As Findler [Findler01] states, many existing contract-checking systems [Duncan98, Gomes96, Karaorman96, Kizub98, Kölling97, Kramer98, MMS00] collect all the assertions of a method and its super-methods. The preconditions are disjointed, i.e., they are checked with a logical or—that is, $pre_{super} \Rightarrow (pre_{super}$ **or** $pre_{type})$—while postconditions are conjuncted, i.e., they are checked with a logical and; that is, $(post_{super}$ **and** $post_{type}) \Rightarrow post_{super}$. Rewriting the preconditions of our BankAccount and SavingsAccount example leads to (amount > 0) $\Rightarrow$ ((amount > 0) **or** (amount > 100)), which of course is always true, although it should not be.

Contract-checking tools that follow the approach sketched above assume that programmers do not make mistakes concerning the relationship of preconditions and postconditions within an inheritance scenario. Instead, these tools assume that the contracts of superclasses are well understood and that only additional specifications are added, i.e., specifications the follow the behavioral subtyping idea also in the specified contracts.

Given our above pair of BankAccount and SavingsAccount classes, the following example shows the problem associated with inheritance:

```
BankAccount account= new SavingsAccount();
account.deposit(10);
```

The expression account.deposit(10) violates the contract of the SavingsAccount class, although the parameter 10 is perfectly suitable for a variable of type BankAccount. This effect occurs not only for implementation inheritance but also in conjunction with interfaces. Rewriting the BankAccount example using interfaces leads to similar problems, as inheritance is also allowed for interfaces:

```
public interface BankAccountIF {
    ...
    public void deposit(float amount) { ... }
        pre: amount > 0
    ...
}

public interface SavingsAccountIF extends BankAccountIF {
    ...
    public void deposit(float amount) { ... }
        pre: amount > 100
    ...
}

public class BankAccount implements BankAccountIF {
    ...
}

public class SavingsAccount implements SavingsAccountIF {
    ...
}

    ...
BankAccountIF account= new SavingsAccount();
account.deposit(10);
```

In the above example, classes BankAccount and SavingsAccount do not rely on implementation inheritance, i.e., the class SavingsAccount does not reuse any code from any superclass. Both classes can be used in all situations where an object of type BankAccountIF is required. Nevertheless, due to the inheritance relationship between the interfaces BankAccountIF and SavingsAccountIF, the above violation of contracts occurs in this case too, i.e., interface SavingsAccountIF is not a behavioral subtype of the interface BankAccountIF.

The reason for this violation is that the contract in interface SavingsAccountIF violates the notion of behavioral subtyping [America91, Liskov94, Liskov99]. According to Findler and Felleisen [Findler01], behavioral subtyping in the context of contracts is defined as follows (without using more precise mathematical notation):

> "An instance of a subtype must be substitutable for an instance of a super type. For pre- and postcondition contracts, behavioral subtyping mandates that the precondition of a method in a type implies the precondition of the same method in each of its subtypes. Similarly, it requires that each postcondition in a subtype implies the corresponding postcondition in the original type."

Given this definition in our above example, the following relation would have to be true:

$(amount > 0) \Rightarrow (amount > 100)$

This is obviously not true, for example, for an amount of value 5. Invariants are special cases of preconditions and postconditions, and with regard to the notion of behavioral subtyping, they have to be treated accordingly.

2.3.2   Contracts, Subtyping, and Correctness

In Sect. 2.2, a definition for correctness based on contracts was given. In this section, we will give two definitions of correctness; that is, a definition for weak correctness, following the proposal by Meyer [Meyer97a], and a definition of strong correctness, founded on the basis of the theory of behavioral subtyping and formulated by Findler [Findler01][5]. This distinction is reasonable if we assume that the programmer is aware of the behavioral subtyping issues and formulates the contracts accordingly. Furthermore, as a number of programming languages and systems follow the weak correctness definition, this definition should be stated clearly, as we will rely on it in Sect. 2.4.

Following Meyer [Meyer97a], weak correctness is defined as follows:

- A class C is given. C_{super} denotes a superclass of C.

- $C_{super}.pre_r$ denotes a precondition of a public method r of a superclass of C.

- $C_{super}.INV$ denotes an invariant of a superclass of C.

- The implementation of a method must fulfill the following condition for preconditions:

    For every public method r and any set of valid arguments x_y:

    $(pre_r(x_r)$ or $\forall C_{super}: C_{super}.pre_r(x_y))$

- The implementation of a method must fulfill the following condition for postconditions:

    For every public method r and any set of valid arguments x_y:

    $(post_r(x_y)$ and $\forall C_{super}: C_{super}.post_r(x_y))$

- The implementation of a class as a whole must fulfill the following condition for invariants:

    INV and $\forall C_{super}: C_{super}.INV$

Given these definitions, a class is correct when, for every exported routine r and any set of valid arguments x_y, the following condition is not violated:

$\{ (pre_r(x_y)$ or $\forall C_{super}: C_{super}.pre_r(x_y))$ and $(INV$ and $\forall C_{super}: C_{super}.INV) \}$
$Body_r$
$\{ (post_r(x_y)$ and $\forall C_{super}: C_{super}.post_r(x_y))$ and $(INV$ and $\forall C_{super}: C_{super}.INV) \}$

---

[5] This Section can be skipped by readers not interested in subtle details of the meaning of correctness in the context of contracts.

Less formally, any subclass has to fulfill three rules (see [Meyer97a]):

- The invariants of all of the parents of a class apply to the class itself.
- Any added preconditions in a subclass are to be OR-ed with the original precondition.
- Any added postconditions in a subclass are to be AND-ed with the original postcondition.

This definition only leads to correct subclasses in cases in which the preconditions are truly weakened and the postconditions are truly strengthened (see above).

The strong correctness implied by the theory of behavioral subtyping can be defined as follows:

- A class C is given. C_{sub} denotes a subclass of C.

- C_{super} denotes a superclass of C.

- $C_{sub}.pre_r$ denotes a precondition of a public method r of a subclass of C.

- $C_{super}.post_r$ denotes a postcondition of an public method r of a superclass of C.

- $C_{sub}.INV$ denotes an invariant of a subclass of C.

- The implementation of a method must fulfill the following condition for preconditions:

    For every public method r and any set of valid arguments x_y:

    $(pre_r(x_y) \Rightarrow \forall C_{sub}.\ C_{sub}.pre_r(x_y))$

- The implementation of a method must fulfill the following condition for postconditions:

    For every public method r and any set of valid arguments x_y:

    $(post_r(x_y) \Rightarrow \forall C_{super}.\ C_{super}.post_r(x_y))$

- The implementation of a class as a whole must fulfill the following condition for invariants:

    $INV \Rightarrow \forall C_{sub}.\ C_{sub}.INV$

Given these definitions, a class is correct when, for every public method r and any set of valid arguments x_y, the following condition is not violated:

$\{ (pre_r(x_y) \Rightarrow \forall C_{sub}.\ C_{sub}.pre_r(x_y))$ and $(INV \Rightarrow \forall C_{sub}.\ C_{sub}.INV) \}$
$Body_r$
$\{ (post_r(x_y) \Rightarrow \forall C_{super}.\ C_{super}.post_r(x_y))$ and $(INV \Rightarrow \forall C_{sub}.\ C_{sub}.INV) \}$

A more formal definition of these correctness criteria, with additional theorems and axioms to enable a proof of whether contracts fulfill them, may be found in Findler and Felleisen [Findler01].

As already mentioned in Sect. 2.2, it is possible to enhance the quality of software by improving its correctness. The problematic issue is again how to transform analysis results, which form the basis of any further design or implementation, into more formally specified contracts that may be checked automatically. This issue will be discussed in detail in the next section.

2.4   The Behavioral Level in Programming Languages and Systems

2.4.1   Introduction

In the preceding sections of this chapter, the idea of contracts was presented, together with some historical background, an explanation of the basic idea of preconditions, postconditions, and invariants, and the presentation of a language for describing contracts. Additionally, the specific problems associated with behavioral subtyping were discussed and a definition of the correctness of a class was developed. There is some evidence (see [Rosenblum95] and [Meyer97b]) that assertions have positive effects on the overall software quality, especially on the correctness of software.

Nevertheless, only a   limited number of programming languages directly support contracts in the way described in the preceding sections. The goal of this chapter is to describe different possible approaches to supporting contracts in a programming language or programming system. Furthermore, we give an overview of programming languages and systems that support assertions in one way or another, and we define criteria for evaluating the level of contract support. The evaluation of the selected systems concludes this section.

In general, three different approaches are possible to technically support assertions in a programming language or programming system:

Built-In: This means that support for contracts is directly included in the programming language. The programming language contains language constructs to formulate assertions in one way or another. The syntactical correctness of assertions is checked directly by the compiler. In addition, a run-time environment must be available to perform the run-time assertion checks. Ideally, the run-time environment should be sufficiently flexible to allow a   fine-grained control of the assertion checking mechanism; that is, it should be possible to selectively enable and disable assertion checking. Examples of programming languages with built-in assertion checking are Eiffel [Meyer92] and Biscotti [Cicalese99], a language extension to the Java programming language, which itself also provides assertion support to some degree—this will be discussed in more detail later. The main advantage of this approach is the homogeneous integration of assertions into the programming language; that is, compiler error messages are consistent and debugging tools can properly consider assertions (e.g., correct line numbers and stack traces).

Preprocessing: This is the most popular kind of support for assertions in a programming language. The general idea is to formulate assertions separately from the program or to include the assertions as special comments. A preprocessor is used to weave the assertions into the program or to transform the comments that contain assertion formulas into native programming language code. The main advantage of this approach is the separation of the programming language and the language for formulating contracts, which is important in cases in which the native programming language does not support, or does not sufficiently support, assertions and in which it must not be altered for various reasons (e.g., conformance to standards, insufficient knowledge available to change the compiler). The main disadvantage of this approach is that the original program code is changed by the preprocessor; that is, the line numbers of run-time errors do not actually fit the line numbers of the program text in a debugger. In case of run-time exceptions misleading line numbers are reported, too. A popular example of a preprocessing language for Java technology is iContract [Kramer98]. Other examples are Design by Contract for C++ [Plösch99] and Jass [Bartezko01].

Metaprogramming: According to Templ [Templ94], metaprogramming refers to "programming at the level of program interpretation, or in other words, to extending the interpreter of a given programming language in an application-specific way. Traditionally, this concept is available only in dynamically typed and interpreted languages" [Templ94]. Programs that include the possibility of reasoning about themselves have so-called "reflective" capabilities. The Java programming language has reflective capabilities, and may access information about elements of a Java program by means of a reflection API. The main advantage of the metaprogramming approach is that no specialized preprocessor needs to be used: the native compiler suffices. Nevertheless, a specialized run-time environment has to be used to enable assertion checking. The metaprogramming approach is especially useful in cases of a dynamically typed interpreted programming language (see, for example, DBC for Python [Plösch97]). Other examples of systems that support assertions using metaprogramming techniques are jContractor [Karaorman96] and Handshake [Duncan98].

2.4.2   Criteria for Evaluating Contract Support

The criteria to be used when different programming languages or programming systems are evaluated may be split into four groups:

- Basic assertion support (BAS).
- Advanced assertion support (AAS).
- Support for behavioral subtyping (SBS).
- Run-time monitoring of assertions (RMA).

The criteria for each group are explained in more detail below. The abbreviation for a group, combined with a criterion identifier, is unique and is used later, in the evaluation of programming languages and systems (see Sect. 2.4.4) to compactly describe the evaluation results. The criteria themselves are explained by means of questions; this is a straightforward and simple approach, and it should clearly show what the respective criteria are about. For simplicity, we will use the term *system*—meaning programming languages and programming systems—when describing the criteria.

Before describing our criteria, we will discuss a couple of terms used in their description. For ease of reading, we will provide some definitions in advance—we do not refer to them explicitly in the criteria section, but we set them in italics:

- *Side effect free methods:* As already mentioned in this chapter, assertions may also use methods. From the point of view of correctness, it is necessary that these methods behave as pure functions; that is, they do not produce any side effects, in the sense that in order to be side effect free a method must not change the state of the object. In the evaluation of contract-supporting systems, we assume a method to be side effect free when it guarantees not to change the state of the object to which it belongs. From an implementation point of view, a const method in C++ fulfills this requirement, as the compiler guarantees that in the body of a const method no instance variables are changed; furthermore, only calls to other const methods are allowed. On the contrary, in the Java programming language no syntactical construct is available that is similar to the C++ approach.
- *Proper checking of assertions in public methods:* In the specification of a contract for a public method, it has to be assured that the only other methods used are side effect free in the sense of the above definition.
- *Proper checking of assertions in private methods:* Private methods typically have no assertions, as they are always called directly and indirectly by other public methods. It is guaranteed that private methods are never used from the outside; that is, from a client class or component.
- *Proper checking of assertions in case of recursion:* For recursive methods, preconditions are only checked the first time a method is entered, and postconditions are checked only at the end of the invocation of the recursive method; that is, when the last recursive method on the stack is executed.

Basic Assertion Support (BAS): This group of criteria forms the basis and should be supported by any system that claims to support a contract style of programming and modeling:

- *BAS-1 (Basic assertions):* Does the system support basic assertion annotations in the implementation of a method?[6]

---

[6]This criterion is aimed at systems that do not directly support preconditions and postconditions as explained in this chapter, but provide simpler approaches only; for example, assertion macros or similar techniques.

- *BAS-2 (Preconditions and postconditions):* Does the system support preconditions? Does the system support postconditions? May assertion expressions access properties of a class? Are properties of a class guaranteed to remain unchanged during assertion checking? May assertion expressions also contain method calls? Is it guaranteed that a method call will not produce any side effects (especially changes in the state of the object)?
- *BAS-3 (Invariants):* Is it possible to formulate invariants? Are there any restrictions in formulating invariants (compared to the formulation of preconditions or postconditions)?

Advanced Assertion Support (AAS): Programming languages and systems that support this group of criteria lead to more expressive contracts that allow us to capture more complex contract situations:

- *AAS-1 (Enhanced assertion expressions):* May assertions contain Boolean implications? May postconditions access the original values of parameters; that is, the values at method entry? May postconditions access the original values of instance variables; that is, the values at method entry?
- *AAS-2 (Operations on collections):* Does the system support assertion expressions on collections? Is it guaranteed that collections will remain immutable in assertion expressions? May universal quantifications be expressed in the expression language? May existential quantifications be expressed in the expression language?
- *AAS-3* (Additional expressions): Does the assertion expression language have additional features? Are these additional features guaranteed to be side effect free?

Support for Behavioral Subtyping (SBS): Most systems that provide assertion support for classes will also take inheritance and interfaces into consideration. As discussed in Sect. 2.3, there are different approaches to subcontracting:

- *SBS-1 (Interfaces):* Is it possible to specify contracts for interfaces? May contracts be added for classes that implement assertion-enriched interfaces?
- *SBS-2 (Correctness I):* Does the system impose any restrictions on subcontracts? Does the system ensure that preconditions may only be weakened? Does the system ensure that postconditions may only be strengthened?
- *SBS-3 (Correctness II):* Does the system impose stronger requirements on subcontracts, as specified in SBS-2? Does the system ensure that the correctness rules for behavioral subtyping are not violated?

Run-Time Monitoring of Assertions (RMA): As already mentioned in Sect. 2.2.6, run-time monitoring of assertions is important, especially from a practitioner's point of view:

- *RMA-1 (Contract violations):* Is an exception handling mechanism available in case of violations of assertions? Are additional features available for dealing with assertion violations (e.g., log files)?

- *RMA-2 (Configurability):* Is it possible to enable and disable precondition checking, postcondition checking, and invariant checking selectively? Is it possible to enable and disable assertion checking at a package, class, or even method level?
- *RMA-3 (Efficiency):* Are there any additional memory requirements when assertion checking is disabled? Is there any additional processor usage when assertion checking is disabled?

2.4.3   An Overview of Selected Systems

In this section, we give an overview of selected programming languages and systems that provide support for contract-based software development. We only present systems that allow us to formulate assertions in the style and manner as described in the previous sections. Approaches that use algebraic techniques or higher-order logics are not considered. Therefore, systems such as Larch [Leavens99a] are not considered in this section: their discussion is postponed until Chap. 8.

Furthermore, we only consider programming languages and systems that have industrial relevance; that is, programming languages and extensions along the line of Eiffel, C++, and Java. Therefore, systems such as Design by Contract for Smalltalk [Carillo96] or Design by Contract for Python [Plösch97] are considered neither in this overview nor in the evaluation.

In this overview section we provide for each system its name, the kind of approach used (programming language, programming language extension, preprocessor, or metaprogramming), an overview, special features, references, and notes about the system's status. A detailed evaluation of each presented system, according to the criteria developed in Sect. 2.4.2, will be carried out in Sect. 2.4.4.

Eiffel:

- *Type of support:* Built-in.
- *Overview:* Eiffel was one of the first mainstream programming languages that supported the idea of contracts, considering object-oriented concepts such as polymorphism and inheritance.
- *Special features:* Does also provide assertions for loops.
- *References:* [Meyer92, Meyer97a, Meyer97b].
- *Status:* Eiffel is still used in education as well as in industrial projects. Given Eiffel's new capability to deploy .net components [Powell01] directly from the Eiffel code, its popularity might increase.

Biscotti:

- *Type of support:* Java language extension; built-in compiler support.
- *Overview:* Biscotti concentrates on enabling behavioral specification of Java RMI interfaces by introducing additional keywords.

- *Special features:* It is not necessary to make any changes to the Java virtual machine, as Biscotti uses reflection facilities to make preconditions, postconditions, and invariants visible at run time.
- *Reference:* [Cicalese99].
- *Status:* The work will be continued.

Java Assertion Facility (JAF):

- *Type of support:* Built-in since the release of Java 1.4.
- *Overview:* Java 1.4 adds an additional keyword assert as well as some configuration flags to the Java compiler and to the Java virtual machine. The Java programming language only supports a simple assertion mechanism that allows us to formulate correctness conditions within methods.
- *Special features:* Assertion checking can be easily enabled and disabled, and traces of assertions may be completely eliminated from class files.
- *References:* [Rogers01a, Rogers01b, Sun02a].
- *Status:* Part of the specified programming language.

ContractJava:

- *Type of support:* ContractJava is a typical preprocessor that generates Java code.
- *Overview:* The preprocessor supports typical kinds of assertions. Assertions are formulated in a similar way to those expressed in previous sections of this book.
- *Special features:* ContractJava supports behavioral subtyping in the sense that the elaborator checks whether a type really is a behavioral subtype of another type.
- *Reference:* [Findler01].
- *Status:* Experimental work, which will probably be continued.

iContract:

- *Type of support:* A preprocessor that generates Java code, which is passed to the standard Java compiler after preprocessing.
- *Overview:* Assertions are described as documentation for a method or class (for invariants) using special documentation tags. These documentation tags are extracted by the preprocessor and converted into Java code. An iContract program is a well-formed Java program and can therefore be translated directly by a Java compiler without assertion support.
- *Special features:* iContract supports operations on collections and provides additional tools for documenting the assertions in a javadoc-like fashion (iDoclet), and for facilitating the redesign of Java classes (iDarwin).
- *References:* [Enseling01, Kramer98].
- *Status:* iContract, as well as the accompanying tools iDoclet and iDarwin, are constantly being enhanced.

Jass:

- *Type of support:* A preprocessor that generates Java code, which is passed to the standard Java compiler after preprocessing.
- *Overview:* Assertions are specified by means of a specific comment for methods or classes. A Jass program is a well-formed Java program and can therefore be translated directly by a Java compiler without assertion support.
- *Special features:* Jass supports universal and existential quantification that range over finite sets. The Jass preprocessor tries to detect violations of subtyping relationships, although there is no sound theory to underlie it (as is the case for ConractJava). Additionally, Jass supports so-called trace assertions to specify the dynamic behavior of a class.
- *Reference:* [Bartezko01].
- *Status:* Jass is constantly being enhanced.

Design by Contract for C++:

- *Type of support:* A preprocessor that generates C++ code, which is passed to the standard C++ compiler after preprocessing.
- *Overview:* The system provides support for Design by Contract in the Eiffel tradition. The assertions are described separately from the C++ classes and are weaved into the C++ code by the preprocessor.
- *Special features:* The preprocessor relies heavily on macros and multiple inheritance to produce easily readable C++ code.
- *Reference:* [Plösch99].
- *Status:* This work has been discontinued.

Handshake:

- *Type of support:* Provides assertion support by means of reflection; that is, uses metaprogramming techniques.
- *Overview:* Contracts are specified in separate contract files. The usual kind of preconditions, postconditions, and assertions may be specified. At class load time, the handshake system combines this contract file with the original class file; that is, the handshake system dynamically changes the byte code of the class.
- *Special features:* Due to the dynamic nature of Handshake, contracts can be added to classes where only the byte code, rather than the source code, is available.
- *Reference:* [Duncan98].
- *Status:* This work has been discontinued.

jContractor:

- *Type of support:* jContractor is a pure library-based approach that utilizes the meta-level information found in Java class files and uses dynamic class loading

to perform reflective on-the-fly byte code modification.
- *Overview:* Contract code (preconditions, postconditions, and invariants) is added to a class in the form of methods, following specific naming conventions.
- *Special features:* Inside a method's postcondition, it is possible to check the result associated with the method's execution with a specified result.
- *Reference:* [Karaorman96].
- *Status:* This work has been discontinued.

Jcontract:

- *Type of support:* A preprocessor that generates Java code, which is passed to the standard Java compiler after preprocessing.
- *Overview:* Assertions are specified by means of a specific comment for methods or classes. Jcontract makes use of the assert command available in Java 1.4.
- *Special features:* Jcontract supports universal and existential quantification of collection types. Additionally, Jcontract is tightly integrated with the test tool Jtest [Parasoft02a]. Jtest examines the specification information contained in the contract, and then creates and executes test cases that evaluate whether the class functions as specified. Jcontract includes a javadoc generation tool that allows us to generate API documentation containing the specified assertions.
- *References:* [Parasoft02a, Parasoft02b].

Of course, a number of other systems exist that will not be evaluated because of lack of space, or because of the fact that these systems had only a minor influence or are now outdated. These systems include class assertions in C++ by Porat and Fertig [Porat95], direct Design By Contract support for the Java programming language by Mannion and Philips [Mannion98], and assertion extension for Java technology by Payne, Schatz, and Schmid [Payne98].

2.4.4   Evaluation of Contract Support

In this section, we will evaluate the systems that have been sketched out in the previous section. The emphasis of this evaluation is to provide a consistent evaluation of the criteria developed in Sect. 2.4.2. A quantitative assessment of the criteria is omitted. Nevertheless, for the sake of simplicity we will make some use of an ordinal scale to express the evaluation result for a criterion. The possible values for a criterion are as follows:

- *1:* excellent support.
- *3:* reasonable support.
- *5:* poorly supported.
- *ns:* not supported.

The evaluation results are presented in a tabular fashion. In order to make the results easily readable, the evaluation results are split into three groups. Each group contains the evaluation results for one type of system. There is one table for systems that provide assertion support that is built into the programming language, or via direct compiler support. Another table describes the evaluation results for systems that provide assertion support by means of preprocessing. A third table shows the results for systems that provide assertion support by means of metaprogramming or reflection. For reasons of readability, the evaluation table for each type of system is split into two; that is, one part that deals with the basic assertion support criteria (BAS) and the advanced assertion support (AAS), and a second part that lists the results for support for behavioral subtyping (SBS) and the runtime monitoring of assertions (RMA).

Each table is accompanied by comments that are intended to justify the evaluation results; that is, the grade on the ordinal scale assigned to a criterion.

BAS and AAS criteria (built-in systems)

System	BAS-1	BAS-2	BAS-3	AAS-1	AAS-2	AAS-3
Eiffel	1	3	1	1	ns	3
Biscotti	ns	3	1	3	ns	ns
JAF	1	ns	ns	ns	ns	ns

Eiffel allows us to formulate correctness conditions on loops and supports a special strip statement. Strip extracts the values of all instance variables of the object (with some possibly excluded). This may be used in conjunction with accessing the value of instance variables at method entry (e.g., equal(strip(), old strip()[7]). Eiffel allows the use of methods in assertion expressions. As Eiffel has no notation for defining side effect free methods, side effects have to be assumed. Bertrand Meyer is aware of this problem as far as correctness is concerned. In the course of writing this book, he has been planning to introduce a notation for pure functions—that is, side effect free methods—in Eiffel.

Biscotti does not guarantee that methods used in assertion expression do not change the state of the object.

JAF provides only   basic assertion support. Preconditions, postconditions, and invariants are not directly supported. Boolean implications are not supported by JAF.

SBS and RMA criteria (built-in systems)

System	SBS-1	SBS-2	SBS-3	RMA-1	RMA-2	RMA-3
Eiffel	ns	1	ns	1	1	1
Biscotti	1	1	ns	1	ns	ns
JAF	ns	ns	ns	1	3	3

Eiffel does not support the idea of interfaces (as proposed by the Java programming language), but uses the idea of multiple inheritance. Nevertheless, the crite-

---

[7]old strip() is Eiffel syntax and is semantically equivalent with strip()@pre.

rion SBS-1 is not fulfilled by Eiffel due to its nature—but this is not to be seen as negative.

Biscotti does not allow the explicit enabling or disabling of assertions. Therefore, assertion checking is always enabled, and this influences the speed of execution as well as the memory usage.

JAF allows us to enable and disable assertions at a package or class level. As JAF does not support true preconditions or postconditions, but only basic assertions, this granularity is reasonable. Using the conditional compilation idiom of the Java programming language (see the Java specification, chap. 14.19) [Gosling96], all traces of assertions can be removed from class files by an optimizing compiler. As this idiom leads to scattered code, we consider the support to be reasonable but not excellent.

BAS and AAS criteria (preprocessors)

System	BAS-1	BAS-2	BAS-3	AAS-1	AAS-2	AAS-3
ContractJava	ns	3	1	ns	ns	ns
iContract	ns	3	1	1	1	ns
Jass	1	3	1	3	1	1
DBC-C++	1	1	1	3	ns	ns

ContractJava allows method calls in assertion expressions, but the system does not ensure that the methods called do not change the state of the object.

iContract allows method calls in assertion expressions, but the pre-compiler does not ensure that the methods called do not change the state of the object. iContract supports operations on Java collections, and also provides universal and existential quantification.

Jass allows method calls in assertion expressions without insuring that the methods called do not change the state of the object. Side effects may be reduced by using change lists in postconditions. A change list allows us to specify which instance variables of this object may be changed. Jass does not allow Boolean implications, but supports access to the original values of instance variables. The developer is responsible for proper cloning of the object. Access to the original values of parameters is not possible. As already mentioned, Jass provides change lists and loop invariants. In addition, Jass allows us to formulate so-called trace assertions that allow us to specify valid sequences of method calls.

DBC-C++ provides assertion for the C++ programming language. It is guaranteed that the methods used in assertion expression do not alter the state of the object, as only methods that are declared to be const (in the C++ sense) may be used. DBC-C++ does not support Boolean implications, but provides access to the original values of instance variables or parameters. The code generated automatically takes care of cloning objects whose initial state (i.e., the state at method entry) is needed in postconditions.

SBS and RMA criteria (preprocessors)

System	SBS-1	SBS-2	SBS-3	RMA-1	RMA-2	RMA-3
ContractJava	1	ns	1	ns	ns	ns
iContract	1	1	ns	1	1	1
Jass	ns	1	5	1	1	1
DBC-C++	ns	1	ns	1	1	1

ContractJava supports behavioral subtyping—it is the major contribution of this work to ensure the correctness of assertions in subtyping situations. The preprocessor is in a prototype stadium and does not offer build options for assertion checking.

iContract allows for a fine-grained instrumentation level; that is, the level can be chosen for each file, enabling fine-grained, vertical (inheritance, implementation) and horizontal (delegation) performance control. Source code that contains assertions remains fully compatible with the Java programming language, without any performance penalties.

Jass considers behavioral subtyping. An abstraction function has to be provided by the implementer, which must return a reference of the type of the superclass. The returned instance must be in an abstract state that is mapped from the concrete state through the abstraction function. This support is rather complicated to use and time-consuming. Additionally, only the superclass of a class is considered, rather than the entire hierarchy. The type of assertion checks that are enabled can be configured easily by means of flags, passed to the preprocessor. As Jass is a typical preprocessor, any traces may be excluded.

DBC-C++ has no special support for interfaces, which is also due to the fact that interfaces as understood in Java technology are not supported by C++. As the instrumentation of the C++ code relies on macros and C++ preprocessing, any traces of assertions may be removed from the C++ source code by the use of conditional compilation.

BAS and AAS criteria (reflective systems)

System	BAS-1	BAS-2	BAS-3	AAS-1	AAS-2	AAS-3
Handshake	ns	3	1	3	5	ns
jContractor	ns	3	1	5	5	ns

Handshake does not ensure side effect free usage of methods in assertions. While Boolean implications are not supported, unlimited access to values of instance variables or parameters at method entry in postconditions is possible. There is no special support for dealing with collections.

jContractor also does not ensure side effect free usage of methods in assertion expressions. Boolean implications are not supported and only values of instance variables at method entry are supported, rather than references to values of parameters at method entry. Assertion expressions in jContractor may be arbitrary expressions; that is, operations on Java collections are possible—a specific syntax for dealing with universal and existential quantification is not provided.

SBS and RMA criteria (reflective systems)

System	SBS-1	SBS-2	SBS-3	RMA-1	RMA-2	RMA-3
Handshake	1	1	ns	1	1	3
jContractor	1	1	ns	1	5	5

Handshake forces the specification of assertions separately from the implementation of the class, using a specific syntax. The Handshake system transforms the assertion specification into Java code and weaves it into the original byte code. Assertion checking can therefore be selectively controlled by commenting and uncommenting assertions, or by replacing assertion specifications entirely. Unfortunately, enabling and disabling are not supported by compiler flags.

jContractor provides full support for contracts in interfaces. jContractor offers two opportunities for run-time instrumentation: (1) by using a special class loader that is responsible for instrumentation; or (2) via a factory-style instantiation of classes. In the latter case, assertion checking can be enabled at the class level. In the former case, assertion checking can be enabled and disabled globally; that is, for one virtual machine only. Assertions—preconditions, postconditions, and invariants—are ordinary Java methods that follow specific naming patterns. These specific methods can either be implemented in the class to be instrumented or in a separate class using—once again—a specific naming pattern. Assertions specified in separate classes do not have any impact on the run-time performance.

3 Contracts and Analysis

Summary: Currently, assertion techniques are used in the implementation phase of the software life cycle, as some programming languages (e.g., Eiffel [Meyer92]) directly support the underlying concepts, or at least provide comparable support (e.g., iContract [Kramer98] for the Java programming language). Since software contracting means adding specification elements to classes, it is ideally suited for object-oriented analysis and design. The advantage of the approach is that when specification and implementation share the same set of behavioral abstractions, system changes will automatically be applied to the specification and implementation models.

The importance of assertions is also understood by the designers of the Unified Modeling Language (UML), as the actual specification of the UML also contains the Object Constraint Language (OCL), which supports the formulation of contracts. Design by Contract and OCL share many similarities. The main differences are (1) the possibility of imposing correctness conditions on collections by means of OCL language features, and (2) the lack of subcontracting in OCL, which is an important concept to ensure the conformance of derived classes with their base classes. However, an assertion technique alone does not provide a methodological framework by means of which it can be applied in the analysis and design phase. In order to guide this process, best practices may be used.

Keywords: Object Constraint Language (OCL), Unified Modeling Language (UML)

3.1 Introduction

Chapter 2 described the theoretic foundations of contracts (assertions) and showed what kind of semantics can usually be expressed using assertion techniques. Chapter 2 also makes clear that only a limited number of programming languages directly support assertion techniques. Nevertheless, a number of extensions are available that add this support to a specific programming language.

As already explained, the basic idea of assertions is to add additional specification elements to software artifacts and therefore to impose obligations on the clients and implementers of these artifacts. In our opinion, it is too late to add these specification elements to classes and methods in the implementation phase: they have to be considered right from the beginning—that is, in the analysis and early design phase. Currently, some analysis and design methods consider assertions in their methodology: examples include BON [Waldén95], Catalysis [D'Souza99], and Syntropy [Cook94].

Object-oriented analysis and design activities are often carried out using the UML notation [UML97] and relying on the Unified Process [Jacobson99]. As part of the UML notation, the Object Management Group (OMG) has standardized the Object Constraint Language (OCL) [OCL97].

In Sect. 3.2 we briefly describe the properties of the OCL language at a technical level (syntax and semantics), and we use the criteria developed in Sect. 2.4.2 to evaluate the assertion support available in OCL. This evaluation should clarify whether a mapping of a UML–OCL model to an implementation model for assertions (e.g., Jass [Bartezko01]) can easily be realized.

In Sect. 3.3, we will try to formulate a number of best practices; that is, hints about how to formulate assertions (what should be specified, and what should be avoided). The best practices formulated in this section will not consider the analysis and design process itself, but will focus generally on the task of formulating assertions. Process issues will be discussed later, in Chap. 6.

3.2   Contracts and UML

The UML notation [UML97] is currently used to capture analysis and design results using a number of types of graphical notation (use case diagrams, class diagrams, sequence diagrams, collaboration diagrams, statechart diagrams, activity diagrams, component diagrams, and deployment diagrams). In order to add constraints—that is, assertions—to these models, the OMG have standardized the Object Constraint Language (OCL) together with the specification of Version 1.1 of the UML. In this section, we describe the basic requirements for the OCL language. Furthermore, we give an overview of the OCL language properties. A detailed description of the OCL language is outside the scope of this book, but can be found in OCL Version 1.1 [OCL97] and Warmer and Kleppe [Warmer99]. This section concludes with an evaluation of the OCL language using the evaluation criteria developed in Sect. 2.4.2. The OMG plans to enhance the OCL specification. Section 3.2.4 gives an overview of the respective Request for Proposal of the OMG.

3.2.1   The Principles of OCL

The OCL specification [OCL97] concisely describes the main reason for developing this language:

> "In object-oriented modeling a graphical model, like a class model, is not enough for a precise and unambiguous specification. There is a need to describe additional constraints about the objects in the model. Such constraints are often described in natural language. Practice has shown that this will always result in ambiguities. In order to write unambiguous constraints, so-called formal languages have been developed. The disadvantage of traditional formal languages is that they are useable to persons with a strong mathematical

background, but difficult for the average business or system modeler to use. OCL has been developed to fill this gap. It is a formal language that remains easy to read and write."

The term "constraint" used in the above quotation is defined as a restriction on one or more values of (part of) an object-oriented model or system [Warmer99]. A constraint can be viewed as an assertion. OCL has a number of interesting properties [OCL97, Warmer99]:

- OCL is a pure expression language. Any OCL expression is guaranteed to be side effect free; that is, by definition it cannot change the state of the system— all operations are purely functional. This is one major difference as compared to the approaches discussed in Sect. 2.4.3. OCL expressions specify which constraints must be fulfilled by the model. If an assertion is not valid, then the model is not valid. In this case, actions must be taken to transform the model into a valid state. The actions to be taken are not specified in OCL. This is a major difference compared to typical assertion languages as discussed in Chap. 2 where, usually, an exception is thrown in the case of an assertion violation.
- OCL is not a programming language, so it is not possible to write program logic or flow control in OCL. Due to its declarative nature, not everything in the language is promised to be directly executable.
- OCL is a typed language, so each OCL expression has a type. In a correct OCL expression, all types used must be type-conformant. OCL is specified in such a way that it is possible to check any OCL expression for validity.

3.2.2   The Basics of OCL

In order to explain the basic capabilities of OCL we will use our bank account example of Sect. 2.2. The class model used is depicted in Fig. 8 a UML class diagram (for details concerning the graphical notation of UML class diagrams, see [Booch99] or [Fowler99]).

Any OCL expression may be included in the graphical notation of, for example, a UML class diagram. In order to enhance readability, we use a textual description for OCL expressions. For these textual descriptions, each OCL expression must be preceded by a context. In the case of an invariant, the context of the OCL expression is a class, whereas for preconditions and postconditions the context is a method. In the following examples, the context is underlined:

BankAccount
customer != null

The above example shows that access to the members of a class is possible. Alternately, any OCL expression may also use operations:

BankAccount
getCustomer() != null

The above example models the aspect that BankAccount objects must always contain a reference to a customer object in order to perform valid operations. Invariants may also specify correctness conditions upon associated classes. In this case, the role name is used to identify the associated object:

BankAccount
customer.lastName <> null and customer.firstName <> null

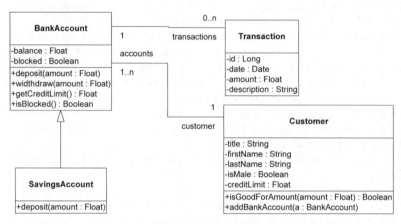

Fig. 8. The class diagram for the bank account example

Without describing and explaining it in detail, it is obvious that any OCL expression may use relational operations, string constants, and numeric constants. Strings provide additional operations, such as extracting substrings, concatenating strings, transforming strings into lower case or upper case, and determining the length of a string. OCL expressions may also contain boolean implications. A conditional operator may also be used, as shown in the following example:

Customer
title = (if isMale = true
          then 'Mr'
          else 'Ms'
       endif)

Preconditions and postconditions may be specified by changing the context of the OCL expression. In other words, the context is not a class, but a method:

BankAccount::withdraw(float amount)
pre: amount > getCreditLimit() implies hasTempOverdraft()
pre: not isBlocked()
post: balance@pre - amount = balance

Postconditions may contain an @pre keyword, which indicates the value of an attribute or association at the start of the execution of the operation.

In Sect. 2.2.4, we defined a number of operations on collections for our contract language. OCL also allows us to deal with collections. It is important that any OCL expression on collections is meant to be side effect free, regardless of whether or not this would be difficult to implement. OCL supports the following types of collection:

- A Set is a collection of an arbitrary number of elements of arbitrary type. Each object contained in a set is unique. Objects in a Set are accessible via typical Set operators.
- A Bag is like a Set, but it can contain duplicate elements.
- A Sequence is like a Bag, but the elements are ordered. The term "ordered" means that each element has a unique sequence number, like array elements in an ordinary programming language.

Figure 9 shows all of the operations that are possible using collections.

Operation	Description
int **size**	Returns the number of elements in the collection.
int **count**(object)	Returns the number of occurrences of an object in the collection.
Boolean **includes**(object)	Returns true if the object is an element of the collection.
Boolean **includesAll**(collection)	Returns true if all elements of the parameter collection are contained in the current collection.
Boolean **isEmpty**	Returns true if the collection contains no elements.
Boolean **notEmpty**	Returns true if the collection contains one or more elements.
iterate(expression)	The expression is evaluated for every element in the collection. The type of the result depends on the expression.
sum()	Returns the addition of all elements in the collection. The elements must be of a type that supports addition (such as real, integer).
Boolean **exists**(expression)	Returns true if the expression is true for at least one element in the collection (existential quantification).
Boolean **forAll**(expression)	Returns true if the expression is true for all elements (universal quantification).
collection **select**(expression)	Returns a collection containing all objects of the original collection for which the Boolean expression is true.
collection **collect**(expression)	This operation iterates over the collection, computes a value for each object in the collection, and puts the evaluated values into a collection to be returned.
collection **reject**(expression)	Returns a collection that contains all objects of the original collection for which the Boolean expression is not true.

Fig. 9. Standard operations on all collections

The following examples illustrate the use of some of the OCL operations defined in Fig. 9:

<u>Customer</u>
accounts.notEmpty

<u>BankAccount</u>
transactions->forAll(t: Transaction | t.date < Date.now)
transactions->includesAll(transactions@pre)

<u>Customer ::addBankAccount(a : BankAccount)</u>
pre: accounts->exists(a: BankAccount | not a.isBlocked())

The operations defined in Fig. 9 basically have the same meaning regardless of the specific type of collection. Figure 10 shows a number of operations that are available in principle for every type of collection, but that have a variable meaning, depending on the specific type of collection.

Operation	Description
Collection = collection	Two sets are equal if all of the elements are the same. Additionally, for bags, the number of times an element is present must also be the same. For two sequences, the order of the elements must also be the same.
Collection **union**(collection)	Combines two collections into a new one. A set may be combined with a bag and vice versa, while a sequence may only be combined with another sequence.
Collection **including**(object)	Adds an object to the collection (by returning a new collection containing the added object). If the collection is a set, the element is only added if it is not already contained in the set. If the collection is a sequence, the object is appended.
Collection **excluding**(object)	Removes an object from the collection (by returning a new collection that does not contain the excluded object). From a bag or sequence, this operation removes all occurrences of the object.
Collection **intersection**(collection)	Returns a collection that contains the objects contained in both collections. Sets or bags may not be combined with sequences.

Fig. 10. Operations on collections with variable meaning

While the operations specified in Fig. 9 are side effect free by their nature, some of the operations specified in Fig. 10 (union, including, excluding, and intersection) change collections. Nevertheless, in OCL these operations are side effect free, as these operations always work on a copy of the original collection. Two examples (that express the same semantics) of the use of some of the operations defined in Fig. 10 are as follows:

Customer::addBankAccount(a: BankAccount)
post: accounts->excluding(a) = accounts@pre

Customer::addBankAccount(a: BankAccount)
post: accounts@pre->including(a) = accounts

Besides these general operations on any collection (with some restrictions, as explained in Fig. 10), some operations are only available for specific collections. Figure 11 gives an overview.

Type	Operation	Description
Set	set – set	The minus operation results in a new set that contains all of the elements that are in the first set but not in the second set.
	set **symmetricDifference**(set)	The operation returns a new set that contains all of the elements that are not in both sets.
Sequence	object **first**()	Returns the first object of the sequence.
	object **last**()	Returns the last object of the sequence.
	object **at**(Integer)	Returns the object at the given index.
	sequence **append**(object)	Adds the object to the end of the sequence
	sequence **preprend**(object)	Adds the object to the beginning of the sequence.
	sequence **subSequence** (lower: Integer, upper: Integer)	Returns a sequence that contains all of the objects in the range [lower..upper].

Fig. 11. Specific operations on collections

Some of the operations specified in Fig. 11 (append and preprend) also change collections. Nevertheless, in OCL these operations are side effect free, as these operations always work on a copy of the original collection. Some examples that illustrate the use of some of the operations listed in Fig. 11 are as follows:

Customer::addBankAccount(a: BankAccount)
post: accounts->last() = a

Customer::addBankAccount(a: BankAccount)
post: accounts@pre->append(a) = accounts

Unfortunately, OCL has no explicit rules to indicate whether or not an assertion in a superclass is inherited by the subclasses. Warmer and Kleppe [Warmer99] suggest giving assertions (invariants, postconditions, and preconditions) a meaningful semantics. They suggest the semantics as proposed by Meyer [Meyer97a] (see Sect. 2.3.1); that is, the Design by Contract principle.

3.2.3   Evaluation of OCL

In Sect. 2.4.2, we defined a number of criteria with which to evaluate the assertion support that is available in current programming languages and systems. In Sect. 2.4.4, we carried out an evaluation of programming languages and systems that support assertion in different ways. In this section, we use the criteria to evaluate OCL.

BAS and AAS criteria (OCL)

System	BAS-1	BAS-2	BAS-3	AAS-1	AAS-2	AAS-3
OCL	ns	1	1	1	1	3

OCL has no implementation perspective. Therefore, it is not possible to provide assertion annotations in the implementation of a method (see BAS-1). OCL is meant to be side effect free, which is one of the major strengths of this language. The number of operations available on collections supersedes the possibilities as described in our language (see Sect. 2.2.4). Nevertheless, OCL does not take into consideration efficiency problems associated with assuring side effect free operations on collections. We have also emphasized this issue in our language. Therefore, we have excluded operations that are difficult to implement free of side effects. OCL also supports operations on enumerations (not explained in this chapter), conditional operations, and operations for various kinds of type tests.

SBS and RMA criteria (OCL)

System	SBS-1	SBS-2	SBS-3	RMA-1	RMA-2	RMA-3
OCL	1	ns	ns	ns	ns	ns

OCL allows us to express constraints—that is, assertions—on arbitrary UML elements. Therefore, it is also possible to express correctness conditions upon interfaces. Unfortunately, OCL does not define at all whether assertions are inherited. Therefore, the correctness requirements as defined by SBS-2 and SBS-3 are not supported. As already explained in Sect. 3.2.1, OCL is not designed to be executable. It is a pure modeling language. In order to ensure that assertions specified during development of a UML model may be transformed into a programming language or into a programming system that supports assertions, only a subset of OCL may be used. We will comment on this later, in the best practice section (see Sect. 3.3).

3.2.4   Further Developments

In September 2000, the OMG issued a Request for Proposal (an RfP) for UML 2.0 OCL [OMG00]. The main reason behind this RfP is to enhance and enlarge the current OCL specification. The goals for this specification enhancement are as follows (see [Boldsoft02]):

- *The introduction of a metamodel for OCL:* Currently, OCL has no metamodel, which makes it difficult to integrate with the UML metamodel. The OCL metamodel to be introduced will define the concepts and semantics of OCL and act as an abstract syntax for the language. Furthermore, on the basis of this abstract syntax, a redefinition of the concrete OCL syntax will be undertaken. This separation of abstract syntax and concrete syntax is important in order to enable alternative concrete syntaxes (e.g., visual constraint diagrams).

- *Enhancing the expressibility and usability of OCL:* As already described in previous sections, OCL allows us to describe constraints. OCL 2.0 will also be a general object query language that can be used whenever expressions over UML models are required.

- *Enhanced preciseness of OCL semantics:* The precise semantics of OCL should be defined to the greatest feasible extent.

There are a number of planned enhancements (compared to the original OCL 1.1 specification [OCL97]) that will also have impact on the usage of OCL as a constraint language (as we see it in this section). The remainder of this section briefly describes some planned vital changes (from the point of view of added syntax and semantics) to OCL [Boldsoft02]. We will not go into too much detail, as the final OCL 2.0 specification, and especially the operations available for collections (see [Boldsoft02]), may yet be changed:

- OCL 2.0 expressions may contain so-called let expressions. Sometimes a sub-expression is used more than once in an expression. The let expression allows us to define an attribute or operations that may be used in a constraint:

```
Customer
let hasTitle(t : String) : Boolean = (self.title = t) in
isMale() implies hasTitle('Mr')
```

- OCL 2.0 will allow us to specify so-called Message expressions. Message expressions will allow us to guarantee that, for example, in a postcondition, a specific message has been sent to a specific receiver. Additionally, even the result values may be accessed. In the example given below, the postcondition ensures that method isGoodForAmount of class Customer was called in the body of the method with the appropriate parameter amount. However, timely ordering of the messages cannot be expressed:

```
BankAccount::widthdraw(amount: Float)
post: let msg: OclMessage= customer^isGoodForAmount(amount) in
    msg.isSent()
```

- OCL 2.0 collections may also contain collections. Previous releases of OCL always flattened collections. This can still be achieved by applying flattening operations explicitly.

- OCL 2.0 collections will provide additional operations; for example, count, one, any, isUnique, and sortedBy. A detailed description may be found in Boldsoft et al. [Boldsoft02].

- OCL 2.0 will support a Tuple as an additional type. It is possible to combine several values into a Tuple. A Tuple consists of named parts, each of which can have a distinct type:

```
Customer
let statistics=
   {
      noOfAccounts: Integer= accounts->size(),
      creditworthy: Boolean= account->exists(a: BankAccount | not a.isBlocked()
   }
```

The submission [Boldsoft02], which is a response to the OMG RfP [OMG00], is currently being reviewed. The OMG plans to adopt the specification in the near future.

3.3 Guidelines and Rules

As already mentioned in the introduction to this chapter, we have tried to set out a number of guidelines—that is, rules—about how to formulate assertions (what should be specified, and what should be avoided). The guidelines set out in this section do not consider the analysis and design process itself, but focus on the task of formulating assertions. The best practices described in this section are a compilation and unification of hints and principles that can be found, explicitly or implicitly, in Coleman et al. [Coleman94], Meyer [Meyer97a], Warmer and Kleppe [Warmer99], Mitchell and McKim [Mitchell99, Mitchell01], Mitchell et al. [Mitchell97], D'Souza and Wills [D'Souza99], Waldén and Nerson [Waldén95], Jézéquel et al. [Jézéquel00], and Cook and Daniels [Cook94].

Methods that rely on assertion techniques should be a major source of guidelines. Methods that explicitly consider assertions (with formal or informal notation) are BON [Waldén95], Catalysis [D'Souza99], and Fusion [Coleman94]. Before presenting our guidelines, we will give a rough overview of the above-mentioned methods with respect to assertions:

- *BON:* This method explicitly supports assertions in its diagrams as well as in the method itself. The syntax and semantics of assertion expressions is equal to Design by Contract as supported by Eiffel [Meyer92] and developed by Meyer [Meyer97a]. Besides general remarks, no specific guidelines can be extracted.
- *Catalysis:* This method emphasizes assertions for specifying the behavior of methods, so-called actions in Catalysis. OCL syntax is used for describing assertions. The approach also extends the OCL language. Catalysis provides a large number of examples of how to specify certain behavioral aspects. Unfortunately, the examples are specific and it is therefore difficult to extract general guidelines.
- *Fusion:* This method propagates an informal style for specifying assertions. Nevertheless, assertions are considered to be key elements of analysis and design models. As with BON [Waldén95], only general remarks can be distilled.

In this section, we introduce two new terms that it is important to understand. A *query* is a method that retrieves portions of the state of an object or that computes and returns a value without changing the state of the object. A *command* is a method that changes the state of an object. This distinction is important for some of the rules that we define in this section.

In order to enhance readability, we use the term *rule* in this section synonymously for best practice, hint, and principle. The description of each rule follows a specific pattern:

- *Name:* The unique name of the rule.
- *Description:* This captures the basic idea of the rule.
- *References:* Where available, references to the origin of the rule are given.
- *Example:* The example may either show how to use the rule or it may illustrate violations of the rule. For the description of examples we will use UML diagrams, as well as OCL syntax for describing the assertions.
- *Discussion:* This section provides an in-depth discussion of the rule. This is an optional part of the description and for simple rules it may be skipped.

R1: Separate queries and commands

- *Description:* Right from the beginning, it is important to distinguish between operations that return values and do not change the state of the object (queries) and operations that change the state of the object (commands). Additionally, in many cases queries can be specified in terms of basic queries. Queries defined in terms of basic queries are called derived queries.
- *References:* The rule can be found as two principles, in Mitchell and McKim [Mitchell99, Mitchell01].
- *Example:*

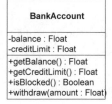

Class BankAccount offers two basic queries; that is, getBalance and getMaxOverdraft. The method widthdraw is an example of a command. The method isBlocked is a derived query, as it can be specified in terms of the basic queries (a BankAccount is blocked when the balance is equal to or less than the credit limit).

- *Discussion:* This is a basic rule that does not directly lead to specific preconditions, postconditions, and invariants. Nevertheless, this rule is fundamental for other rules, such as **R6** and **R7**. Additionally, it leads to a better understanding of the interrelationships in a class.

R2: Avoid complex navigation expressions

- *Description:* Assertion expressions may contain navigation expressions that involve large portions of the class model. First, this makes assertion expressions difficult to understand. Secondly, this makes details of distant objects

visible to the object where the navigation starts. Assertion expression should therefore be limited to the directly associated classes of a type.
- *Reference:* [Warmer99].
- *Example:*

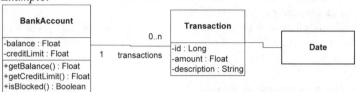

Given the above diagram, we could express the fact that the date of all transactions must be in the past in the following way:

```
BankAccount
transactions->forAll(t: Transaction | t.date <= Date.now)
```

Alternately—that is, bearing this rule in mind—we could achieve the same effect by adding an invariant to the type Transaction:

```
Transaction
self.date <= Date.now
```

- *Discussion:* This rule facilitates the understanding of behavioral properties of classes and also makes it easier to change assertions, as the assertions are more local to their associated classes.

R3: Avoid complex assertions

- *Description:* Use of the and operator allows us to formulate complex assertions. Avoid the and operator and split assertions.
- *References:* [Coleman94, Warmer99].
- *Example:* In our BankAccount example (see rule **R1**), the postcondition of the command isBlocked may be expressed as follows:

```
BankAccount::isBlocked(): Boolean
post: result = (getBalance() <= getCreditLimit()) and not isBlocked()
```

Alternately—that is, bearing this rule in mind—we should split this postcondition into two separate postconditions:

```
BankAccount::isBlocked(): Boolean
post: result = (getBalance() <= getCreditLimit())
post: not isBlocked()
```

- *Discussion:* Each assertion becomes less complex and therefore easier to understand. Additionally, it is easier to find out at run time (provided that you transform your OCL assertions in such a way that they become available in the implementation) which assertion was violated, as the run-time checking mechanism usually states which assertion was broken. For complex assertions, therefore, the real problem cannot be directly localized—any of the expressions concatenated by the and operator could be the source of the problem.

R4: Ensure proper use of design patterns

- *Description:* Design patterns [Gamma95] play in important role in modern software engineering, as they allow us to capture complex concepts easily, and assign unique names; for example, Factory, Visitor, and Mediator. In order to ensure that the properties inherently associated with a pattern are fulfilled, it is crucial to capture these properties by means of assertions.
- *Reference:* [Jézéquel00].
- *Example:* Jézéquel et al. devoted an entire book to this topic [Jézéquel00]. Detailed examples of the usage of contracts in the context of patterns can be found there.

R5: Check preconditions properly

- *Description:* It is difficult to state useful rules for preconditions, as the proper use of preconditions depends heavily on the specific problem. The general rule (formulated by Meyer [Meyer97a]) says that no precondition should be too large or too small. The use of a large number of preconditions for routines implies a rather demanding style of programming, as clients have to ensure that they properly fulfill the obligations imposed on them by the preconditions. On the other hand, a tolerant style uses few preconditions. A precondition may only be included in the specification of a method if it is possible to justify the need for the precondition in terms of the specification.
- *Reference:* [Meyer97a].
- *Example:* Meyer gives an example of a square-root method from a mathematical library. In this context, either a demanding or a tolerant style can be followed. An example of the demanding style is given below—the tolerant style would omit any precondition:

```
MathLib::sqrt(x: Float): Float
pre: x >= 0
```

Another example is a push method in a Stack. For this push method, the following precondition seems to be reasonable:

```
Stack::push(o: Object)
pre: not isFull()
```

Nevertheless, this precondition only makes sense when your specification forces you to guarantee that the number of elements stored in the Stack is limited.

- *Discussion:* In the above square-root example, it is obvious that the demanding style must be followed, as by definition the square root of a negative number is undefined. The stack example shows that whether or not the precondition is correct depends on the requirements. Therefore, it has to be decided for each case whether the requirements imply preconditions.

R6: *Express results of derived queries by means of basic queries*

- *Description:* Derived queries should be expressed in terms of basic queries (see rule **R1**). Therefore, it is possible to write a postcondition for each derived query that specifies the result of the query in terms of basic queries.
- *References:* [Mitchell99, Mitchell01].
- *Example:* In our BankAccount example (see rule **R1**), the postcondition of the derived query isBlocked may be expressed as follows:

```
BankAccount::isBlocked(): Boolean
post: result = (getBalance() < getCreditLimit())
```

- *Discussion:* This rule leads to a better understanding of the dependencies in a class.

R7: *Specify effects of commands on basic queries*

- *Description:* A command is method that changes the state of the object (see rule **R1**). The state of the object is made visible to clients by means of queries and derived queries. Therefore, it is essential to describe the effect of a command in its postcondition by means of the changes that it makes to the basic queries. Often, commands do not have an effect on all basic queries, but only on a subset of them. Of course, only the effect of changes on the affected basic queries should be part of the postconditions.
- *References:* [Mitchell99, Mitchell01].
- *Example:*

BankAccount
-balance : Float
-creditLimit : Float
+getBalance() : Float
+getCreditLimit() : Float
+isBlocked() : Boolean
+withdraw(amount : Float)

The method—that is, the command withdraw—only changes the state of balance. The creditLimit is not changed:

```
BankAccount::withdraw(amount: Float)
post: getBalance() =
    (if isBlocked()
        then getBalance()@pre
        else getBalance()@pre - amount
    endif)
```

The above postcondition considers that balance is only changed in cases in which the account is not blocked. The above postcondition does not explicitly state that creditLimit must be unchanged. Therefore, there is no guarantee that creditLimit will remain unchanged. In order to ensure this, it is necessary to include it in the postcondition:

```
BankAccount::withdraw(amount: Float)
post: getCreditLimit() = getCreditLimit()@pre
```

- *Discussion:* Consequently, application of this rule leads to a deep understanding of how commands change behavior. When a command does not change a basic query (see the creditLimit example above), this fact need not necessarily be expressed in the postcondition.

R8: *Ensure side effect free queries*

- *Description:* One important criterion for assertions is that they are side effect free. This is the reason why languages for expressing assertions usually do not contain operations that allow assignments to instance variables. Nevertheless, assertion expressions may contain method calls. Any assertion expression should only call queries; that is, methods that inherently do not change the state of the object. Thus every query should explicitly state in its postcondition that it does not alter the state of the object.
- *Example:* In our BankAccount example (see rule **R1**) the postcondition of, for example, the query getBalance may be expressed as follows:

```
BankAccount::getBalance(): Float
post: getBalance() = getBalance()@pre and
              getCreditLimit()= getCreditLimit@pre
```

- *Discussion:* In principle, the approach presented here ensures side effect free queries, with the negative effect of a substantial increase in postconditions. As a compromise, it would be sufficient to explicitly mark queries during analysis and the early stages of design. Later in the development process, the assertions have to be included in the programming language used. At that stage, these postconditions can be added manually or by means of tool support to the implementation. In cases in which the underlying programming language can ensure side effect free operations (e.g., C++ offers so-called const methods), the postconditions described above can even be omitted. This has the additional positive effect that side effect free queries are guaranteed by the compiler. The Java programming language offers no language construct that guarantees side effect free operations.

R9: *Ensure proper object creation*

- *Description:* Often, operations on objects create new objects. These objects are either returned by that operation or are added to the state of the original object or those of associated objects. For such operations, it should be systematically checked whether the objects were properly created by that operation. Additionally, it may be checked whether that object has been properly initialized.

- *Example:* In our BankAccount example (see rule **R2**) the postcondition of, for example, the operation withdraw may be expressed as follows:

    BankAccount::withdraw(amount: Float)
    post: not isBlocked() implies
               ((transactions->Size() – transactions@pre->Size() = 1 and
               transactions->last().getAmount() = amount))

    As stated in rule **R4**, design patterns play an important role. For the factory pattern (see [Gamma95]) the creational operations should, for example, be guarded by appropriate postconditions. Here is an example of a GraphicObject factory in a drawing program that uses a makePolygon factory method:

    GraphicObjectFactory::makePolygon(): Polygon
    post: return != null

- *Discussion:* As long as the operation changes the state of the object, this rule is a specialization of rule **R7**. Consequently, application of this rule leads to a better understanding of the object creation processes inasmuch as they are relevant to the model (temporary object creations should not be considered).

3.4   The Impact of Contracts on Quality

The aim of providing guidelines and best practices for formulating assertions is to enhance the quality of the products to be developed. The emphasis of assertions is on specifying the behavior of software components more precisely than without use of the technique. In Chap. 1 we gave an overview (see Fig. 3) of the positive effects of assertion and scenario techniques on quality.

In Chap. 2 we identified a number of quality criteria that it is important to consider when developing a product. We believe that using assertions throughout the development process has positive effects on a number of these quality criteria:

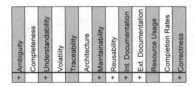

- *Ambiguity:* Assertions clearly have a positive effect on reducing ambiguity, as they are specified in a more formal manner, and therefore they reduce the ambiguity that is inherent in textual prose specifications.
- *Understandability:* Assertions enhance understandability for designers and implementers, as aspects of behavior (both at the class and at the method level) are defined in a less ambiguous way—which makes them easier to understand.

Furthermore, if a contract-based development process is followed—that is, a process in which it is important to clearly specify more elaborate interfaces (i.e., interfaces beyond ordinary signatures in the Java programming language or C++)—project members tend to capture essential constraints at the class and method level. Furthermore, designers and implementers are used to more formal descriptions and should experience no difficulty in reading and understanding assertions—at least when the complexity of the assertions language is low, as is the case for OCL [OCL97].

- *Maintainability:* Maintainability is clearly supported by the use of assertions, for various reasons. (1) In an error situation you can first check whether the client that is using a class is adhering to the contract; that is, whether it assures that the preconditions are fulfilled or whether the implementation conforms to the specification (postconditions). This is often sufficient to locate the error. (2) It is primarily not necessary to understand the code, but only to understand the contracts that are related to the error situation—this facilitates localization of the error. (3) For all other error situations, the maintenance personnel definitely know that the client and the postconditions are adhering to the specification, and that therefore the error must be something different—this helps much in localizing the error. (4) Furthermore, fixing an error may possibly lead to an adjustment of the postconditions, as the reason for the error may be a misunderstood implementation guarantee (postcondition). If this is not the case (that is, the specific error was not captured by the postconditions) additional postconditions can be added to make the specification more complete.

- *Reusability:* The application of assertions facilitates reusability. (1) The behavior of a class can be more easily assessed, as its interface is described more clearly than with an ordinary textual comment. (2) Directly reusing a class means putting it into a special context. The preconditions specified for the reused class assure that it is correctly used; that is, according to its specification. (3) In other situations, reusing a class means extending it by adding additional behavior or by changing the initial behavior. During this task, the postconditions specified for the class assist in this process, as they assure that the correctness conditions imposed by the superclass are also valid for the newly created subclass.

- *Internal documentation:* The internal documentation is enhanced, as not only is the principal functional behavior described using text, but the additionally available formal descriptions lead to a more precise understanding of the behavior of the class. This is especially important when reusing classes by means of subclassing.

- *External documentation:* The assertions of a class are usually made available to reusers and therefore provide an enhanced description about how to use the class (preconditions) and what to expect from this class; that is, what functional behavior to expect (postconditions).

- *Correctness:* Assuming that the assertions specified for a system reflect the desired behavior (from the user's perspective), assertions are an important step toward more correct software. Although it is not yet possible to verify (in the mathematical sense) the correctness of classes, the assertions provided enhance the testability. There are even tools available (e.g., [Parasoft02a, Parasoft02b]) that try to automatically derive test cases, taking the pre- and postconditions of a class into consideration, in order to show that a class does not fulfill its obligations (although a client fulfills the preconditions); that is, the contract is broken due to violation of the postconditions. For more details of this important issue, see Sect. 6.3.4.

4 Scenarios

Summary: The gathering, definition, and specification of requirements is a difficult task. A number of techniques support the documentation of these requirements—for example, requirement lists, data-flow diagrams, and entity/relationship diagrams—and each has its specific advantages and disadvantages. Use cases were introduced by Jacobson [Jacobson92] in 1992; they have now become part of the Unified Process [Jacobson99] and can be expressed using UML syntax. A number of published reports ([Achour99], [Cox00], [Cox01], [Lilly99], and [Palph02]) indicate that use cases are easy to understand and can be utilized for requirements validation by domain experts or users. Furthermore, use cases facilitate communication with customers and therefore often lead to more complete and more correct requirements specifications. This makes them better suited for documenting requirements than traditional techniques.

The term "scenario" as used in this book is a synonym for the term "use case". The term scenario is used throughout this book to indicate that the emphasis is on the concepts and ideas that underlie use cases, rather than on the specific use case approach as understood by the Unified Process or UML. Scenarios may capture local or global behavior; they may present an external or an internal view of a system. Scenarios may be abstract in the sense that they capture the general interaction of system components or the interaction of specific instances of the system. Scenarios may be documented by using pure textual descriptions or tabular representations, or by means of time-line diagrams.

Keywords: Scenario, Interaction, Parallel interactions, Timing issues, Notation for describing scenarios

4.1 Introduction

A scenario is a typical interaction between a computer system and its clients. A client may be either a physical person or another computer system. As Fowler [Fowler99] points out, scenarios are not an invention of modern software engineering approaches, but have always been used to capture user requirements. Figure 12 shows a typical scenario for scheduling an appointment between a customer and a designer, using a tabular representation (a detailed discussion of notational issues is given in Sect. 4.4):

Scenario Name:	Schedule Customer Appointment
Overview:	Enter an appointment with the designer and customer to take initial measurements and to determine the best design for the customer.
Basic Course of Events:	- The office administrator, using date/time parameters supplied by the customer, requests a list of available times at which the designer and customer can have a consultation. - The system responds with a list of available appointment times. - The office administrator picks one of the times or enters a different time based on the customer's preference. - The system records the appointment time and later notifies the designer of the upcoming appointment.

Fig. 12. An example scenario

Defining the requirements of a system that is to be designed and implemented is a difficult task. A number of challenges are associated with this early phase of activity concerning requirements elicitation and definition [Kulak00]. In this introductory section, we discuss some of them to provide better motivation for why it is important to use scenarios throughout the entire software development process. Besides the issues discussed, others—such as traceability, conciseness, redundancy, and modifiability—play important roles in the analysis phase. A comprehensive and general discussion of the problems associated with requirements gathering and specification can be found in the requirements engineering literature (see, e.g., [Davis93], [Kotonya97], [Robertson99], and [Sommerville97]).

How do we Find Out what Future Users Really Need? This is a difficult problem, which is related to the complexity of challenging systems combined with inappropriate approaches to requirements gathering. This is an issue where scenarios contribute a great deal, as we will see in the remainder of this chapter.

Are there any Conflicting Requirements? As long as the requirements are not specified using a defined syntax with clear underlying semantics, automatic detection of conflicting requirements using proofing tools is practically impossible. Here, scenarios contribute just a little, as the documentation of major parts of the requirements using scenario approaches leads to more easily reviewable documents, thus facilitating the detection of conflicting requirements.

What is the Proper Structure for Documenting Requirements? Current standards, such as IEEE 830-1998 [IEEE98], have a functional approach to the structuring of software requirements documents. According to this standard, a requirements document is divided into two major parts: a general part, with sections devoted to the aim of the project, definitions, acronyms, the system context, assumptions, and dependencies; and a second part that contains the specific requirements. The typical structure of a specific requirements section that adheres to the IEEE 830-1998 standard would be as follows:

3 Specific Requirements
    3.1 External Interfaces
        3.1.1 User Interfaces
        3.1.2 Hardware Interfaces
        3.1.3 Software Interfaces
        3.1.4 Communication Interfaces
    3.2 Functional Requirements
        3.2.1 Mode A
            3.2.1.1 Functional Requirement 1
            3.2.1.2 Functional Requirement 2
            ...

        ...
    3.3 Performance
    3.4 Logical Database Design
    3.5 Design Constraints
    3.6 Characteristics
        3.6.1 Availability
        3.6.2 Security
        ...
    3.7 Other Requirements

Obviously, this structure is highly systematic and facilitates the work of system designers and implementers, as it reflects the needs of these project participants. Unfortunately, it is not suitable for a customer who has to review these requirements [Kulak00]. The major drawback of this structure—from the customer's point of view—is that the processes that are usually supported by the software are not directly visible to the customer.

In a banking system with an automated teller machine, for instance, the customer is interested in reviewing whether the process of, say, the withdrawal of money was well understood, with all its subtleties, by the analysts. A structure as depicted above does not support him or her in this review task. On the contrary, it is a hindrance, as—in order to be able to seriously check whether the requirements were well understood by the analysts—the customer may have to scan a number of disjunctive functional requirements, spread throughout the document, to find out whether any misunderstandings or misinterpretations still exist. Therefore, the documentation of requirements using scenario approaches leads to a more natural organization of the requirements document. We will discuss this issue in detail in this section.

During design and implementation, it is a challenging task to define a class structure (assuming object-oriented implementation). Here again, scenarios are a good starting point for the definition of this structure. In our opinion, the contribution of scenario approaches to high-quality design cannot be overestimated.

Scenarios play a major role in integration and acceptance tests. As a scenario is a step-by-step description of the interaction of the system with its environment, this is the perfect basis for deriving test cases, and later test scripts, for integration testing. The advantage is that the test scripts can be more or less directly derived from the scenarios of the requirements specification. This means that the scenarios that the customers and developers agreed upon in the early phases of the development process really are the basis for checking the correctness of the software.

To summarize, there are a number of reasons why scenarios should be used throughout the software development process. Authors such as Holbrock [Holbrock90], Firesmith [Firesmith95], Jacobson et al. [Jacobson92], Wilkinson [Wilkinson95], Kulak and Guiney [Kulak00], and Cockburn [Cockburn00] share our opinion (see also [Behringer97]):

- Scenarios facilitate the breaking-up of a system into meaningful pieces, by concentrating on an external view of the software system.
- Scenarios (regardless of their notation) are easy to understand and to validate by users. Therefore, they support and enhance communication with different stakeholders in a software project.
- Scenarios can be used in integration testing both to define the requirements and to test subsystems, and to test the final system.
- In a project with an incremental development process, the increments can be defined in terms of scenarios; that is, the most important scenarios for the daily business of a customer can be implemented first.
- Scenarios are a starting point for deriving an object-oriented design for the system.

As already mentioned, scenarios have always been used (more or less informally) to elicit and document user requirements. Nevertheless, Ivar Jacobson has systematized these approaches [Jacobson92], and has coined the term *use case* for scenarios. Nowadays, scenarios can also be specified by means of the UML notation.

In the remainder of Chap. 4, we describe and illustrate the basic concepts, enhanced concepts, and notation in a general way. In this chapter, we concentrate on the general concepts that underlie scenario techniques, but we do not compare them with the popular UML concepts and notation. A discussion of the UML approach is postponed until Chap. 5.

4.2 Basic Concepts

As already mentioned in the introductory section, scenarios are useful for capturing and documenting user requirements. In this section, we will try to describe the concepts that underlie scenario techniques. The descriptions given here are independent of any specific notation or method. The organization of the concepts presented in this section partially follows the structure given by Behringer [Behringer97]. Scenarios describe the behavior of a system, or of parts of a system. There are of course different approaches to describing behavior. To some extent, the contract approach described in Chaps. 2 and 3 also captures parts of the behavior of a system. The emphasis of the scenario approach is on capturing the interactions between system properties; that is, the objects of a system. We will concentrate on these kinds of interaction in this section.

4.2.1   Internal and External Views of Behavior

At a conceptual level, object interactions can be viewed in either an internal or an external perspective.

The external view emphasizes all of the interactions between the system and its participants. A participant can be a physical person, but it can also be an abstract organization or a computer system. The system is described by a number of single scenarios. Variants of external view descriptions [Hsia94] concentrate on a single participant and all of its interactions.

The internal view not only shows the interactions between the system and its environment, but also the interactions between the different parts of a system. Figure 13 visualizes the difference between external and internal views.

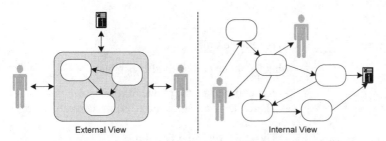

Fig. 13. External and internal views

The external and internal views of a system are complementary; that is, the external view tries to capture and visualize the "big picture" of a system, while the internal view usually concentrates on the parts of a system. An internal view typically captures the details of one single scenario.

4.2.2   Types of Interaction

As already mentioned in the introduction, a scenario shows a typical interaction between the objects of the system or between the system and its environment. Therefore, an interaction is a message from one object to another object (or to itself). Interactions between objects can be described at different levels of abstraction; that is, at the technical level or at the conceptual level:

- *Technical level:* A technical interaction corresponds to a certain construct in the final software system. A technical interaction could be a procedure call, a remote procedure call, or the sending of a message from one object to another.
- *Conceptual level:* A conceptual interaction does not consider the technical interaction at all, but focuses on the interaction itself, without considering how to technically implement the interaction.

Both technical events and conceptual events may be specified at different levels of abstraction. Figure 14 shows an example of a scenario for making a phone call at a abstract level, while Fig. 15 shows the same scenario at a more detailed level.

Scenario Name:	Make Phone Call
Overview:	Make a phone call to another person.
Basic Course of Events:	- The caller takes the phone off the hook and receives the dialing tone. - The caller dials the number. - ...

Fig. 14. Make Phone Call (abstract)

Scenario Name:	Make Phone Call
Overview:	Make a phone call to another person.
Basic Course of Events:	- The caller takes the phone off the hook - The caller waits until he or she receives the dialing tone. - The caller dials the first digit. - The dialing tone is stopped. - The caller dials the remaining digits until the whole number has been dialed. - ...

Fig. 15. Make Phone Call (abstract)

Both use case descriptions describe part of the phone call process, but at different levels of abstraction. The determination of which representation is more suitable depends on the specific situation (e.g., familiarity with the application domain, or progress in the analysis phase). We will discuss this issue in more detail in Sect. 4.4.

Besides this distinction between technical and conceptual interactions at different levels of abstraction, we can also distinguish between *notifications* and *requests*:

- *Notification:* A notification (or one-way message) is a message that is sent to another object (or to itself), optionally passing additional data with this message but not waiting for any confirmation or return value from the receiver of the notification. At a technical level, inter-process or intra-process notifications are possible; that is, the receiver of the message either resides in the same address space (e.g., as an operating system thread) or resides in a different operating system process. This distinction implies different implementations of notification services.
- *Request:* A request implies a client–server relationship between two objects; that is, the sending object waits for a reply from the receiving object. Comparable to notifications, the receiver of a request resides within the same operating system process or can only be received remotely. Therefore, a typical technical solution for implementing requests is either a procedure (method) call for intra-process communication or a remote procedure call (remote method invocation) for the inter-process case.

When describing scenarios using a text notation (see, e.g., Fig. 15), a distinction can be made between these different types of interaction (notification versus request) through the use of appropriate phrases. For example, in step 2 of Fig. 15, "The caller waits until he or she receives the dialing tone" explicitly states that something is awaited; that is, the reply to a request. When time-line diagrams are used to document scenarios (see Sect. 4.4), different shapes for interactions can usually be used to distinguish between notifications and interactions.

4.2.3   Single-Object and Inter-Object Scenarios

In principle, a scenario might either show the interactions between several objects or, alternately, the interaction between one object and its environment. In the first case (the inter-object scenario), the objects taking part in the interaction may be of different classes. They may be either physical people or another computer system or subsystem.

Usually, scenarios show inter-object interactions. Nevertheless, scenarios showing the interactions between one object and its environment can be used when the focus of the scenario is on capturing the interactions of one specific object. Furthermore, focusing on one object has the advantage that the interactions can be divided into input and output interactions, thus capturing the global behavior of one object with its environment.

4.2.4   Scenario Instances and Scenario Types

Scenario instances show one specific interaction between specific objects, taking part in this interaction. Typically, the objects that take part in the scenario have specific names, and specific values are used in the interaction, rather than abstract parameters. Figure 16 shows an example of a phone call scenario between John and Paul.

Scenario Name:	John Calls Paul
Overview:	John makes a phone call to Paul.
Basic Course of Events:	- John takes the phone off the hook. - John waits until he receives the dialing tone. - John dials "1". - The dialing tone is stopped. - John dials 237890. - ...

Fig. 16. Making a phone call (Scenario Instance)

While a scenario instance describes one specific interaction, a scenario type specifies a set of possible scenario instances—in this case, abstract object names and abstract values are used as interaction parameters. Figure 15 is a good example of a scenario type, describing at a more general level the scenario of making a phone call. In order to be able to express all possible interactions of a scenario type, sequence information—that is, iteration, alternation, and concurrency (see Sect. 4.3)—has to be added to the interactions.

In the general case, scenario types are more interesting than scenario instances, as they capture a set of possible interactions in a compact way. Nevertheless, scenario instances are useful in the elicitation phase, as partners in the analysis process might not be used to abstract formulations; they can better understand and validate scenarios using concrete examples.

4.2.5   The Scope of Scenario Types

The scope of a scenario type has two dimensions: the lengths of the scenario instances and the number of possible scenario instances captured by a single scenario type. Concerning the length of a scenario, different approaches can be followed. One business case (e.g., making a phone call—see Fig. 15) might be captured using one single scenario, or by splitting up the large scenario into a number of distinct separate scenarios. Figure 17 shows our phone call example split up into three scenarios.

Scenario Name:	Start Phone Call
Overview:	Initiate a phone call to a callee.

Basic Course of Events:	- The caller takes the phone off the hook and receives the dialing tone. - The caller dials the first digit. - The dialing tone is stopped. - The caller dials the rest of the number. - If the callee is busy, then the caller receives the busy tone; else, the callee's telephone rings and the caller receives the ringing tone.

Scenario Name:	Answer Phone Call
Overview:	The caller answers the phone call.
Basic Course of Events:	- The caller answers the call. - The line is connected. - ...

Scenario Name:	The Caller Ends the Phone Call
Overview:	The caller ends the phone call.
Basic Course of Events:	- The caller ends the call. - If the call was connected, disconnect all. - If the call was ringing, stop ringing. - ...

Scenario Name:	The Callee Ends the Phone Call
Overview:	The callee ends the phone call.
Basic Course of Events:	- The callee ends the call. - If the call was connected, disconnect all. - If the call was ringing, stop ringing. - ...

Fig. 17. Phone call scenarios (split)

Splitting up one large scenario makes it possible to reuse the smaller scenarios in other parts of the system. On the other hand, understanding one large scenario possibly gives the reader a better feel for the complexity of the process captured by the scenario. In Chap. 5, we will give some advice for splitting up large scenarios properly.

4.2.6   Modeling Dynamic and Static Aspects

According to IEEE 610.3 [IEEE89], a dynamic model explicitly shows which state of the system is changed at which time, while static models show aspects that explicitly do not change over time. This distinction between static and dynamic aspects is also relevant for scenarios. When scenarios are described using textual representations (see, e.g., Fig. 15), the sequence of phrases defines a partial order of events. Nevertheless, whether or not interactions take place concurrently may still remain open in a textual representation; that is, textual representations sometimes describe a fully dynamic model, or at least a partially dynamic model.

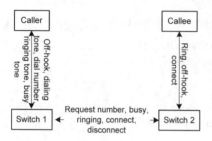

Fig. 18. A static interaction diagram

Scenarios can also be described using graphical notation (see Sect. 4.4). This notation can describe the kind of interaction that takes place in a system without considering the timely ordering of events. Figure 18 is an example of an interaction diagram, where the emphasis is on understanding the principal flow of control and data between participating objects without taking into consideration the timely ordering of interactions.

4.2.7   Object Interactions and State Transitions

Up to now we have said that interactions take place between objects; that is, the emphasis here is on the flow of messages between the participating objects of a scenario.

On the other hand, we could view the sending of a message as a special kind of event that leads to a state transition. When the focus is on the events and on the state transition associated with them, typically, a different kind of notation is used. One visual notation for a state transition oriented view of a system, called statecharts, has been developed by Harel [Harel87]. Figure 19 shows a simple statechart for modeling the high-level states of an airplane, using Harel's notation. Figure 19 shows a system with three possible states—that is, cruise, navigate, and on-ground—and the possible transitions between these states. The arrows indicate the directions of the state transitions and can be named. In our example, a touchdown event leads to a state transition from navigate to on-ground.

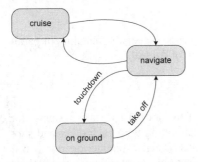

Fig. 19. An avionic system (statechart diagram)

Both object interactions and state transitions describe the behavior of an object or of a set of objects; nevertheless, the focus is different. State transition diagrams show the entire life cycle of one object; that is, all events that an object possibly experiences and all of its possible states. Additionally, a statechart diagram explicitly shows under which circumstances a state transition occurs. Figure 20 [Behringer97] shows the difference between object interactions and state transitions, and gives examples of methods and types of notation that provide support for a specific view.

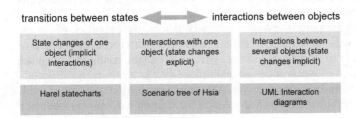

Fig. 20. Interactions versus state transitions

In object-oriented analysis and design, both views are necessary in principle. Focusing on object interactions leads to a better understanding of the collaboration issues of a system, while focusing on state transitions leads to a detailed understanding of the behavior of one object. Both approaches lead to the same result—nevertheless, the focus differs.

   In this chapter, we concentrate on object interactions, since we use contracts for the behavioral specification of a single class. For a more detailed discussion on how to integrate object interactions—that is, scenarios—with contract specifications, see Chap. 6. Behringer [Behringer97] explicitly mentions assertions and

rules as an alternative way of specifying the behavior of a single object; see also
Graham [Graham94a, Graham94b, Graham96].

4.3 Advanced Concepts

In this section, we discuss some advanced concepts, especially modeling of parallel interactions, timing issues, and issues of flow of control.

4.3.1 Interactions in Parallel

Interactions in parallel play an important role in modern software systems; for example, a number of server applications collaborating with each other and supporting a number of different client applications. Usually, distinct operating system processes cannot be distinguished at a notational level. Objects modeled as separate operating system processes play an important role, even when a scenario is described at an abstract level.

Especially when describing the internal view of a scenario (see Sect. 4.2.1), it is not sufficient to distinguish between different operating system processes, but it is also necessary to distinguish and model a system as a network of communicating threads. A thread defines its own flow of control, but resides within an operating system process. At the conceptual level, it is important to be able to model a number of aspects of parallel execution:

- The creation of processes and threads.
- The destruction of processes and threads.
- Support for describing different communication models; that is, synchronous and asynchronous communication.
- The synchronization of processes and threads; that is, the definition of certain points in a scenario at which execution of one thread or process can only proceed when another thread or process fulfills a certain condition—in other words, some kind of synchronization takes place.
- Dealing with mutual exclusion; that is, it must be possible to use different models to solve this problem. A typical solution for dealing with mutual exclusion in object-oriented systems is to attach a synchronization property to operations of classes.

    - *Sequential:* This approach assumes that the coordination takes place outside the object. In case of multiple flow of controls, the integrity of the object cannot be guaranteed.
    - *Guarded:* The guarded approach guarantees that in case of multiple flows of control all calls to an operation are sequentialized; that is, exactly one operation at a time can be invoked on an object. A message queue (see [Sun02b]) is one typical approach in distributed systems to ensure guarded operations on objects.
    - *Concurrent:* This approach guarantees the integrity of an object by treating

an operation as atomic. This allows a better control of concurrency issues, as some (uncritical) operations may be executed in parallel. Some programming languages directly support concurrent execution (e.g., Java technology, using the synchronized keyword [Gosling96]).

- Systems with parallel interactions need not necessarily be executed on a single machine, but the execution may be spread over a network of computers. It must therefore be possible to specify the location of processes and threads.

Typically, graphical notation for describing scenarios provides support to deal with parallelism (see Sect. 4.4). Pure textual descriptions are not suitable for dealing with parallelism. In this case, the phrasing of scenarios has to be highly formalized.

4.3.2   Timing Issues

Timing issues play an important role when modeling real-time systems. A system has real-time properties if certain actions must be carried out at a precise absolute or relative time and within an (often) constrained duration. Hard real-time systems require complete, repeatable, and predictable behavior within nanoseconds or milliseconds. At the other extreme, soft real-time systems also need predictable and repeatable behavior, but of the order of seconds or longer.

Timing issues also play an important role for distributed systems; that is, for systems in which services are spread over a network of computers. Those systems, by their nature, are not hard real-time systems, but may have soft real-time capabilities.

Regardless of the kind of real-time systems, it must be possible to define timing constraints for parts of a use case; that is, a precise description of the maximum time available for a specific behavior.

Some forms of graphical notation provide support to deal with timing issues (see Sect. 4.4). Pure textual descriptions can also contain timing issues, although it is more difficult to present them in a consistent way. Figure 21 shows a variant of our "Make Phone Call" scenario that includes timing constraints.

Scenario Name:	Make Phone Call
Overview:	Make a phone call between two persons.
Basic Course of Events:	- The caller takes the phone off the hook and receives the dialing tone. - The caller dials the first digit. - The dialing tone is stopped. - The caller dials the remaining digits of the phone number until the phone number is complete. The maximum time interval between two dialed digits is 30 seconds. - If the callee is busy, then the caller receives the busy tone; else, the callee's telephone rings and the caller receives the ringing tone at the same time. In any case, feedback must be provided within 0.5 seconds.

Fig. 21. The Make Phone Call scenario with timing constraints

4.3.3   The Flow of Control

Mere interactions between objects—that is, a sequence of requests or notifications—are only sufficient for scenario instances or for simple scenario types. For more complex interactions, additional control structures have to be expressed:

- *Conditional interaction:* This allows us to specify that an interaction only takes place when a specified condition is fulfilled.
- *Selection:* Semantically, selection for scenarios resembles the if–then–else construct in typical algorithmic description languages or programming languages, and allows us to formulate more complex conditional interaction constructs than with simple conditional interaction.
- *Iteration:* As in algorithmic description languages and programming languages, at least a simple iteration (a while-loop) has to be supported. In order to enhance the readability and expressiveness of scenario descriptions, repeat-until loops and for-loops should also be supported by the underlying language.
- *Return values:* In many cases (especially when the level of detail of the scenarios increases), it should be possible to explicitly state which values are returned from the receiver of a request.

Graphical notation uses different shapes of arrows as well as additional graphical symbols to express conditional interaction, selection, iteration, and return values: see Sects. 4.4.1 and 4.4.2 for examples at a general—that is, not method-specific—level. Section 5.2 shows the notational solution for the UML diagrams.

Nevertheless, for textual or tabular documentation of scenarios, specific wording has to be used in order to be able to properly and uniformly express flow of control. Figure 22 gives some examples of a possible wording for expressing flow of control.

Scenario Name:	Make Phone Call
Overview:	Make a phone call between two persons.
Basic Course of Events:	- The caller takes the phone off the hook and receives the dialing tone. - The caller dials the first digit. - The dialing tone is stopped. - The caller dials the remaining digits of the phone number, until the number is complete. - If the callee is busy, then the caller receives the busy tone; else, the callee's telephone rings and the caller receives the ringing tone at the same time.

Fig. 22. The flow of control in verbal descriptions of scenarios

- caller dials the remaining digits of the phone number, until the number is complete: This is a good example of an iteration. The phrase even expresses quite clearly when the iteration is finished.
- If the callee is busy, then the caller receives the busy tone ...: This is an example of a selection with one then and one else clause.
- the callee's telephone rings and the caller receives the ringing tone at the same time: This is a good example of a description of parallel action.

4.4 Describing Scenarios

The emphasis of this section is not on special notation, but on more general concepts concerning how to document scenarios. The capabilities of UML with respect to the modeling of scenarios are presented in detail in Chap. 5. In principle, we can distinguish between time-line notation and two-dimensional object models.

4.4.1 Time-Line Notation

The general characteristic of time-line notation, regardless of the specific kind of notation used, is that the vertical axis represents the time line. Optionally, the objects involved in the scenario are listed horizontally.

Tables: The principal idea of using tables is that only text is used to capture and describe scenarios. Different approaches exist about how to use tables. OBA

[Rubin92] uses tables, and Fig. 23 shows part of a scenario using a tabular representation as proposed by Rubin.

Initiator	Action	Participant	Service
User	select D1	Spreadsheet	select a cell
User	type text NEW	D1	set content to text
User	set text style to bold	D1	set text style to bold
User	select Row 2	Spreadsheet	select a row

Fig. 23. A tabular representation of scenarios—detailed level (Rubin)

The "vertical" axis shows the progress over time, while the table columns represent participating objects. The column entitled "Action" describes in a general way what happens at a certain point in time. The example given in Fig. 23Fig. 23 describes a scenario at a detailed level. It is of course also possible to describe a scenario at a more abstract level.

Kulak [Kulak00], Cockburn [Cockburn00], and others also propose a tabular documentation of scenarios. Figure 24 shows an example that follows the structure proposed by Kulak [Kulak00]. The structures proposed by other authors are directly comparable. Nevertheless, we present the structure proposed by Kulak, as we are used to it from our everyday work.

Scenario Name:	Schedule Customer Appointment
Iteration:	Finished.
Overview:	Enter an appointment with the designer and customer to take initial measurements and to determine the best design for the customer.
Basic Course of Events:	1. This use case begins when the office administrator, using date/time parameters supplied by the customer, requests a list of available times at which the designer and customer can have a consultation. 2. The system responds with a list of available appointment times. 3. The office administrator picks one of the times or enters a different time based on the customer's preference. 4. The system records the appointment time and later notifies the designer of the upcoming appointment.
Alternative Paths:	In step 1, if the office administrator has more than

	one appointment to record, the system allows multiple appointment entry.
Exception Paths:	In step 3, if the time that the office administrator chooses conflicts with another appointment, or with the designer in completing another costumer, the system warns the office administrator. The office administrator can respond by overriding the system and entering the appointment, by shuffling this and other appointments until the appointment fits, or by choosing another appointment day.
Trigger:	The customer requests an appointment.
Assumptions:	None.
Preconditions:	Basic information about the customer already exists in the system.
Postconditions:	The appointment is stored, and the system alerts the designer before it comes to pass.
Related Business Rules:	None.
Author:	Tammie Thurber.
Date:	June 3, 2000 (Facade), June 7, 2000 (Filled), June 13, 2000 (Focused), June 22, 2000 (Finished).

Fig. 24. A tabular representation of scenarios (due to Kulak) [Kulak00]

This approach is well suited for typical requirements analysis and documentation. The main advantage of this representation is that (1) the documentation is well structured and (2) a frame is provided that can be used by analysts during elicitation and documenting requirements. The objects involved in a scenario (persons, or other systems), are not explicitly modeled—nevertheless, this information can be extracted from the text later. We believe that this representation is especially valuable for requirements elicitation, since it encourages feedback from the participants, as hardly any formalisms are used. Furthermore, even at this level more advanced issues, such as parallelism, flow of control, and timing issues, can be documented in a consistent way. In Sect. 4.3 we have already shown which phrases can be used to systematically and consistently describe these issues.

The example given in Fig. 24 gives an idea about what should be documented for a use case. More generally, Kulak proposes the following structure and therefore content for a scenario:

- *Name:* The unique name of the scenario, which gives an idea about what is described in this scenario.
- *Iteration:* This indicates the level of maturity of the scenario. Kulak proposes

different stages of maturity levels; that is, Facade, Filled, Focused, or Finished. More information can be found in Kulak and Guiney [Kulak00]. This information is especially important for project managers, to give them some idea about the progress of the project.

- *Summary:* This contains a short description of the scenario. One or two sentences should be sufficient in most cases to capture the principal purpose of a scenario.
- *Basic course of events:* This is the most important part of the description. It describes in a stepwise manner—that is, with a timely ordering—what has to be done in order to achieve the goals of the scenario. As already explained, even more complicated issues, such as timing, flow of control, or issues of parallel actions, can be consistently described by adhering to a standard patterns for describing them (see Sect. 4.3).
- *Alternative paths:* While the "Basic course of events" section typically describes what is going on in 90% of the cases, this section concentrates on alternatives.
- *Exception paths:* This section describes how to deal with exceptional situations; that is, situations that should not happen but still occur. Typically, here it is described how to deal with error situations.
- *Trigger:* This describes the situation that leads to "execution" of the scenario.
- *Assumptions:* This section is quite critical, as it contains things that an analyst assumes, but that need not necessarily be true.
- *Preconditions:* This section describes which preconditions have to be fulfilled before this scenario can start. This is important information that can be used later in the development process, as the preconditions specified here can be transformed into contracts later in the process (see Chap. 6).
- *Postconditions:* This section describes which postconditions have to be fulfilled after termination of this scenario. This is important information that can be used later in the development process, as the postconditions specified here can be transformed into contracts later in the process (see Chap. 6).
- *Related business rules:* The typical approach here is not to describe the business rules directly, but to refer to them unequivocally. Business rules often lead to contracts in the course of the software development process (see Chap. 6). Examples of business rules are as follows [Kulak00]:

  - *BR 1 (Selling and buying property):* The fees that the customer is charged are based on the number of interactions with an agent. Each interaction that requires an agent will be charged to the customer as a one-hour minimum. If the agent spends more than one hour on an interaction, the customer will be charged in quarter-hour segments.
  - *BR 2 (Selling and buying property):* The number of counter-offers between buyer and seller is limited to ten for the buyer and ten for the seller.

Time-Line Diagrams: Time-line diagrams are two-dimensional graphs. The vertical axis represents the time, and on the horizontal axis the objects involved in the scenario are listed. Arrows are usually used to indicate the flow of messages. Different arrow shapes indicate different types of communication (e.g., synchronous versus asynchronous communication). Usually, additional (graphical) syntax is provided to show the flow of control or to indicate parallel actions. Figure 25 shows an example of a time-line diagram (without any specific notation in mind). We will not discuss notational issues (e.g., how to express asynchronous messaging) in this section. We will discuss and demonstrate this in detail in Chap. 5.

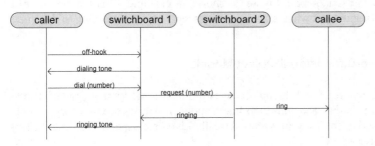

Fig. 25. Time-line notation

Figure 25 shows parts of our phone call scenario. Without going into detail, the diagram clearly shows the participants in the scenario (Caller, Switchboard 1, Switchboard 2, and Callee), as well as which kind of interaction takes place at which time. Notational issues for expressing repetition, conditional execution, and so on are omitted for sake of understandability.

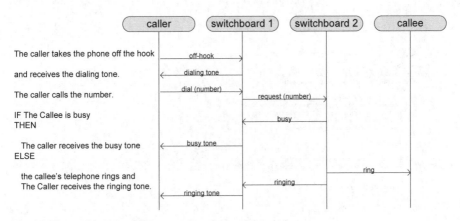

Fig. 26. The combination of diagrammatic and textual description

Time-line diagrams have the advantage that they emphasize time-related aspects, and that they principally allow us to formulate complex interactions in a concise and precise way. We believe that time-line diagrams are useful in a project for selected, more complicated use cases. All use cases should be captured using a tabular representation, but some of them are refined and transformed into time-line diagrams (see Chap. 5 for details). These time-line diagrams, combined with assertions, can be used for the prototype construction as well as during implementation and testing (see Chap. 6).

Behringer [Behringer97] combines the typical graphical notation used in time-line diagrams with pseudo-code. Figure 26 shows an example. This notation gives a better understanding of what is going on in a scenario without having to document it separately.

4.4.2   Two-Dimensional Object Models

Object diagrams represent the objects as two-dimensional symbols, rather than as mere lines (as is the case with time-line diagrams). Arrows are used between objects to describe the flow of events. Usually, dynamic aspects are described by numbering the arrows.

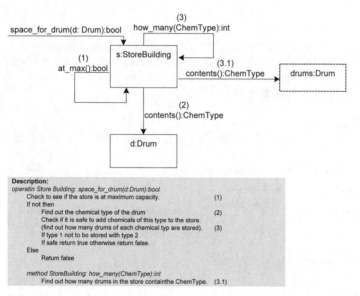

Fig. 27. Object diagrams in Fusion

One advantage (in our opinion) of these diagrams is that they look quite similar to class diagrams—so people need not to become accustomed to different kinds of notation. Nevertheless, the dynamic information is not obvious. In addition, due to the limitations of numbering schemes, only simple timing information can be directly expressed in the diagram. To overcome this problem, these diagrams are often enriched with a textual description of the main flow of events. This leads to redundancy, which might be a problem when changes to an object diagram are not made consistently; that is, both on the textual and the graphical part. Figure 27 shows an example of an object diagram as proposed by Coleman [Coleman94] in his Fusion method. As shown in Fig. 27, the flow of the event cannot be captured at a glance. The additional textual information makes the order in which the operations are carried out quite clear.

5 Scenarios and Analysis

Summary: Chapter 4 emphasized conceptual and notational issues of scenarios without relating them to a specific methodology. A number of published reports [Cockburn00, Regnell95, Rolland98] and books [Kulak00, Regnell99] show how the scenario technique may be used to its utmost in analysis; that is, by using it in a manner that makes requirements easy to understand by customers and that also supports concise and precise documentation. We show that the general scenario concepts developed in Chap. 4 can easily be mapped onto the UML syntax.

The general framework for using scenarios in analysis is: (1) customer investigation; (2) the development or adaptation of scenarios; and (3) presenting the results to customers and deciding whether to iterate once more or to stop the analysis process. This general, and therefore always applicable, approach model proves unsatisfactory for analysts. As scenarios have been employed successfully since their introduction in 1992 by Ivar Jacobson [Jacobson92], a number of reports of experiences using the technique have been published to date. These best practices can be used throughout analysis to guide this process, which is much more effective than following complicated process models.

Keywords: Scenario, Use case, Interaction diagram, Actor, Use case diagram, Activity diagram, Statechart diagram, Sequence diagram, Collaboration diagram

5.1 Introduction

The UML notation [UML97] is currently used to capture analysis and design results using a number of types of graphical notation (use case diagrams, class diagrams, sequence diagrams, collaboration diagrams, statechart diagrams, activity diagrams, component diagrams, and deployment diagrams). Some of these diagrams can be used directly to capture scenarios at a more formal level; that is, by using time-line diagrams or two-dimensional object diagrams (the properties of these principal kinds of notation are explained in Chap. 4).

This section is divided into two major parts. Section 5.3 presents the syntax and semantics for specifying scenarios in UML, while Sect. 5.4 tries to capture best practices when working with scenarios. Scenarios as we understand them in this book can be compared with use cases in UML. In this section, we will use the UML terminology—that is, use cases instead of scenarios—although we mean the same thing. Some authors claim that (in the context of UML) a scenario in UML is one specific instance of a use case (this is comparable to our scenario instances;

see Chap. 4). The description of the UML notation concerning scenarios is divided into three parts:

- Section 5.2 provides an overview of the diagrams that capture (parts of) scenarios. In this section, we also present the use case diagram that gives an overview of actors and use cases (scenarios) in a system, and how these use cases are related to each other. The use case diagram therefore provides the "big" picture for a system under development. Besides that, we give overviews of the collaboration diagram, the statechart diagram, and the activity diagram. We have discussed this in Chap. 4. We also try to capture the advantages and disadvantages of these diagrams from our point of view, and to show the limitations of these kinds of notation. We explicitly do not present the UML interaction diagram in section 5.2—this is postponed to section 5.3.
- Section 5.3.1 concentrates on the basic syntax and semantics of interaction diagrams. In our experience, they are best suited to refine a verbally described scenario, as the graphical notation is both compact and lucid.
- Section 5.3.2 deals with advanced specification issues of interaction diagrams, such as threading, object destruction, and timing and distribution constraints.

5.2   Describing Behavior Using UML—An Overview

5.2.1   Use Case Diagrams

Use case diagrams are central to modeling the behavior of a system, as they make a number of aspects visible to the analysts: (1) they show the major tasks that have to be fulfilled by a system, considering (2) which users (roles) are involved in the fulfillment of each task; and (3) they show the boundaries of the system—that is, they clearly show what is part of the system and what should not be considered.

Therefore, use case diagrams show the overall structure of a system under investigation. The two major elements of a use diagram are actors and use cases:

- *Actor:* An actor represents a user of the system—or, more precisely, the role that a user of the system plays. The term "user" is not person-centered; a user may also be a hardware device or another system. In Fig. 28, Scheduler is an example of a role, where a member of the administrative staff of a clinic is responsible for scheduling patient appointments. The same physical person may also play the role of a Patient in the event that he or she is ill, and may also need an appointment. Finally, the Scheduler might also be a smart application capable of dealing with the management of patient appointments.
- *Use case:* A use case has a unique name and identifies a number of actions in which a number of actors may be involved; that is, a use case also comprises interaction between the use case and its actors. A use case is the specific UML term for a scenario (as defined in Chap. 4). As we will see later, a UML use case has additional properties, such as generalization, extension, and inclusion.

In Chap. 4 we concentrated on a single use case (scenario), while the emphasis of the use case diagram is to capture a set of use cases together with their interrelations. Therefore, each use case identified and captured in the use case diagram must be refined later on, using either of the general techniques presented in Chap. 4. Alternately, the respective UML diagrams (e.g., an interaction diagram) can also be used to refine the use cases.

Figure 28 shows an example of a use case diagram with a number of actors (Scheduler, Patient, and Doctor) and use cases (Make Appointment, Cancel Appointment, Request Medication, and Pay Bill).

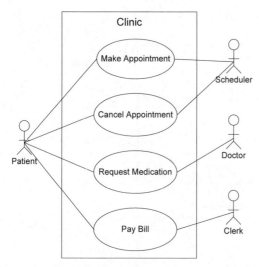

Fig. 28. A basic use case diagram

The lines between the use cases and the actors denote general communication, without specifying in detail how this communication is carried out technically. All of the use cases of this example belong to the system Clinic. For large (real-world) systems, it is not sufficient to have just one system view with a number of use cases inside; instead, a structuring of subsystems must be possible. To achieve this, each use case can be the name of a subsystem; that is, a group of closely related use cases that can be refined in another use case diagram.

Besides this basic semantics as described above, a number of properties can be described using a visual notation (see Fig. 29). A more detailed discussion of the semantics can be found in Hitz and Kappel [Hitz02]:

- *Generalization:* Generalization may be used for actors as well as for use cases. Generalization means that the more specific element is fully consistent with the more general element and may contain additional information. Generalization always implies substitutability; that is, any specific element may replace a more general element. In our example (see Fig. 29), Bill Insurance is a specialization of the Pay Bill use case. Generalization may also take place for actors (which is the more common usage of generalization with use case diagrams).

- *Include:* This relationship means that a use case contains the behavior defined in another use case. In our example (see Fig. 29), the use cases Make Appointment and Request Medication both make use of (i.e., include) the use case Check Patient Record. The notation does not allow us to specify at which point in the use case the included use has to be "inserted".

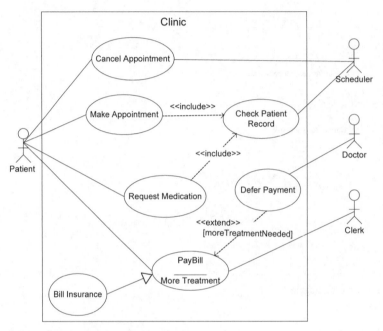

Fig. 29. A more complex use case diagram

- *Extend:* According to this relationship, a use case may be augmented with additional behavior defined in an extending use case. In our example, Defer Payment is an optional extension of the Pay Bill use case. Each extension relationship may also define the condition that must be fulfilled in order to make the extension valid. In our example, Defer Payment extends Pay Bill if the patient needs more treatment (moreTreatmentNeeded). The extension point defined in the use case Pay Bill indicates the point (more or less exactly) in the Pay Bill uses case at which the extended use case (Defer Payment) provides an extension.

5.2.2   Activity diagrams

An activity diagram combines ideas from several techniques—event diagrams [Odell93], SDL [ITU99], state modeling techniques, and Petri nets. These diagrams are useful for describing behavior that has a lot of parallel processing. Figure 30 gives an example of an activity diagram that deals with order processing.

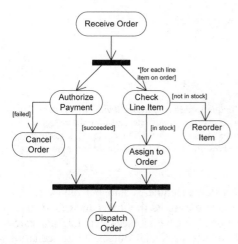

Fig. 30. An activity diagram in UML

An activity diagram shows the flow from activity to activity. An activity is denoted by a box with rounded corners and may either be quite abstract (e.g., Receive Order in Fig. 30) or very specific. Horizontal bars indicate synchronization points in the activity diagrams; that is, locations at which parallel execution either starts or finishes. The principal usage of activity diagrams is to model a workflow, as shown in Fig. 30. Nevertheless, operations can also be modeled using this approach. Figure 31 [Booch99] shows an example of an operation that determines the intersection point of two lines. This example illustrates the use of actions at a low level; that is, at the statement level.

   While interaction diagrams are especially useful for describing a single use case, activity diagrams can be useful in the following situations [Fowler99]:

- *Analyzing a use case:* Activity diagrams are useful in cases in which the modeler wants to gain an understanding of the use case without having to deal with allocating methods to classes, since the actions can be described at an abstract level.
- *Workflows across many use cases:* Interacting use cases are best visualized using activity diagrams.
- *Multi-threaded applications:* Issues of parallel execution can be easily modeled using activity diagrams.

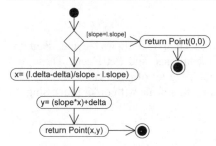

Fig. 31. Modeling an intersection operation

5.2.3   Statechart Diagrams

"Statechart diagrams are a familiar technique to describe the behavior of a system. They describe all the possible states a particular object can get into and how the object's state changes as a result of events that reach the object. In most OO techniques, statechart diagrams are drawn for a single class to show the lifetime behavior of a single object."[8] [Fowler99]

A statechart diagram is used to describe a state machine. A state machine specifies the transition of an object from state to state during its lifetime. Changes to states are triggered by events. As already mentioned in Chap. 4 (see Sect. 4.2.7), a statechart diagram focuses on the life cycle of one particular object, while scenarios emphasize the description of collaborations of objects. In object-oriented systems both views are important, although we feel—that especially for business software—the collaborative view is more interesting. On the other hand, statechart diagrams are certainly a good choice for modeling embedded systems, as in many cases a number of meaningful states are inherently built into the hardware or into the low-level control software.

Figure 32 shows an example of a state machine that uses substates [Booch99]. The example models parts of an automated teller machine (ATM). The system consists of three principal states—Idle, Active, and Maintenance. The transition between, for example, the Idle state and the Active state occurs by means of the cardInserted event. The Active state itself is a state that is modeled as a unique state machine with the initial status Validating and a number of subsequent states, such as Selecting, Processing, and Printing. The expression [continue] denotes a guard; that is, the transition from the Processing state into the Selecting state can only occur when the guard—the condition [continue]—is true. A substate (in our example, Printing) can directly trigger an event that leads to the transition into an upper state (in our example, Idle). The Active state is left as soon as a cancel event occurs, regardless of the current substate in the Active state.

---

[8] In the original quote the term "state diagram" is used instead of the term "statechart diagram" that is commonly used in the UML word. In order to avoid misunderstandings we use the UML term "statechart diagram"

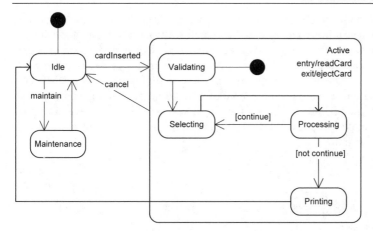

Fig. 32. A statechart diagram with substates

The above example should give you a rough understanding of the principles of statechart diagrams. A more detailed discussion of this important UML diagram can be found in Booch et al. [Booch99], Fowler et al. [Fowler99], or Hitz and Kappel [Hitz02].

5.3   Scenarios and UML

UML [Booch99] is often used for structural modeling of classes and their relation-ships. Besides diagrams for structural modeling, UML also provides a number of diagrams for supporting behavioral modeling—use case diagrams, interaction diagrams, activity diagrams, and statechart diagrams. In the previous Section we concentrated on selected UML diagrams for specifying the behavior of object-oriented systems. Sections 5.3.1 and 5.3.2 concentrate on modeling issues associ-ated with interaction diagrams. We will concentrate on interaction diagrams, as they can be used directly to capture scenarios (in textual notation) at a more for-mal level.

5.3.1   Basic Interaction Diagrams

Fowler's definition [Fowler99] (already quoted in the introduction to this section) captures the essence of interaction diagrams:

> "Interaction diagrams are models that describe how groups of objects collaborate in some behavior. Typically, an interaction diagram captures the behavior of a single use case."

Alternately, we could say that each high-level use case can also potentially be described using a UML interaction diagram, giving us a more formal description of the collaboration of objects. As we will see in Chap. 6, we believe that this opportunity plays an important role in the overall software development process.

An interaction diagram in UML can either be a sequence diagram or a collaboration diagram. Basically, this is a matter of notation. As described in Sect. 4.4.1, the UML sequence diagram uses the time-line notation, while UML collaboration diagrams are a typical example of a two-dimensional object model (see Sect. 4.4.2). Figure 33 shows the interaction of several objects involved (a variation of an example given in [OMG01]) using a sequence diagram and using a collaboration diagram.

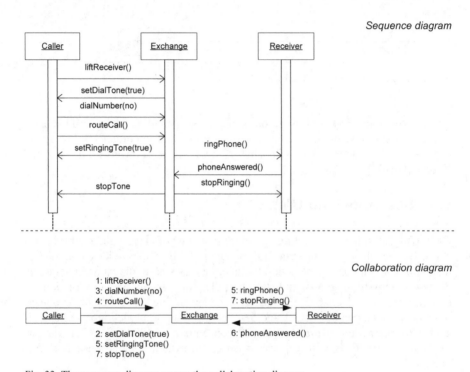

Fig. 33. The sequence diagram versus the collaboration diagram

The sequence diagram clearly shows the timely ordering of communication that is taking place between the collaborating objects. The collaboration diagram shows this aspect using a numbering scheme. The numbering scheme used in Fig. 33Fig. 33 is simple—it visualizes the timely ordering by means of ascending numbers. Alternately, a hierarchical decimal numbering scheme could also be used.

Semantically, both kinds of diagram can express the same facts. Nevertheless, in the remainder of this section we will use sequence diagrams to show the capabilities of UML interaction diagrams, as we think that they visualize the timely ordering of collaborations better than collaboration diagrams. Other authors (e.g., [Fowler99]) also share our opinion.

A sequence diagram consists of a number of basic elements that we briefly describe in the following paragraphs. We give a comprehensive annotated example (in the context of the Insight agent system—see Appendix A) after this brief theoretic overview.

- *Objects:* On the horizontal axis of a sequence diagram, all of the objects that take part in the communication are listed. Besides the name of the object (e.g., c in Fig. 33), the type of the object is also listed. Therefore, typically a sequence diagram describes one instance of a scenario (see Sect. 4.2.4). Nevertheless, it is also possible to show the type names only—that is, to capture a more general behavior based on the types involved in the collaboration (see Sect. 4.2.4).
- *Messages:* The vertical axis represents time. Along this general time axis (which spans all of the objects involved in the sequence diagram), messages are exchanged between distinctive objects. According to Booch [Booch99], a message is a specification of a communication amongst objects. A message is therefore a rather abstract concept (compare Sect. 4.2.2) that results in an action at the receiver. UML distinguishes different kinds of message:

  - *Call:* Invoking an operation; that is, a method on an object. The invocation may either take place locally (local method call) or remotely (remote method invocation).
  - *Return:* Returns the value of an operation to the caller.
  - *Send:* Sends a signal—that is, an asynchronous message—to the receiver. This type of communication can only take place between objects with a separate flow of control; that is, objects that reside in different threads or operating system processes.
  - *Create:* Creates a new object of a specified type. A created object may also run as a separate process. Generally, the objects of a sequence diagram—that is, the objects that take part in the collaboration—exist *per se*; in other words, it is not specified how they come into existence. For some objects, a message can lead to the explicit creation of an object (as explained above).
  - *Destroy:* Destroys an object explicitly. Not all objects of a scenario have to be destroyed—in many cases, the emphasis of the scenario is not on the proper cleanup of objects; nevertheless, situations often occur in which the creation and destruction of objects is important for an understanding of the overall behavior of a scenario.

- *Lifeline:* Every object has a distinctive lifeline that lasts from the (implicit or explicit) creation of the object until it is destroyed explicitly. For objects that are not destroyed explicitly, it remains unspecified at which point in time they get destroyed. Therefore, the lifeline models the vertical time axis of a sequence diagram.
- *Activation:* An activation shows the focus of control; that is, an activation (denoted by a rectangle on a lifeline) indicates which objects have the focus of

control at which periods in time. This is especially interesting for objects working in parallel, as it facilitates the understanding of concurrent activities and of the problems associated with concurrent activities (e.g., deadlocks).

Figure 34 shows an example of a basic interaction diagram, from the deployment of components to a target system in our monitoring and control example (see Appendix A). It is important at this point that you are familiar with the basic requirements of our system, as this example will be used in the remainder of the book; that is, to discuss the UML properties of interaction diagrams in our approach to the combination of scenarios and assertions (Chap. 6), and in our section about tool support for assertions and scenarios (Chap. 7).

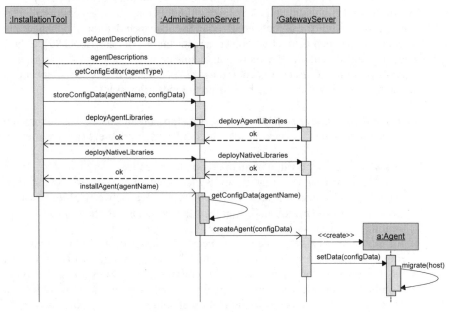

Fig. 34. An interaction diagram (Install Agent—basic version)

In Fig. 34, the objects involved in the interaction diagram are marked by boxes that contain the type of the object and (if necessary) the name of the object. The objects of type InstallationTool, AdministrationServer, and GatewayServer are unnamed, while the object Agent has the name a, which could be used in the diagram to identify it unequivocally. Usually, it is not possible to show in an interaction diagram how objects come into existence. In our scenario—which is visualized as an interaction diagram—it is not clear how and when the main objects of the scenario, of type InstallationTool, AdministrationServer, and GatewayServer, begin to exist; we just assume that they have been properly created and initialized.

As already explained, the vertical axis defines a timely ordering of messages. We can have different levels of formality when using messages. We can have message names only (e.g., deployNativeLibraries) or we can have more complete messages with parameters (e.g., createAgent(configData)), or even type names for parameters and return values. In our example, four special kinds of message are used:

- *Call:* The message getAgentDescriptions() is an example of a message call that has synchronous messaging semantics.
- *Send:* The message installAgent(agentName) is an example of a message send operation that has asynchronous messaging semantics. This means that the message is sent to the object of type AdministrationServer without awaiting any confirmation. This is due to the fact that the installation process may last for a longer time; blocking a client for (in a worst-case scenario) a couple of minutes is not possible—therefore, only an asynchronous message is sent to the AdministrationServer and the agent to be installed will confirm its proper installation later (not visualized in Fig. 34).
- *Return:* The return message (a dotted line with an open arrow) may contain the name of the parameter that is returned from the message receiver. Return messages are optional—for example, for the message getConfigEditor(agentType), sent from the InstallationTool object to the AdministrationServer object, no explicit return message is drawn. Depending on the kind of message, it is obvious whether a return message is awaited by the caller. In our example, the messages getConfigEditor(agentType) and storeConfigData(agentName, configData) are examples of (synchronous) call messages—that is, a return message is awaited by the caller, regardless of whether or not it is drawn in the diagram. The message installAgent(agentName) is an asynchronous message; that is, no return message is awaited. This is also clearly indicated in our example, as the activation bar for the object InstallationTool ends directly after sending the message installAgent(agentName).
- *Create:* During the installation process, the GatewayServer creates a new Agent object. This creation process is visualized using a creation message. The receiver of the message is a new object. In our example (see Fig. 34) not additional parameters can be set, although this is possible in principle. It is also common to use a new operation with parameters.

The vertical axis is also called the lifeline and shows how long the objects exist. In Fig. 34, nothing special is indicated about the lifetime of the objects involved in the interaction diagram. As we will see later, the destruction of objects can be modeled using an interaction diagram (see Fig. 35), indicating that the lifeline of an object terminates.

As long as an object performs an operation, the lifeline is thickened—this thickened lifeline is called an "activation bar". When an object sends a message to itself during execution (e.g., getConfigData(agentName)), an additional activation bar is drawn.

5.3.2   Advanced Interaction Diagrams

The basic syntax and semantics presented in the previous section are sufficient for simple scenarios, and capture participating objects, timely ordering of messages, and some aspects of object creation. Nevertheless, UML provides a number of additional properties for interaction diagrams that allow us to capture some aspects of behavior more precisely:

- *Active objects:* Active objects are objects that have their own flow of control. Marking an object as active means, technically speaking, that the object runs as a separate operating system process, or at least as a thread. Marking an object as active (i.e., using a box with a thicker line) does not at all indicate whether the object runs as a separate operating system process or as a thread (for how to accomplish this, see later). Some authors (e.g., [Hitz02]) propose that active objects are active in principle (i.e., have an activation bar). We do not follow this suggestion, but we use activation bars in the same way as in a sequential program, in order to make clear where the focus of the operation is at a specific point in time.
- *Conditional messages:* Each message can have a conditional expression (in square brackets, before the message name). Depending on the value of the expression (true or false), the sending of messages takes place. It is important here that the names used in the expressions are either names of objects or names of parameters that can be accessed at this point in time by the sending object.
- *Object destruction:* A cross on a lifeline indicates that an object is destroyed. The semantics depends on the kind of object and on the underlying programming language. If the object is active, destroying such an object means destroying the thread or the operating system process. Depending on the programming language, either an explicit release of this allocated memory is necessary (e.g., in C++) or the object de-allocation can take place at any time via the garbage collector (e.g., in Java technology). The symbol for object destruction is often combined with a destruction message; that is, a special message that shows which object initiated the destruction process.

In Fig. 35, we show an elaborate version of the Install Agent use case. As you can see, all of the objects involved in this use case are active objects—that is, have their own flow of control—without specifying more precisely whether they should be implemented as threads or as operating system processes.

Furthermore, we have introduced return messages for all messages in this scenario. This makes the synchronous behavior of the call messages more explicit and gives a better expression of the kind of data that is returned by each message.

The messages deployNativeLibraries and installAgent(agentName) are conditional messages. The condition is in both cases the simple expression [ok]. For the deployNativeLibraries message, [ok] means the value of the return message associated with the storeConfigData message. For the installAgent(agentName) message, [ok] refers to value of the return message associated with the deployNativeLibraries message. The conditional message does not allow us to specify alternative paths; that is, we cannot describe (yet) what should happen if a specific condition is not fulfilled.

In Fig. 35, at the end of the use case, the agent migrates itself to a new host, confirms the migration to the GatewayServer, and is afterwards explicitly destroyed by the GatewayServer. To achieve this, the GatewayServer sends a special destroy message to the Agent. The destruction of the agent is visualized by a crossed lifeline.

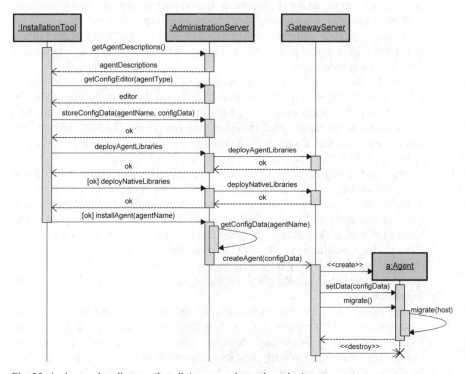

Fig. 35. An interaction diagram (Install Agent—enhanced version)

UML offers a number of additional capabilities that we will discuss in the following paragraph. Nevertheless, we first want to mention that these additional features should always be used carefully, as they might lead to interaction diagrams that are difficult to read and understand. We will refer to this issue in more detail in Sect. 5.4:

- *Selection:* While conditional messages (see above) only allow us to specify under which condition a message has to be executed, the selection also allows us to specify alternatives; that is, which message should be sent when the condition is not met. Nested selections cannot be expressed in UML, but it is possible to have an arbitrary number of alternatives at a specific point in time.

Alternative messages are drawn from one origin, at which each message has a condition (in square brackets) that makes clear which condition must be fulfilled to send this message. Each alternative message also has an associated condition. What happens if, for a number of alternatives, overlapping conditions exist is not specified.

- *Iteration:* Iterations allow us to specify which messages have to be executed repeatedly. A box is drawn around those messages that are to be repeated. Additionally, it is possible to formulate conditions that specify more precisely how often the messages have to be repeated. It is important that all expressions used in looping conditions are accessible at the point of evaluation.
- *Alternative lifelines:* Alternative lifelines are used to visualize different flows of control within one object. Alternative lifelines are often used in conjunction with selections (see above).
- *Parallel messages:* Parallel messages allow us to specify that messages can be sent at the same time. This is indicated by drawing the message lines from the same conceptual point in time (i.e., from one origin). In principle, the notation is equivalent to the notion used for describing selections. The only difference is that parallel messages do not have guarding conditions. In order to achieve parallelism, parallel messages can only be asynchronous.
- *Distribution of objects:* For distributed applications, it is important to know where the objects are placed during execution. This is important for all objects in the system, regardless of whether or not they are active. The location properties can be expressed using tagged values with objects. The tagged value location (as well as the value of the property) is written in curly brackets.
- *Constraints:* Constraints are formulated using the OCL syntax—they are placed in curly brackets and they may refer to any variables that are visible in the interaction diagram. Typically, they are placed near the spot to which they belong semantically.
- *Timing constraints:* Timing constraints are specialized constraints that can be used to formulate timing constraints. Any message can have a timing mark (in front of the message, separated from the message by a colon). Timing constraints are conditions (in curly brackets) that refer to these timing marks. It is therefore possible to express different timing constraints for different types of message (identified by different timing marks).

Figure 36 applies a number of these advanced features of UML for the deployment process of a native library (see Appendix A):

- (1) {libraryDescriptions.size()>0} is an example of a constraint formulated using the OCL language. Note that this is just an ordinary constraint, without specifying in more detail whether it is a precondition, a postcondition, or an invariant—furthermore, it is not clear where to put this constraint. We will come back to this issue is Chap. 6.
- (2) {t1.executionTime < 60s} is an example of a timing constraint. This constraint is valid for all messages that are associated with the timing mark t1.
- (3) This is an example of a selection. Depending on the return value of the

deployLibrary(library, platform) message, different branches at the AdministrationSrv
object are executed. In our example, only two branches are shown—[ok] and
[!ok]; in principle, an arbitrary number of branches is possible.

- (4) This shows an alternative lifeline for the AdministrationSrv object. This lifeline is activated when not all of the libraries could be deployed successfully to
the GatewayServer.
- (5) These are examples of iterations. Both iterations show an iteration condition: forall libraryDesc in libraryDescriptions and forall libraryDesc in missingLibraries. It
is important here that all of the variables used in the expressions (libraryDesc,
libraryDescriptions, missingLibraries) are accessible at iteration entry.

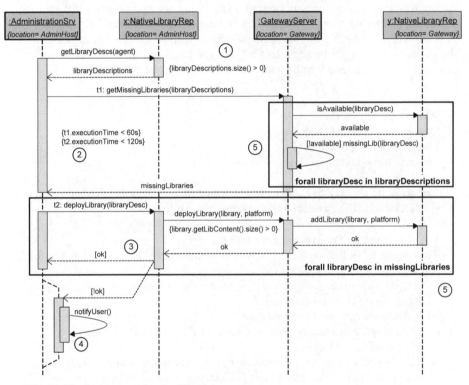

Fig. 36. The deployment of native libraries

Up to now, we have presented the capabilities of interaction diagrams. One obvious conclusion here is that it is important to keep interaction diagrams simple. In
the following section, we will try to identify guidelines that should be used when
developing interaction diagrams, and when working with use cases and use case
diagrams.

5.4   Best Practices

As already mentioned in the introduction to this chapter, we have tried to formulate a number of guidelines—that is, rules—about how to deal with use cases, use case diagrams, or interaction diagrams (what should be specified, and what should be avoided). The guidelines formulated in this section do not consider the analysis and design process itself, but focus on the task of formulating use case and interaction diagrams. The best practices described in this section are a compilation and unification of hints and principles found explicitly or implicitly in the literature.

In Chap. 4, we identified a small number of precise rules for dealing with assertions. In this section, we will present a larger number of guidelines that can be considered when working with use cases and interaction diagrams. In many cases, it is sufficient to briefly describe these guidelines without any further explanation. In other cases, it might be important to give good and/or bad examples, to make clearer how guidelines are to be understood. We will group the guidelines into the following categories:

- Writing guidelines (W).
- Quality management guidelines (Q).
- Process-related guidelines (P).
- Diagramming guidelines (D).

We will use the abbreviations given in the above list (in brackets) to identify each kind of guideline. The structure for describing the guidelines is as follows:

- For each category, we give a short overview.
- This overview is followed by a tabular presentation of the guidelines, the following content being provided for each one:
  - A unique identifier for the guideline; that is, an abbreviation for the category name and consecutive numbers.
  - A short description of the guideline.
  - Bibliographic references; that is, details of the source(s) in which we found this guideline.
  - Hints (using pictograms) to indicate that further information is provided following the table. The pictograms indicate the kind of information that will be provided; that is, it is possible to combine more pictograms here—just to make clear that this kind of information is available to the reader. The pictogram ⌂ indicates that additional information or comments are available. The symbol ⇑ indicates that a good example will be given, while ⇓ indicates a bad example; that is, an example that violates the guideline.
- After the tabular representation of the guidelines, comments (⌂), good examples (⇑), and bad examples (⇓) are given for selected guidelines.

In some cases, it is difficult to assign a guideline to a specific category—nevertheless, we have tried to assign them to the categories into which they fit best.

5.4.1   Writing Guidelines (W)

Writing guidelines aim at enhancing the content and style by giving hints about how sentences should be formulated and how to emphasize certain aspects of use cases (e.g., exceptional cases); they also give hints about which style to use in the description of use cases.

ID	Guideline	References	Details
W-01	The structure of the sentences used to describe use cases in textual form should be simple.	[Achour99, Cockburn00, Cox00,Cox01, Palph02, Rolland98]	▯
W-02	Always make clear which actors are involved in an action.	[Cockburn00, Lilly99, Wirfs-Brock02a, Wirfs-Brock02b]	–
W-03	Only include conditions (with alternative branches) if it is really necessary.	[Cockburn00]	▯ ⇧ ⇩
W-04	For exceptional cases, always make clear the condition under which the exceptional case occurs.	[Cockburn00]	▯ ⇧
W-05	All use cases should be written in such a way that the user can understand them.	[Kulak00]	▯
W-06	Use strong verbs in use case names.	[Kulak00, Wirfs-Brock02a, Wirfs-Brock02b]	▯ ⇧ ⇩
W-07	Try to write scenarios, not requirements.	[Lilly99, Rosenberg01]	▯
W-08	Don't write too tersely.	[Rosenberg01]	▯
W-09	Don't write in the passive voice.	[Achour99, Lilly99, Rosenberg01]	▯
W-10	Avoid synonyms and homonyms.	[Achour99, Lilly99, Rolland98]	▯
W-11	You should mention your assumption explicitly when some action is carried out under certain conditions.	[Rolland98]	▯ ⇧
W-12	You should mention the condition for stopping repeated actions explicitly.	[Rolland98]	▯ ⇧
W-13	You should mention the co-occurrence of several actions explicitly.	[Rolland98]	▯ ⇧
W-14	Avoid the use of negations, adverbs, and modal verbs in the description of an action.	[Achour99]	–

The following list gives more detailed information about the guidelines (the type of information provided can be seen from the overview table):

W-01   ▯   The basic structure is subject – verb – direct object – prepositional phrase. The subject (noun) should be stated anyway, to make clear who controls the action; that is, is the driving force for this action.

Some authors (e.g., [Achour99], [Cox00], [Cox01], [Palph02], and [Rolland98]) propose an even stricter structure for the sentences that can be used for describing action steps in a use case. These linguistic approaches deliver a use case specification as an unambiguous natural language text. This is done by a stepwise process that progressively transforms natural language descriptions into well-structured use case specifications. There is some empirical evidence that this approach leads to a better overall quality of the use cases (see [Achour99], [Cox00], [Cox01], and [Palph02]). Nevertheless, additional efforts have to be made to reformulate the use case descriptions according to the guidelines provided—additionally, tool support (some kind of verifier) has to be used that facilitates this transformation process.

W-03   ⬜   A typical step in a scenario is to verify that some business rule is satisfied. A typical error here is to use phrases such as "if the system detects ...". This leads to less legible texts and also imposes an obligation upon the writer to state what happens if the condition is not fulfilled.

⬇   The system checks whether the password is correct.

If it is, the system presents the available actions to the user.

⬆   The system validates that the password is correct.

The system presents the available actions for the user.

W-04   ⬜   Exceptional cases should be documented separately from the main course of events (see also the general template for describing scenarios in Sect. 4.4.1). In the description of the exceptional cases, you should clearly identify the step at which the exception occurs, as well as the exact condition that leads to alternative behavior. If an alternative may occur at any time during the basic course of events, it should be documented by using an asterisk.

⬆   *a. Network goes down: <description>

2a. Insufficient funds: <description>

2b. Network down : <description>

W-05   ⬜   In particular, this means that no computer terminology (e.g., "LAN", "WAN", "GUI elements", or "server") should be used. Furthermore, no pseudo-code should be used to describe use cases. Preconditions and postconditions could (in principle) be described using OCL—nevertheless, we recommend that you do not include OCL in the textual use case description, as it is also usually not readable as far as the user is concerned.

W-06   ⬜   Strong verbs are more meaningful than generalized weak verbs. Tend to use strong verbs, since they capture the purpose of a use case in a better way.

⬆   Examples of strong verbs in use case names: merge, defer, switch, calculate, combine, migrate, receive.

⬇   Examples of weak verbs in use case names: make, report, find, list, copy, record.

W-07   ⬜   Requirements are usually stated in terms what the system shall do. Use cases – on the other hand – describe actions from the perspective of the actors involved in the use case.

W-08   ⬜   Of course, use cases should be formulated concisely and precisely—nevertheless, it is important to describe all of the actions of the actors and all system responses in sufficient detail. The omission of details might lead to gaps that have to be filled later.

On the other hand, this does not mean that this information has to be packed into the use cases at once, but that additional details have to be added in the course of writing the use cases (see also guideline P-04).

W-09   ◌   Use cases should always be described from the user's perspective (see guidelines W-01 and W-07) in order to enhance the readability of the document.

W-10   ◌   Synonyms should not be used; that is, all objects and actors involved should always be named identically. Homonyms are words that are identical but have a different meaning; homonyms lead to even more misunderstandings than do synonyms.

W-11   ◌   The description of conditions should follow the pattern "if <condition> then <action>". This contradicts guideline W-04. Guideline W-04 deals with exception situations that should be documented separately from the basic course of events. Nevertheless, situations often occur in which conditions must be stated— but there is not "enough" exceptional logic that would force us to put into the exceptional path of the use case description.

    ⇧   From our deployment example in Appendix A—Use Case "Deploy Agent Libraries": *If the agent needs a user interface library for configuration purposes, the AS retrieves this library from the local JCR and transfers it to the GS.*

W-12   ◌   The description of conditions for stopping repeated actions should follow the pattern "Repeat <action> until <condition>", or similar patterns such as "While <condition> <action>" or "For <condition> <action>".

    ⇧   From our deployment example in Appendix A—Use Case "Deploy Native Libraries": *For each missing library (see the previous step) the AS retrieves the native library from the NLR at the AS (based on the description) and transfers it to the GS.*

W-13   ◌   The description of co-occurring actions should follow the pattern "while <action>, <co-occurring action>".

    ⇧   While the system is trying to establish a speech connection between the caller and the callee, the caller hears a ringing tone.

5.4.2 Quality Management Guidelines (Q)

While the writing guidelines emphasize how the content—that is, the description of use cases—should be presented, quality management guidelines define what should and what should not be included. In our opinion, quality management guidelines are like checklists, to which every writer of use cases must adhere.

ID	Guideline	References	Details
Q-01	Don't include interface detail descriptions.	[Cockburn00, Firesmith99, Rosenberg01]	◌ ⇧ ⇩
Q-02	Include a reasonable set of actions in one step of a use case.	[Cockburn00]	◌ ⇧
Q-03	Don't create inside-out use cases; that is, use cases that are written from the perspective of the application rather than the user.	[Kulak00, Lilly99]	◌ ⇧ ⇩
Q-04	User interface details are not part of the use case description.	[Kulak00, Lilly99, Rosenberg01]	◌
Q-05	Avoid cross-references in the use case text.	[Kulak00]	◌
Q-06	Exception logic should not be included	[Kulak00]	◌

	in the basic course of events.		
Q-07	Try to extract common parts of use cases.	[Andersson95]	▯
Q-08	Name entities consistently.	[Achour99, Ambler02, Firesmith99, Lilly99, Wirfs-Brock02a, Wirfs-Brock02b]	▯
Q-09	Describe only functional requirements.	[Firesmith99]	▯

The following list gives more detailed information about the guidelines (the type of information provided can be seen from the overview table):

Q-01 ▯ It is a common and serious mistake to include user interface elements in a use case (see also guideline Q-03). Another typical mistake (addressed by this guideline) is to show the kind of interaction between the actor and the system at a low level of detail; that is, at the level of interface descriptions.

⇩ 1. The system asks for a name.
2. The user enters a name.
3. The system prompts for an address.
4. The user enters an address.
5. The user clicks "OK".
6. The system presents the user's profile.

⇧ The user enters a name and address.

The system presents the user's profile.

Q-02 ▯ As Jacobson [Jacobson92] states, one step in a use case represents a transaction. A transaction is a compound interaction with the following typical steps. (1) The primary actor sends a request and data to the system. (2) The system validates the request and the accompanying data. (3) The system changes its internal state. (4) The system responds to the actor with a result. Each part of the transaction can be described as a separate step in the scenario, but several steps may also be combined. Whether or not to prefer the more detailed versions depends on the complexity of the use cases.

⇧ The customer enters the order number.

The system detects that it matches the winning number for this month.

The system registers the user and order number as this month's winner, sends an email to the sales manager, congratulates the customer, and gives him or her instructions about how to collect the prize.

Q-03 ▯ It is important to consider use cases as black boxes, which means that use cases do not include any implementation details. At this stage in the development process in particular, the partners involved in the use case elicitation and documentation process are not interested in finding out how a specific use case will be implemented. These details are of concern later in the development process. Typical terms that are specific to implementation are as follows:

▪ Specific people—instead of roles.
▪ User interface widgets.
▪ Assumptions about where the work is being done physically.
▪ If–then–else statements.
▪ Pseudo-code.
▪ The use of any kind of constraint language (e.g., OCL) in the use case text.

⇓   The clerk pushes the "OK" button.

The account holder folds the envelope that contains the cash or check and deposits it into the slot of the automated teller machine (ATM).

⇑   The clerk signifies completion of the transaction.

The account holder provides the deposit, including the cash, check, and deposit summary data.

Q-04   ▢   During the requirements gathering phase, no user interface details should be included in the use case text, as they distract the reader from the core purpose of a use case; that is, describing which actions have to be fulfilled in which order.

Q-05   ▢   In Sect. 4.4.1 we proposed the use of a template for documenting use cases. In principle, additional information could be inserted; for example, actor lists, included use cases, sequence diagrams, and subordinate use cases. Usually, this information should not be provided, as it has to be maintained throughout the entire software development process. The general rule here is that you should only enforce information that is of value to you—the more information you gather, the more information you will have to maintain later.

Q-06   ▢   The use case template proposed in Sect. 4.4.1 distinguishes, amongst other things, between the basic course of events and the exception paths. It is important that the description of the basic course of events does not contain descriptions of the exception paths, as this will distract the readers of the use case. See also guideline W-04.

Q-07   ▢   In order to avoid redundancy in use case descriptions, it is important to identify common blocks and to extract them as separate use cases. Those common blocks can be set in relation to each other by using the generalization, include, and extends mechanisms. Nevertheless, don't overuse these relations (see guidelines D-02 and D-03).

Q-08   ▢   It is important to name use cases, actors, and so on consistently in all documents. You should therefore ensure that the same names are used for actors and use cases in use case diagrams, use case descriptions, and interaction diagrams. Avoid synonyms and homonyms (see guideline W-10).

Furthermore, it is import to provide unique, meaningful names for actors, interactions, and use cases.

Q-09   ▢   The emphasis of a use case based approach to the capturing of requirements is on a user-centered approach to documenting them. However, quality requirements cannot be reasonably stated in terms of interactions.

5.4.3   Process-Related Guidelines (P)

Process-related guidelines help to guide the process of use case gathering and documentation. In many cases, it is not clear when to include certain details or when to carry out certain tasks. The guidelines summarized below might give some advice on such questions:

ID	Guideline	References	Details
P-01	Don't expand the system boundaries by chance.	[Firesmith99, Kulak00, Lilly99]	▢
P-02	Assign one owner to each use case or to a group of use cases.	[Kulak00]	▢

P-03	Start with the use cases that provide the most value to the actors.	[Kulak00]	–
P-04	Clearly distinguish between scenario instances and scenario types.	[Kulak00]	◻
P-05	Use an iterative approach to the description of use cases.	[Kulak00, Wirfs-Brock02a, Wirfs-Brock02b]	◻ ⇧
P-06	Provide an overview for each use case.	[Firesmith99, Lilly99, Wirfs-Brock02a, Wirfs-Brock02b]	◻ ⇧
P-07	Systematically capture relevant assertions.	[Firesmith99, Wirfs-Brock02a, Wirfs-Brock02b]	◻ ⇧
P-08	Ensure proper granularity of use cases.	[Lilly99], [Anda02]	◻
P-09	Package use cases properly.	[Lilly99, Wirfs-Brock02a, Wirfs-Brock02b]	◻ ⇧
P-10	Focus on primary actors.	[Wirfs-Brock02a, Wirfs-Brock02b]	◻
P11	Provide and maintain glossary definitions.	[Wirfs-Brock02a, Wirfs-Brock02b]	◻ ⇧

The following list gives more detailed information about the guidelines (the type of information provided can be seen from the overview table):

P-01 ◻ The developer of the system always has to keep the scope of the system in mind. You always have to keep the goals of your project in mind. Nevertheless, during system analysis it is sometimes unclear whether a subsystem is part of the system to be developed—that is, within the system boundaries—or whether it is an actor. It is important to be precise on this question; otherwise, the system cannot be realized within the proposed budget (too much has been included in the system) or interfaces to external systems don't get clearly identified (the system is not recognized as an actor).

P-02 ◻ Use cases usually evolve over time; that is, several iterations are necessary until a use case captures the basic course of events as well as alternative paths, exceptions, and so on correctly. In order to assure that changes to the use cases are made in a consistent way, it is inevitable that each use case or use case group must be assigned to an owner who is responsible for assuring that the use cases get modified consistently throughout the iterations.

P-04 ◻ Use cases in the sense of UML are scenario types—that is, they represent a fairly abstract actor interaction—while scenario instances are instantiations from use cases with specific actors and with a specific interaction.

P-05 ◻ Use cases are typically started within the analysis phase, where the necessary information is gathered gradually. In order to work in a concentrated and focused way, we suggest that you follow guidelines as to which steps of the use case development process should be carried out. We feel that the overall process described by Kulak and Guiney [Kulak00] is suitable for this purpose.

Additionally, clearly indicate for each use case how complete it is; that is, its stage in the development process.

⇧ Kulak proposes different stages of maturity level; that is, Facade, Filled, Focused, and Finished. More information can be found in Kulak and Guiney [Kulak00].

Facade: In this early stage, use cases are identified and described at a general level. Usually, they only contain the name of the use case, together with a short description of each one. Additionally, the major actors should be identified.

Filled: The objective of this iteration is to define a comprehensive set of use cases and business rules that comprise the application. The major task is to gather information about the requirements and to find possible interactions to model the process under investigation. All details (functional requirements, nonfunctional requirements, and business rules) should be documented.

Focused: The emphasis of the focused iteration is on separating essential use cases from those that are just nice to have. The emphasis here is to define the system—especially the boundaries of the system. This is a difficult task, as you have to ensure that the solution does not solve unnecessary problems.

Finished: In this phase, the emphasis is on refining the developed use cases; that is, clarifying details with the customer, enhancing the description of the use cases, and so on.

P-06   □   For each use case, an overview should exist that captures its functional abstraction and external goals.

    ⇧   In Sect. 4.4.1, we presented a tabular representation for describing use cases, proposed by Kulak [Kulak00]. The template is also used for the description of the use cases for our mobile agent example (see Appendix A).

P-07   □   For each use case, systematically capture (and refine) which preconditions and postconditions are relevant. Preconditions are important to be able to determine under which circumstances a use case can be executed. The postconditions tell us what must have been achieved upon successful completion of a use case.

Furthermore, these assertions give us valuable hints for later phases of the software development process. Ultimately, during class design it is possible to systematically check whether all of the relevant assertions are included as preconditions, postconditions, or even invariants in the designed classes. Although the textual representation in the use case descriptions does not explicitly help us to assign assertions to specific classes, it gives us a hint as to the actors or system components for which they are important. Bear in mind that not every assertion has to be finally transformed to a formal precondition or postcondition, as some of these assertions also deal with checks that have to be guaranteed by external actors, or by other systems that are not part of the system under development.

Additionally, these assertions give us hints for the specification of associated test cases.

We think that it is important to capture preconditions and postconditions in textual form—at this stage of development, the use of a more formal language such as OCL [OCL97] to capture those preconditions and postconditions is not suitable.

    ⇧   In Appendix A, we give an overview of the deployment process for a mobile agent system. Besides this overview, we describe the process of agent deployment by means of use cases. Some of these use case descriptions contain preconditions and postconditions in textual form.

P-08   □   A large number of use cases is an indicator that the granularity of the use cases is not appropriate. You should always bear in mind that use cases should reflect "results of value" to the system's users; that is, the attainment of real user goals.

To reduce the number of use cases, you can combine use cases with trivial or incidental behavior. Additionally, you can try to remove use cases that describe purely internal system processing—where "internal" has to be understood with respect to the system boundaries.

P-09   □   In cases in which the granularity of the use cases is correct (see guideline P-08) but the system is large, it is important to partition the use cases.

    ⇧   In Appendix A, we describe some use cases for the deployment of a mobile agent.

The entire system consists of many more use cases. It certainly would be a good idea to put all of the use cases related to the deployment into one package: the remainder of the use cases would also have to be packaged properly; for example, "Agent configuration" and "System monitoring".

P-10   ▭   An emphasis on primary actors automatically leads to a reduction in the number of use cases (see guideline P-08) and automatically focuses on use cases that provide the most value to the actors (see guideline P-03).

P-11   ▭   The purpose of a glossary is to clarify terms, so that team members can know what they are agreeing or disagreeing on. A glossary should be built incrementally and should be developed to accompany a use case model.

A good glossary entry should follow the form: "Name of concept" related to "a broader concept" + any distinguishing characteristics.

⇧   In our mobile agent example (see Appendix A), we could give a definition of the term "native library" as follows:

Native Library: A native library is a software library in binary format for a specific platform (a combination of an operating system and a processor) that can be linked to an application dynamically; that is, during execution of the application.

5.4.4   Diagramming Guidelines (D)

UML use case diagrams and interaction diagrams are employed to capture the relationship between use cases and actors (the use case diagram) and to show more formally the flow of messages and control within a use case (the interaction diagram). As UML offers a variety of diagramming options for use case diagrams and interaction diagrams, we consider it to be important to define how these diagrams should be used. The guidelines listed below should help you to draw diagrams that are easy to understand, and that capture important aspects of use cases:

ID	Guideline	References	Details
D-01	When the use case diagram gets too complex, split it up.	[Kulak00]	▭
D-02	Use include and extend correctly and consistently.	[Ambler02, Anda02, Hitz02, Jonathan99, Kulak00, Rosenberg01, Simons99]	▭
D-03	Don't overuse generalization, include, and extend relationships in use case diagrams.	[Ambler02, Booch99, Kulak00]	▭
D-04	Use the sequence diagrams and collaboration diagrams depending on the emphasis of the interaction.	[Booch99]	▭
D-05	Show only those properties of messages in interaction diagrams that are important with regard to understanding the interaction in its context.	[Booch99]	▭⇧
D-06	Minimize crossing lines in interaction diagrams.	[Booch99]	–
D-07	Emphasize important aspects of diagrams.	[Booch99]	▭

D-08	Lay out the elements in use case diagrams with meaning.	[Booch99]	🗋
D-09	Use branching sparingly in interaction diagrams.	[Booch99, Fowler99]	🗋
D-10	For active objects, distinguish explicitly between processes and threads.	[Booch99]	⇧
D-11	Use time and space properties sparingly in interaction diagrams.	[Booch99]	🗋
D-12	In sequence diagrams, the main message flow should be from left to right.	[Ambler02]	–
D-13	Avoid the modeling of object destruction.	[Ambler02]	🗋
D-14	Use prose for interactions with physical actors.	[Ambler02]	🗋
D-15	Only model return values when necessary.	[Ambler02]	🗋⇧
D-16	Try to imply timing considerations by stacking use cases.	[Ambler02]	🗋⇧
D-17	Put primary actors in the top left corner of use case diagrams.	[Ambler02]	⇧
D-18	Actors must not interact directly with other actors.	[Ambler02]	–
D-19	Use structured message flow only.	[Simons99]	🗋⇧

The following list gives more detailed information about the guidelines (the type of information provided can be seen from the overview table):

D-01   🗋   In most cases, it is not reasonable to show all of the use cases and their relationships in one use case diagram. Instead, the entire system should be grouped logically (from the point of view of the use cases) and one diagram should exist for each subsystem.

Additionally, keep in mind (see [Jonathan99] for details) that the semantics of the extends relationship implies that the basic flow of control, as well as the general aims of a use case, must not be touched or altered by extension. In a comparable way to behavioral subtyping [Liskov94], the general behavior and semantics must not be altered.

D-02   🗋   Unfortunately, different definitions of the include and extend features can be found in the literature. We have provided some definitions in Sect. 5.2, which you should adhere to. In addition, don't overuse these relationships, since this makes use case diagrams difficult to understand (see guideline D-03).

D-03   🗋   Essential include, generalization, and extend relationships should be visualized in the use case diagram. Nevertheless, keep in mind that the emphasis of use cases and use case diagrams is on gathering requirements and not on design issues. This is especially true for the generalization and extend relationships.

D-04   🗋   If it is important to show the ordering of messages, sequence diagrams should be used. If it is important to show the structural organization of objects, collaboration diagrams are the correct choice. There is no possibility of emphasizing both aspects in one diagram.

D-05   🗋   Depending on the granularity of the use case to be described, it is sufficient just to show the name of the interaction. If you want to be more precise, you can also include names and types of parameters as well as names of return values. On the other hand, if you use the return value of a message in the following communication, you must make clear where this value comes from; the same applies to parameters.

rameters.

⇧   Figure 36 is an example of a sequence diagram in which details of interactions are included. In this diagram these details are necessary, as the parameters and return values are used in consecutive interactions.

D-07   ▭   Emphasize important aspects of diagrams (use case diagrams and interaction diagrams) by means of color or by adding notes.

D-08   ▭   Behaviors and roles that are semantically close should also be spatially close in the use case diagram. This facilitates the understanding of use case diagrams.

D-09   ▭   Simple branching—as shown, for example, in Fig. 36—can be used without any problems in interaction diagrams. Nevertheless, avoid complex branching situations, as they make interaction diagrams difficult to understand.

Typically, use an interaction diagram to capture the behavior of a use case more precisely. If you follow guidelines Q-06 and W-03, the main course of events should contain only sparse branching. Therefore, the branching problem should not arise in the corresponding interaction diagram.

Only include alternative paths in the interaction diagram as long as it does not get too complex (from the point of view of branching). Alternately, capture the behavior described in one use case (including alternative paths) in several interaction diagrams.

D-10   ⇧

Process: Thread:

D-11   ▭   Timing and space properties are important in describing timing constraints, as well as the location of processes. Space properties should in any case be used as soon as processes are involved (see guideline D-10). Timing constraints should only be used for extraordinary timing situations; that is, when it is really crucial that an operation returns a result within a specified period of time.

D-13   ▭   In the normal case, don't model the destruction of objects explicitly. First, during analysis this implementation issue is not yet important. Secondly, many object-oriented programming languages (e.g., Java and C#) offer automatic garbage collection mechanisms.

For active objects (processes or threads), it might be important to clearly specify when these objects come into existence and when they are terminated. Therefore, for active objects it might be useful to model the destruction (and possibly the creation) of the active object.

D-14   ▭   This is important, to distinguish it from more formal communication with other systems of subsystems.

D-15   ▭   Only use return values for synchronous messages when the value returned is needed in consecutive interaction steps.

⇧   In Fig. 36 return values are used, as the return values are either used in further interactions (*missingLibraries* and *ok*), in constraints (*libraryDescriptions*), or in conditions (*available*).

D-16   ▭   Basically, use case diagrams do not reflect any timing issues. Nevertheless, the understanding of use case diagrams can be facilitated by arranging the use cases in the diagram into a logical—that is, timely—order.

⇧   Figure 64 shows a use case diagram for deploying mobile agents. Here we give an example of the same use case diagram, considering the timely ordering of use cases:

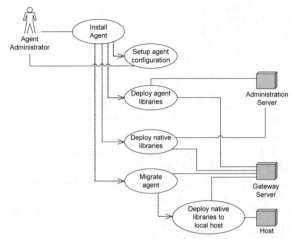

D-17   ⇧   See Fig. 64 or the example given in guideline D-16.

D-19   ⬚   The UML notation for sequence diagrams does not impose any limitations on how
to draw the message flow. It is therefore possible to "jump" into arbitrary loops, to
draw the message flow across other messages. Nevertheless, you are encouraged to
use disciplined message flows—comparable to the discipline of structured (GOTO-
less) programming.

⇧   Both Fig. 35Fig. 35 and Fig. 36Fig. 36 are examples of interaction diagrams that
adhere to this principle.

5.5   The Impact of Scenarios on Quality

As already mentioned in the introduction to Sect. 5.3, the aim of providing guidelines and best practices for use cases, use case diagrams, and interaction diagrams
is to enhance the quality of the descriptions, in order to enhance the overall quality
throughout the entire software development process. In Chap. 1, we gave an overview (see Fig. 3) of the positive effects of assertion and scenario techniques on
quality.

In Chap. 2, we identified a number of quality criteria that it is important to
consider when developing a product. We believe that applying use cases, and use
case diagrams throughout the development process has positive effects on a number of these quality criteria. There is some empirical evidence (see [Achour99],
[Cox00], [Cox01], [Lilly99], and [Palph02]) that measurable enhancements can be
obtained when applying these techniques:

Ambiguity	Completeness	Understandability	Volatility	Traceability	Architecture	Maintainability	Reusability	Int. Documentation	Ext. Documentation	Resource Usage	Completion Rates	Correctness
	+	+		+		+						+

- *Completeness:* The use of scenarios in software development processes leads to a more complete specification of the intended behavior of the system. This is mainly due to the fact that scenarios try to focus on the system behavior from the viewpoint of the users of the system. Turning the typical system-centered approach upside down enables the domain experts, and later users, to identify wrong or missing behavior, as the document that describes this behavior is written from their perspective.

- *Understandability:* Focusing the description of scenarios on the user's perspective leads to a better understanding of the documented behavior, as the process-oriented view facilitates the understanding process of the domain experts. Additionally, use case descriptions contain a variety of detailed information (preconditions, postconditions, assumptions, and business rules) that also serves as a basis for further design and implementation tasks.

- *Traceability:* As scenarios document business processes, they can be more easily mapped with the source of the information, as organizations tend to document their overall processes but not the individual steps in the process. Therefore, scenarios support backward traceability. Forward traceability—that is, the ability to trace from the scenarios to design or implementation—cannot be directly achieved. Forward traceability is achievable in an iterative, prototyping-oriented project setting (see Chap. 6).

- *Maintainability:* Maintainability is enhanced to a large degree, as it is easier to understand the impacts that changes in one part of the system might have on the entire system. At the very least, it is possible to perform a risk analysis: changes to the system that affect scenarios that are used directly in many other scenarios probably involve higher risks than changes that only affect "solitaire" scenarios. Besides risk management, a scenario-based approach reduces the time necessary for new developers and maintainers to become familiar with a project, as the scenario-based description always shows the context within which a system function is used.

- *Correctness:* Correctness is supported in the sense that system developers can show that the software complies with the specified scenarios. This can either be shown by hand or—in the case of a prototyping-oriented project setting (see Chap. 6)—it can also be supported at the tool level.

6 Contracts and Scenarios in the Software Development Process

Summary: Software development processes play an important role in the successful and timely delivery of software. There are different approaches to software development processes—more traditional approaches following and extending the spiral model (e.g., the Rational Unified Process—RUP) and more agile approaches such as Scrum, that try to integrate ideas from extreme programming (XP) and extreme modeling. Regardless of the software development process, the application of contract and scenario techniques is possible in all major tasks involved with software development (analysis, design, implementation, and testing).

Keywords: Unified Process (UP), Rational Unified Process (RUP), Scrum, Agile, Agile models, Quality assurance

So far, we have followed a product-oriented perspective on contracts and scenarios. In Chap. 2, we presented the technical foundations of contracts as we understand them in this book. Chapter 3 related the general principles of contracts to the techniques available in UML, and presented guidelines about how to formulate contracts. In Chap. 4 we presented the technical foundations of scenarios, while Chap. 5 related the general principles of scenarios to the techniques available in UML (e.g., use case diagrams and interaction diagrams) and presented guidelines about how to formulate use cases, use case diagrams, and interaction diagrams.

The emphasis of Chaps. 3 and 5 was on relating general concepts to the techniques available in UML. Implicitly, we assumed that the presented techniques could be applied successfully in the early phases of the software development process. But what is a software development process? In general, a software development process is a set of activities that are needed to transform a user's requirements into a software system. A software development process [Jacobson99]:

- Provides guidance to order a team's activities.
- Directs the tasks of individual developers and of the team as a whole.
- Specifies what artifacts should be developed.
- Offers criteria for monitoring and measuring a project's products and activities.

One general model for describing software development processes is the waterfall model as described by Boehm [Boehm76], which specifies the production of software as a sequence of phases. Numerous variations of this model exist, some even offering the possibility of jumping back to a previous phase. Typical phases according to the waterfall model are requirements analysis and definition, design, implementation, testing, deployment and operation, and maintenance. In the waterfall model, the end of a phase also marks an important milestone at which certain products and documents must be available. For example, the analysis and design phase ends with the availability of the software requirements specification. In real projects [Parnas85] this is problematic, as only parts of the requirements can be captured accurately at the beginning of the project. In a real-world project, the requirements change and evolve in the course of the project. The same problem occurs in the later phases of the software development process.

It is now commonly understood (both in industry and academia) that software development processes have to be iterative. However, some quite different approaches to the software development processes can still be identified. The spiral model [Boehm88] is an enhancement of the classical waterfall model, as it supports an iterative approach; that is, the phases as defined by the waterfall model can be passed several times. However, the waterfall model still concentrates on the production of one defined product, rather than considering several versions—such activities would be postponed to the maintenance phase, or in the case of major revision of a product would lead to a new product.

On the contrary, in an incremental approach, differing versions of the software are considered right from the beginning, The STEPS approach [Floyd89], as well as other more agile process models such as Scrum, explicitly support incremental development. This seems to be a key approach to managing complexity, as the planning horizon always is the next version; that is, the next increment. This approach gives us the additional opportunity to roll out products earlier, as a version of a software product is always considered to be fully functional and stable— but with missing functionality that has to be added in later versions of the product. Nevertheless, if this version supports the users' work, it still makes sense to make it available to them (obviously, roll-out can also take place when all increments are consolidated at the end of the process).

The Unified Process (UP) [Jacobson99] is an example of an iterative process. It is quite popular, as it is tightly tied to UML; that is, the UP is the surrounding process for the development and refining of UML models. The UP still is a rigid process with clearly defined workflows, and with typical activities known from classical software development processes. Basically, the UP is a more modern version of the spiral model. The Rational Unified Process (RUP) [Kruchten00] is a specialized form of the UP. While the UP remains at a somewhat general level, the RUP is a web-enabled product of Rational Software, Inc. According to Rational [Rational03b]:

> The Rational Unified Process, or RUP, is a web-enabled set of software engineering best practices that provide you with guidance to streamline your team's development activities. As an industry-wide process platform, RUP enables you to easily choose the set of process components that are right for your specific project needs. You will achieve more predictable results by unifying your team with common processes that improve communication and create a common understanding of all tasks, responsibilities, and artifacts. On one cen-

tralized web exchange, Rational Software, platform vendors, tool vendors and domains experts provide the process components you need to be successful.

On the other hand, agile methods and techniques such as XP [Beck99a, Beck99b], Feature Driven Design [Palmer02], DSDM [Stapleton97], the Chrystal family of methodologies [Cockburn02], and Scrum [Schwaber02] are gaining widespread use. Currently, no agreement exists on what the "agile" concept actually refers to. Nevertheless, it has been widely acknowledged that the introduction of the extreme programming method [Beck99b] was the starting point for various agile software development approaches. The "Agile Software Development Manifesto" [AgileManifesto02] states a number of values that are the driving forces for developing techniques and for organizing software development processes:

- Individuals and interactions over processes and tools.
- Working software over comprehensive documentation.
- Customer collaboration over contract negotiation.
- Responding to change over following a plan.

As McCauley [McCauley01] and Glass [Glass01] state, there is a need for both agile and process-oriented methods, as there is no software development model that suits all imaginable purposes. A good overview of agile methods can be found in Abrahamsson et al. [Abrahamsson02].

Scrum [Schwaber02] is an example of a software development process that aims at supporting the construction of software in an agile way. We have chosen Scrum in this book as it is one of the most promising developments in the field of agile models. There are some developments under way [XPScrum03], such as refactoring, pair programming, and collective code ownership, that are attempting to integrate the Scrum management practices with XP practices [Cockburn02].

In this chapter, we give an overview of the Rational Unified Process (RUP) as well as of the Scrum process, in order to give the readers an idea of typical up-to-date software process models. We prefer the RUP over the UP, as the RUP is more dynamic and open to changes. As this book focuses on quality, we also describe the role of quality assurance in these software development processes; that is, which technical and methodological approaches are followed to enhance software quality. For each typical activity in a software development process, we will show how contracts and scenarios can be applied and how they fit into the specific processes (RUP and Scrum).

6.1 An Overview of the Software Development Process

6.1.1 The Rational Unified Process (RUP)

The RUP is an iterative approach for object-oriented systems. The RUP is use-case driven; that is, use cases are a central part of the modeling requirements and of building the foundation for a system. The RUP is divided into four phases (see

Fig. 37), called "inception", "elaboration", "construction", and "transition". Each phase is split into iterations, each of which serves the purpose of refining the expected results of a phase in an iterative way. It is important to understand that the deployment of the software product is in the transition phase; that is, there is no incremental software development where a preliminary version with, for example, 40% of the intended functionality is available—at project half-time. We will give a short overview of the phases and key workflows—a more detailed description can be found in Abrahamsson et al. [Abrahamsson02] and Kruchten [Kruchten00].

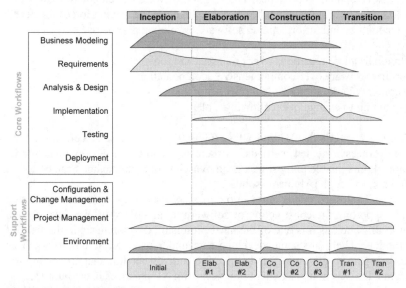

Fig. 37. The Rational Unified Process (RUP)

Inception: During the inception phase, the vision of the end-product and its business application—that is, the scope of the project—is defined. The outcomes of the inception phase are a number of artifacts: a vision document (the project requirements, key features, and main constraints), a use case model (which contains all of the identified use cases and actors), an initial business case, an initial risk assessment, and a project plan (which contains the main phases and iterations).

Elaboration: In general, elaboration is the process of developing something in greater detail. For the RUP, this means that all necessary activities and required resources are planned. All features are specified and the architecture is designed. The outcomes of the elaboration phase are a number of artifacts: a use-case model (quite complete, with all actors and use cases identified), supplementary requirements (to capture nonfunctional requirements or requirements that are not related to use cases), a description of the software architecture, an executable architectural prototype, a revised risk list, and a development plan for the overall project.

Construction: In this phase, building of the product and evolution of the vision, architecture, and plans takes place. At the end of the construction phase, a first release of the product has to be available. The outcomes of this phase are the aforementioned software product, integrated on an adequate platform, the user manuals, and a description of the current release.

Transition: Transition is the process of delivering the product to the customer. This process encompasses manufacturing, delivering, training, supporting, and maintaining the product until users are satisfied.

Each phase can be carried out in several iterations. Kruchten [Kruchten00] gives an example of the timely distribution of the phases for a 2-year project: "inception", 2.5 months; "elaboration", 7 months; "construction", 12 months; and "transition", 2.5 months.

In general, throughout these phases (see Fig. 37) a number of workflows are taking place. The RUP distinguishes between core workflows and supporting workflows. The core workflows are Business Modeling, Requirements, Analysis and Design, Implementation, Testing, and Deployment. The supportive workflows are Configuration and change management, Project Management, and Environment. The contribution of particular workflows varies over time; that is, it depends on the actual phase and iteration of the project. As you can see in Fig. 37 , for example, the emphasis of the deployment workflow is on the transition phase, while deployment does not play any role during the inception and elaboration phases.

Business Modeling: The general goal of this workflow is to understand the structure and dynamics of the organization in which a system is to be deployed. Furthermore, current problems in the target organization and improvement potentials have to be identified. Another important goal of this workflow is to ensure that all stakeholders taking part in the project have a common understanding of the target organization. Finally, system requirements have to be derived in order to support the target organization.

Requirements: The main goal is to establish and maintain agreement with the customer and other stakeholders on what the system should do. The gathering and documentation of requirements has to provide system developers with a better understanding of the system requirements, has to define the boundaries of the system, has to provide the basis for planning the technical contents of iterations, and has to provide a basis for estimating the cost and time needed to develop the system.

Analysis and Design: The purpose of this workflow is to translate the requirements into a specification that describes how to implement the system. The goal is to derive an analysis model and to later transform it into a design model; that is, a model that can be directly used in implementation. We do not discuss how to differentiate between analysis and design models, but we refer to Kruchten [Kruchten00], who presents the RUP view on this issue.

Implementation: The implementation workflow serves a number of purposes. First of all, the general organization and packaging in terms of systems and subsystems has to be defined. Furthermore, the implementation workflow is responsible for implementing the system; that is, providing the necessary classes and components. The testing of individual units, as well as system integration, completes the goals of this workflow.

Testing: The major goal of this workflow is to ensure that the developed software is correct; that is, that it fulfills the specification. Additionally, the testing workflow has to identify any defects, and ensure that all discovered defects are addressed before the software is deployed.

Deployment: The general purpose of deployment is to turn the finished software product over to its users. This involves activities such as beta testing, packaging of the software for delivery, software distribution, software installation, and the training of the end users.

Configuration and Change Management: The purpose of configuration and change management is to track and maintain the integrity of evolving project assets; that is, of all artifacts that are created and changed during the project.

Project Management: The project management workflow as understood by the RUP provides a framework for managing software-intensive projects, provides practical guidelines for planning, staffing, executing, and monitoring projects, and provides a framework for managing risk. The RUP explicitly excludes issues such as managing people, budgets, and contracts.

Environment: This supportive workflow is responsible for providing the development organization with processes and tools. This support includes tool selection and acquisition, process configuration, and improvement, as well as typical technical services to support the process.

6.1.2 Scrum

The Scrum methodology is a typical representative of so-called agile methods. The main reasons why we have chosen Scrum as an alternative approach here are as follows:

- Scrum is a kind of project meta-model that allows us to decide how analysis, design, implementation, and testing have to be carried out—this is not tied to any specific process or method, but is free to the applicants of this meta-model. It is therefore possible to use techniques from the XP toolbox, as well as to introduce proven methodologies or techniques from the RUP.

- Scrum represents a modern style, the agile style, of software development that is suitable for small to medium-sized projects, where incremental software development with easy-to-grasp tasks and functionality is the core planning mechanism. The approach delivers software to the customer in an incremental way and therefore introduces productive feedback mechanisms early in the software development process.
- Scrum integrates well with agile-style software development. Efforts are under way [XPScrum03] to integrate Scrum with XP.
- We believe that scenario-based and contract-based prototyping offer optimal payback in an incremental project setting, as—due to the incremental nature of behavioral changes—contracts are invalidated, outdated, have to be extended, and so on. Both contracts and scenarios support this process, as we will describe in Sect. 6.3.

The Scrum process is person-centered (in the positive meaning of the agile manifesto [AgileManifesto02], as it concentrates on how the team members should function in order to produce the system flexibly. Scrum, as already mentioned, does not define specific software development techniques for the implementation phase—it can be applied regardless of the implementation techniques to be used (object-oriented development or classical module-oriented software development).

The general assumption that underlies the Scrum process is that the development of a system is unpredictable due to a number of variables (e.g., the requirements, the time frame, the resources, and the technology), which are likely to change during the process. According to the proponents of Scrum, this implies a flexible process that can adapt itself according to the changes that take place. Figure 38 visualizes the Scrum process.

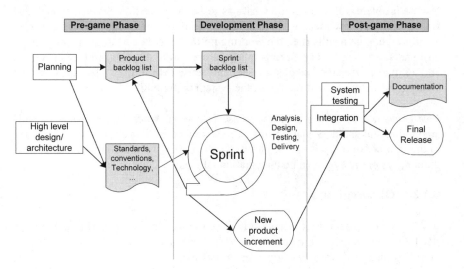

Fig. 38. The Scrum Process

The Scrum process consists of three major phases—the pre-game phase, the development phase, and the post-game phase.

Pre-Game Phase: In the pre-game phase, two major activities take place. (1) Planning activities have to be carried out in order to define the system to be developed. This is achieved by creating a backlog list; that is, a list that contains all known requirements. The backlog list is changed throughout the entire software development process—as soon as new knowledge is available, the backlog list is improved to reflect the current requirements for the product. The backlog list is a central planning instrument, as it serves as the principal means of updating estimations and establishing priorities about the requirements to be implemented in the next increment.

The pre-game phase also incorporates an architecture phase, in which the high-level architecture of the system is developed and changed; that is, changes to the backlog list are also reviewed from a design perspective. The main emphasis here is on how additional or clarified requirements make changes necessary in the design.

Development Phase: The development phase is carried out in Sprints. Sprints are iterative cycles in which the functionality is developed or enhanced to produce new increments. Each Sprint includes the traditional phases of software development; that is, requirements elicitation, analysis, design, implementation, testing, and delivery. A Sprint typically lasts for 30 days. It is current practice that the functionality of an increment is determined in a Sprint planning meeting, where customers, users, and management decide upon the goals and the functionality of the next Sprint. During execution of the Sprint, there are daily Scrum meetings that are organized to keep track of the progress of the Scrum team continuously, to discuss problems, and to decide what has to be done next. A Sprint is concluded with a Sprint review meeting, held on the last day of the Sprint, where the Scrum team presents the results (i.e., the working product increment) to the management, customers, and users. The Sprint review is used to assess the product increment and to make decisions about subsequent activities. It may also happen that changes are made to the direction of the system being built.

Post-Game Phase: The post-game phase is entered when agreement is reached among the stakeholders that no more requirements are left or should be included in the release. In the post-game phase, typical deployment activities such as integration, system testing, and documentation take place.

6.1.3   Observations

In the previous sections, we have briefly presented the Rational Unified Process (RUP) as well as the Scrum approach. While the RUP is a typical representative of more classical software development approaches (in the tradition of the spiral model), Scrum is a "new age" approach to support agile concepts. Some observations that are of importance in the remainder of this chapter are as follows:

- Typical activities, which are already known from the waterfall model or from the spiral model, can also be found in the RUP and in the Scrum software development process—these activities are requirements elicitation, analysis and design, implementation, testing, and deployment. The RUP has additional supportive workflows that are not directly related to core software development (configuration and change management, environment, and project management), and a business modeling workflow that also goes beyond core software development. Business modeling as understood by the RUP concentrates on finding out the structure and dynamics of the organization in which a system is to be deployed. Furthermore, current problems in the target organization and the potential for improvement have to be identified.
- Both approaches are iterative, which means that, for example, the developed specifications, models, and implementations evolve over time—hopefully in a consistent way. In the RUP, the iterations are concentrated on the main products of the actual phase; that is, on the analysis model during the analysis and design phase and on implementation in the construction phase. In the Scrum model, it is obligatory that one iteration covers requirements elicitation, analysis, design, implementation, and testing, which means that usually in every iteration changes to the analysis model, the design, the implementation and to the test environment are necessary.
- The RUP (and also the more general Unified Process—UP) rely heavily on use cases and on the UML. Therefore, our approaches to prototyping with contracts and scenarios are applicable in principle, as both components form part of the UML, by means of the OCL for contracts and interaction diagrams for scenarios.
- Scrum is independent of any specific implementation techniques. It is therefore feasible to integrate contract approaches and scenario approaches—regardless of the technology used (UML-based or not)—into the Scrum process.

6.2   Quality Assurance and Software Development Processes

The emphasis of this book is on providing and explaining techniques to enhance the quality of software products, with a focus on contracts and scenarios. Nevertheless, we will briefly describe how the software development processes described in this chapter attempt to enhance the quality of software from the point of view of the process.

Quality Assurance in the Rational Unified Process (RUP): The RUP is a software development process that is also suitable for large teams. Nevertheless, the RUP does not anticipate a team or a distinctive workflow to ensure quality (as is the case is the V model [VModel03]). The RUP distinguishes between product quality and process quality. Process quality (according to [Kruchten00]) is the degree to which an acceptable process was implemented and adhered to during the manufacturing of the product. The RUP itself focuses on verifying whether a product meets the expected quality level. For this purpose, a test workflow is available that tries to ensure a proper quality level. In the RUP, testing is a workflow that occurs in parallel with the implementation workflow. The RUP systematizes the dimensions of testing—the quality dimension (e.g., reliability and performance), the stages of testing (e.g., the unit test and the integration test), and the types of test (the benchmark test, the function test, and the load test)—and provides a principal test model that can be used in any project. A test model defines what will be tested and how it will be tested. A test model includes test cases, test procedures, test scripts, test classes and components, and notes, and is the basis for carrying out testing. At the general process level, the RUP tries to ensure quality by means of iterative development for the distinctive phases of the software development process.

Quality Assurance in the Scrum Process: At the process level, the most important aspect for quality assurance is the daily Scrum meeting during a Sprint. These daily meetings ensure that the entire development team is on track, that they work focused for the next increment; that is, they try to work off the actual Sprint backlog list.

Another important issue is the continuous involvement of the stakeholders (users, managers, and clients). The main difference compared to classic methods is that the stakeholders get a better feeling about the product capabilities, as they can directly see at the end of a Sprint what could be achieved, and how the software behaves or misbehaves. This is a valuable input for the next planning phase; that is, for adapting and enhancing the product backlog and for planning the next Sprint backlog.

According to the Scrum approach, it is important that there are no interruptions from outside during a Sprint. It is therefore not possible to change a Sprint backlog during execution of a Sprint. We think that this is an important issue, as efficient software production can only take place when the software development team has the time to concentrate on the problems to be solved, without being forced to continuously react to exterior inputs.

In the development phase of Scrum in particular, there no specific development techniques are favored. Nevertheless, as Scrum is an agile process model it perfectly complements agile software development approaches such as XP [Beck99a]. As already mentioned, work is under way [XPScrum03] to integrate XP into the Scrum process model. There are some XP practices that have a positive impact on software quality, such as test-driven development (write tests before you implement the software to be tested), continuous refactoring, continuous integration (code is integrated into the code-base as soon as it is ready), and on-site customer integration (the customer has to be present and available full-time for the team).

6.3 Contracts and Scenarios in the Software Development Process

In the previous sections, we have presented and discussed two typical software development processes, the Rational Unified Process (RUP) and the Scrum approach. While the RUP is a consequent development of the spiral model, the Scrum approach is a representative of an agile process that can easily be complemented by agile techniques.

Regardless of the type of software development model, a number of tasks always occur in software development processes—requirements elicitation, analysis, design, implementation, and testing. In the following sections, we will briefly describe the role of scenarios and contracts in the software development process. We will concentrate on the scenario and contract approaches because we have described them in the early chapters of this book. In this chapter, we will not take necessary tool support into consideration—the discussion about tool support is postponed until Chap. 7. The description in this section has the following pattern:

- *The role of contracts:* This subsection describes how contracts can be applied to the specific task.
- *The role of scenarios:* This subsection describes how scenarios can be applied to the specific task.
- *Methodological issues:* In this subsection we discuss general methodological issues; that is, issues that are independent of any specific software development model.
- *RUP/Scrum issues:* In this subsection we discuss (if applicable) special issues that are related to particular aspects of the RUP or Scrum process.
- *Example:* In this subsection we show, by means of our mobile agent example (see Appendix A), how to use contracts and scenarios.

6.3.1 Contracts and Scenarios for Analysis

Analysis is the task of finding out what exactly a software program should do. This involves tasks such as gathering and documenting requirements. The gathering and documenting of requirements takes place at different levels of abstraction. From the point of view of a customer, features or a list of features are typically the subject matter of interest. For software developers, the detail level of feature lists is too coarse—therefore, the software requirements have to be captured and described in much more detail. With regard to the RUP, the analysis task comprises the requirements workflow as well as parts of the analysis and design workflow. With regard to the Scrum process, the analysis task takes place during the pregame phase (planning and enhancement of the backlog list) and during the development phase—here, an explicit analysis task is anticipated.

The Role of Contracts: During analysis, general, business-related rules are often captured and documented. On the whole, we believe that the use cases to be developed are the driving force for the subsequent development of business rules. Use case descriptions usually have sections that describe preconditions and post-conditions for use cases, and separate tabular representations of business rules (see [Kulak00]). During the analysis process, a model (by means of a class diagram) is developed to capture core elements and their relations. In the course of defining and refining this model, assertions have to be added step by step. As we pointed out earlier in this book, it is not appropriate to capture the assertions at the use case level by means of a formal language such as OCL; the same applies to the business rules. Nevertheless, when a certain degree of maturity is reached in the analysis phase, these formal approaches can be used to capture the assertions (in use cases and business rules) in a more precise way.

The Role of Scenarios: Scenarios play an important role in capturing the requirements of a system—this is true for systems in which business processes play an important role. The approach is not so suitable, in our opinion, for capturing the requirements of typical software tools, such as graphics editors or word processors. The technique can be used from first rough sketches of what has to be achieved right up to detailed descriptions of a scenario. In Chap. 4, we presented a tabular representation for scenarios that is valuable during the analysis task, as additional information can be added in the course of development of the scenarios. For selected use cases, a more formal description by means of interaction diagrams can be developed.

Methodological Issues: As described above, scenarios and contracts are developed in parallel, where the scenarios are the driving force for capturing and documenting the system and software requirements. Figure 39 shows a principal process that contract-related and scenario-related activities follow during analysis.

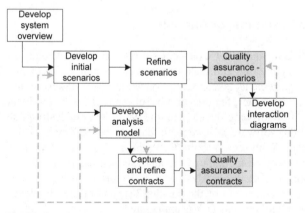

Fig. 39. Contracts and scenarios for analysis

Development of the system overview has something to do with finding out what the customer wants in the larger perspective—What's the business case? What is the aim of the project? What does the customer want the product to do in general? One principal idea about how to capture and document the system overview is to use high-level use case diagrams. The use of this approach helps to identify system boundaries as well as the actors needed to fill in more details.

On the basis of this general understanding of the system, initial scenarios are identified and described. At this stage of the project, it is important not to go into too much detail. It is more important here to identify all of the relevant scenarios and to understand them in principle. It is a good idea at this point to concentrate on good names for scenarios, as well as on good overview descriptions.

After these initial scenarios have been approved by all of the stakeholders who are interested in this system, the scenarios are refined and an analysis model of core parts of the system is developed. The refinement of scenarios, as well as the development of an analysis model, is itself an iterative process, and it might also require us to step back, and to enhance and change the initial set of scenarios, due to additional insights gained during the analysis phase (this explicit iteration leads back to other tasks, as shown by the dotted line in Fig. 39). The process of refining scenarios means to incrementally fill in the missing parts of a textual scenario description (see Sect. 4.4.1); that is, the basic course of events, alternative paths, preconditions, postconditions, and so on. The more insight that the analysts gain in the system to be developed, the more elaborate the analysis model will be. The development of the analysis model comprises the definition of core elements of the system as well as their relationships. This analysis model can also be enhanced using contracts that describe—at the class level (invariants) or at the method level (preconditions and postconditions)—aspects of the behavior of the elements. Refining the analysis model in this way, as well as refining the scenarios, leads to changes (visualized in Fig. 39 using dotted lines). In this context of constant iterations and changes, we believe that contracts are an excellent tool, as they support consistent changes—that is, either you find out that the changes that you make violate existing contracts and therefore are not allowed, or you find out that the contracts have to changed in order to capture the behavior more precisely.

Quality assurance for scenarios and contracts is an important issue. In Chaps. 3 and 5, we developed a number of guidelines for the development of assertions and scenarios. It has to be assured that the contracts and scenarios adhere to these guidelines. These quality assurance tasks definitely have a loop back to the "refine scenario" task, as well as to the "capture and refine contracts" task. We will model this explicitly in order to emphasize it better.

For selected scenarios, event interaction diagrams will be derived on the basis of textual description. For cost reasons, this can only take place for selected scenarios. In order to ensure good quality, the developed interaction diagrams also have to adhere to the developed guidelines—especially the guidelines for drawing interaction diagrams (see Sect. 5.4.4).

RUP/Scrum Issues: The process described in the above subsection can be applied for the RUP as well as for the Scrum approach. Nevertheless, we believe that the payback in the Scrum approach is even higher. In the RUP approach, the analysis task is carried out in several iterations, but always for the entire scope of the project, while with the Scrum approach new requirements are added in each iteration. This incremental approach followed by Scrum imposes additional challenges on the analysis task, as new requirements always lead to changes of requirements or of the analysis model. These changes can more easily be made when parts of the behavior are captured using assertions, as it is possible to find out in a structured way (by systematically reviewing existing and newly added assertions) whether the changed model is still consistent.

Example: The system overview can best be provided by means of a use case diagram. Figure 64 shows such an example for our deployment example (see Appendix A). Usually, such a diagram is developed in several iterations—the diagram as presented in Fig. 64 shows the result of this process. The next important step is the development of initial scenarios; that is, of scenarios that only contain the overview. The following descriptions show the overview for selected scenarios:

Scenario Name:	Install Agent
Overview:	Installs an agent along with its initial configuration at a specified host, and ensures that all agent and native libraries necessary for execution at the target system are transferred to the gateway server.

Scenario Name:	Deploy Agent Libraries
Overview:	Deploys the agent code library, and optionally the user interface library, for the agent in the Java code repository (JCR) at the administration server (AS) to the JCR at the gateway server, if it is not yet available there.

Scenario Name:	Deploy Native Libraries
Overview:	Deploys all required native libraries that are available to the agent in the native code repository at the administration server (AS) to the native library repository (NLR) at the gateway server (GS).

During the process of refining the scenarios, additional parts are filled in: "Basic Course of Events", "Alternative Paths", "Exception Paths", "Trigger", "Assumptions", "Preconditions", "Postconditions", and "Related Business Rules". In Sect.

4.4.1 we described the structure and expected contents. Below you can see the result of the iterative process; that is, a well-described scenario:

Scenario Name:	Deploy Native Libraries
Overview:	Deploys all required native libraries that are available to the agent in the native code repository at the administration server (AS) to the native library repository (NLR) at the gateway server (GS).
Basic Course of Events:	1. The AS retrieves descriptions of all available native libraries for the agent to be installed from the NLR at the AS. 2. The AS sends a description of each native library to the GS. 3. The GS returns a list of libraries that are missing in the NLR of the gateway server. 4. For each missing library (see the previous step), the AS retrieves the native library from the NLR at the AS (based on the description) and transfers it to the GS. 5. The GS stores each received native library in its local NLR and acknowledges proper receipt of the library to the AS.
Alternative Paths:	None.
Exception Paths:	Throughout the scenario, any errors are logged and the system tries to carry on with the installation process. If any missing library cannot be installed properly, the GS signals an error to the AS.
Trigger:	The AS receives the request to deploy the native libraries of a specific agent to a specified target system.
Assumptions:	» The GS is up and running. » No version conflicts can occur, as the version information for a native library is coded into the library name.
Preconditions:	» All native libraries required by an agent are at least available for one platform (e.g., the Win32 platform).
Postconditions:	» Each library whose proper deployment was acknowledged by the GS is guaranteed to be available in the NLR of the GS.
Related Business Rules:	» Naming conventions for native libraries: Each native library name consists of the name of the library plus a version number. The version

number is obligatory and consists of one or two digits. The first digit represents the major release number, and the second digit the minor release number. The library extension terminates the name of the library. The library extension has two to four letters and is separated from the rest of the name by a dot (e.g., "dll" is a valid extension for a Win32 library).

» Compatibility of native libraries: Each native library is backward compatible with any library with a lower minor version digit. Native libraries with differing major version digits are incompatible.

The understanding gained during elicitation and documentation of the use cases enables us to develop an analysis model; that is, a class diagram that shows the main elements of our problem. The analysis model is shown in Fig. 62. On the basis of the knowledge that is now available, we can define a number of initial contracts for this system:

```
Agent
inv: javaArchive != null
inv: nativeLibrary.canLoad()


GatewayServer::storeNativeLibrary(NativeLibrary lib)
pre: !nativeLibraryRepository.contains(lib)
post: nativeLibraryRepository@pre +1 = nativeLibraryRepository.size()
post: nativeLibraryRepository.contains(lib)
```

These activities are all carried out in parallel and must be accompanied by the quality assurance tasks as shown in Fig. 39; that is, quality assurance of scenarios and of guidelines. It makes sense to describe some selected scenarios in more detail using interaction diagrams (Fig. 35 and Fig. 36 are examples of interaction diagrams for the installation of an agent and for the deployment of native libraries).

6.3.2   Contracts and Scenarios for Design

During analysis and requirements elicitation, the emphasis of the activities is on understanding and capturing the problem. In design, a general architecture (e.g., client–server) and an associated design are developed that consider and reflect all functional and nonfunctional requirements. Important aspects to be considered during design are [Jacobson99] as follows:

- Acquisition of an in-depth understanding of the requirements and technologies that are relevant for this project.
- Decomposition of the implementation work into manageable segments that can

be handled by different implementation teams.
- Definition of the major interfaces between subsystems.

The Role of Contracts: As contracts partly capture functional requirements, it is important to transform the contracts developed during analysis (see the previous section) into design. The design process itself is iterative in nature, and starts with the analysis model, which is transformed step by step into the physical design, with different class names, additional or changed interfaces, divided functionality, and so on. Each change in the design model also has to take into consideration the changes in the contracts. Consideration of the contracts in redesign tasks ensures that the design model remains compatible with the analysis model (from the point of view of the behavioral specifications).

The Role of Scenarios: While contracts are a good basis with which to ensure that the specification of selected classes and interfaces is adhered to, scenarios allow us to reflect whether the developed design model can be used in the context of a specific application, where core parts of the functionality (in the sense of how to use the system) are captured in the scenarios.

Methodological Issues: Figure 40 sketches the principal process during design, with an emphasis on contracts and scenarios.

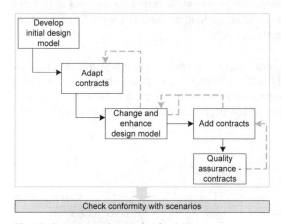

Fig. 40. Contracts and scenarios for design

On the basis of the analysis model, an initial design model has to be derived. In the course of deriving the design model, the contracts have to be adapted to this model—usually by means of simple adaptations, such as name changes, the division of contracts, and so on. Obviously, this task can also be carried out step by step, the contracts being adapted systematically in each step.

During the changes to the design process, enhancements and more details are added to the design model. This is a highly iterative approach (depicted explicitly in Fig. 40) and it naturally implies changes in the contracts. Additionally, by gaining a deeper understanding of the problem domain, additional contracts can be added to the existing ones. This is also an iterative approach, and it has to be ensured that added contracts do not conflict with the additional ones developed during analysis. Quality assurance for contracts is an important issue. In Chap. 3 we developed a number of guidelines for the development of contracts. It has to be assured that the contracts adhere to these guidelines. These quality assurance tasks definitely have a loop back to the "add contracts" task. We will model this explicitly in order to emphasize it better.

In parallel with these activities, the designers always have to check whether their changes conform to the requirements for the system. Parts of the functional requirements are captured by means of scenarios. The designers therefore always have to check whether their design is valid in the context of the developed scenarios.

RUP/Scrum Issues: The role of contracts and scenarios during design is the same as depicted in Fig. 40—regardless of the type of process followed. The RUP, as well as the Scrum approach, are iterative by nature, which means that any changes applied to the design of the system have to be checked in terms of contracts and scenarios. This is even more important in the Scrum approach, as an entire Sprint—in which, for some reason, design decisions might be lost—usually takes place between two design enhancements: as long as contracts were formulated for these decisions, they won't be lost after all.

Example: Figure 62 shows a typical analysis model of our problem domain. During design, this model probably will be changed. Figure 41 shows portions of a design model based on the above-mentioned analysis model. Note that we have only presented one small portion of the design model—the overall design model would be far more complex.

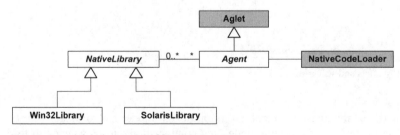

Fig. 41. A partial design model of an agent system

In this design model, the Agent class is now a subclass of an Aglet class [Lange98]; that is, an agent of a specific agent platform. Furthermore, each Agent references a

NativeCodeLoader that is responsible for loading a required native library from the GatewayServer (as described in Appendix B, our deployment process ensures that all required libraries are at least available at the GatewayServer). During the analysis process, we developed (superficially) some contracts for the Agent class:

Agent
inv: javaArchive != null
inv: nativeLibrary.canLoad()

From a design point of view, the Agent class does not necessarily hold a reference to a nativeLibrary at any time, but this association is established when the agent needs this library for the first time during execution. In this event, the library is loaded by the NativeCodeLoader (either directly from the NativeLibraryRepository at the Host or from the NativeLibraryRepository at the GatewayServer). Additionally, we can also say that a native library (once loaded) may not be altered. These insights can be captured using the following contracts:

Agent
inv: javaCodeArchive != null
inv: nativeLibrary != null implies nativeLibrary.canLoad(platform)

Agent::setNativeLibrary(NativeLibray library)
pre: nativeLibrary = null

NativeLibrary
inv: libraryName != null
inv: platform != null

NativeLibrary::canLoad(PlatformDesc platform)
post: result = true implies getPlatform() = platform

The precondition in the setNativeLibrary method ensures that this method can only be called once (assuming that no other method resets the nativeLibrary variable to null—but even in this erroneous case, it would be acceptable to reset the nativeLibrary). We could also capture additional assertions in the newly introduced NativeCodeLoader class:

NativeCodeLoader::getNativeCode(String name, String platform)
post: result != null

This postcondition reflects the fact that a NativeCodeLoader must always find a valid NativeLibrary for a given name and a given platform. This is a restrictive requirement for the getNativeCode method, and it could not be accomplished by the method in a general way. However, in our specific context the postcondition is valid and correct. This example also shows that the contracts expressed in a class need not necessarily be independent of any context. The higher the potential for reusability, the less specific are the assertions formulated. On the other hand, specific contracts describe the specification of a class much better and therefore provide more "guarantees".

6.3.3   Contracts and Scenarios for Implementation

The general goal of the implementation phase is to transform the derived design in such a way that the individual system components are executable in a certain environment. Typical activities during implementation are (1) refinement of design and algorithms, (2) coding, and (3) testing at the unit level. The major artifacts developed during implementation are the source code of the developed classes, as well as the test classes needed for unit testing. Additionally, the results of the unit-testing activities must also be available.

The Role of Contracts: Contracts play an important role, as they guide the implementers during implementation and unit testing. In the implementation phase, invariants and postconditions are important, as each implementation has to show that it meets these assertions.

The Role of Scenarios: In our opinion, scenarios play a minor role during implementation (compared to the role of contracts). They act as a source of clarifications concerning functional requirements.

Methodological Issues: Figure 42 sketches the principal process during implementation, with an emphasis on contracts (scenarios are not included, as they do not have a distinctive role).

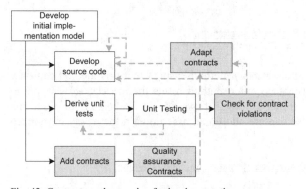

Fig. 42. Contracts and scenarios for implementation

On the basis of the design derived in the design phase, an initial implementation model has to be derived. In our case, the implementation model not only contains the set of classes developed during design but also the contracts initially captured during analysis and refined during design. Unit tests are derived before, during, or after the development of the source code for a unit. Both activities (developing the source code and deriving the unit tests) should be contract-driven:

- The implementation can rely on the contracts—other sources of information (scenarios and requirements documents) also have to be considered. Nevertheless, the implementer need not handle situations that are explicitly captured by the preconditions, although he or she always has to ensure that the implementations do not violate any invariants of the postconditions.
- The contracts specified for a unit (e.g., a class) are an excellent source for deriving test cases. Every precondition reduces the possible combinations of input values and should therefore be used carefully in order to check whether the implementation conforms to the specification in general, and to the postconditions and invariants in particular.

The unit-testing activities may reveal errors that indicate inadequacies in the implementation, as postconditions or invariants are violated. If this is the case, the source code has to be changed accordingly to reflect the correct behavior (in the sense of the specified contracts) of the class. It may also happen that the implementation is acceptable but the specified contracts are wrong. Therefore, it is also necessary to adapt (alter or enhance) the contracts in order to better reflect the behavior of a class.

Additionally, it will always be the case that while developing the source code and deriving the unit tests, new contracts come to mind as the implementers gain a deeper understanding of the problems to be solved. Obviously, these contracts should be added to the existing contracts, insuring that they comply with the quality requirements for contracts and that they do not conflict with existing contracts.

RUP/Scrum Issues: The role of contracts and scenarios during implementation is the same as depicted in Fig. 42—regardless of the type of process followed. The RUP, as well as the Scrum approach, are iterative by nature, which means that any changes have to be checked in terms of contracts.

Example: During the design process, we developed some contracts for the Agent class:

```
Agent
inv: javaCodeArchive != null
inv: nativeLibrary != null implies nativeLibrary.canLoad(platform)

Agent::setNativeLibrary(NativeLibray library)
pre: nativeLibrary = null

NativeLibrary
inv: libraryName != null
inv: platform != null
```

On the basis of this information, the implementer has to ensure that the constructors of the Agent class always set the nativeLibrary instance variable to null. Additionally, we can use the precondition information to construct proper test cases for unit testing.

6.3.4   Contracts and Scenarios for Testing

The goal of testing (beyond ordinary unit tests) is validation of the system, and the detection of as many errors as possible. Integration tests and system tests are the most important types of test.

According to Jacobson et al. [Jacobson99], integration test cases are used to verify that the components interact properly with each other after they have been integrated into a build. Most integration tests can be derived from scenarios, as they describe how the entities of the system interact.

System tests [Jacobson99] are used to test whether the system functions properly as a whole. Each system test primarily tests combinations of scenarios under different conditions. These conditions include different hardware configurations, different levels of system loads, different numbers of users, and so on.

The Role of Contracts: As already mentioned in the introduction to this section, contracts play a subordinate role, as the driving force for developing integration and system tests is the developed scenarios. Nevertheless, the specified contracts support this test process. In case of thorough unit testing during implementation, violations of postconditions should not occur. However, as the individual classes are now tested together, it will happen that some classes violate preconditions, or that special (valid) constellations occur that lead to errors in the postconditions or invariants. In the case of violations of preconditions, the caller has not fulfilled its contract, while in case of postcondition violations the callee has not fulfilled its contracts—therefore the sources of the errors can more easily be traced. It will also happen that errors occur that are not covered by existing assertions. In this case, it has to be decided whether new assertions should be included in order to capture these error situations.

The Role of Scenarios: Scenarios are the primary source for composing interaction tests. Regardless of the representation, the scenarios are used to construct test scripts. Standardized descriptions of scenarios (e.g., using interaction diagrams) facilitate this process. Typically, type scenarios (see Sect. 4.2.4) are used—therefore, from one scenario, a number of test scripts that are suitable for integration or system testing can be extracted.

Methodological Issues: Figure 43 sketches the principal process during testing.

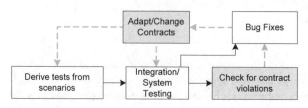

Fig. 43. Contracts and scenarios for testing

The scenarios have to be worked through systematically, in order to derive tests from scenarios for integration and system testing. Typically, one scenario yields a number of different tests. The integration and system testing activities will reveal errors in the implementation. In the case of contract violations, either the contracts have to be adapted (due to incorrectly specified assertions) or the implementation has to be changed. Of course, errors can also occur that are not related to any contract. In these cases, the errors have to be fixed and possibly new assertions have to be added that better reflect the requirements associated with the discovered errors.

RUP/Scrum Issues: The role of contracts and scenarios during implementation is the same as depicted in Fig. 43—regardless of the type of process followed. The RUP, as well as the Scrum approach, are iterative by nature, which means that any changes have to be checked in terms of conformance with the underlying specification and the specified contracts.

7   Prototyping with Contracts and Scenarios

Summary: Prototyping without appropriate tool support is a cost-intensive task and therefore should be avoided. General requirements for prototyping tools include openness, quick turnaround cycles for editing and execution of prototypes, and appropriate easy-to-use user interfaces. The toolset presented in this chapter fulfills the general requirements and provides the following principal prototyping functionality:

- The editing and browsing of classes, methods, inheritance relationships, and assertions (i.e., invariants, preconditions, and postconditions).
- The drawing of interaction diagrams where the types involved are assertion-enriched classes.
- On-the-fly transformation of scenarios into executable prototypes.

There has to be the possibility of (semi)automatically transforming substantial parts of the prototype into a target platform (e.g., Java technology or C++) for system implementation. First, this requirement is pragmatic, as reusable prototypes (in contrast to throwaway prototypes) are favored in order to reduce development costs and development time. Secondly, and more importantly, the formal specifications derived through analysis and expressed by means of assertions must not be lost; as these partial behavioral specifications are of vital importance for the overall software development process, since they facilitate the derivation of test cases and contribute to general quality attributes such as maintainability and correctness.

Keywords: ContractBuilder, ScenarioBuilder, Contract2C++ Transformer, Contract2Java Transformer, Executable scenarios, Evolutionary prototyping

7.1   Prototyping

There is a common understanding of the terms "prototype" and "prototyping", although some minor differences can be observed in the research community. In general, a prototype is model that is used to gain experience in order to reduce errors in the final product. This meaning of the term "prototype" is true for all kinds of prototypes, including software prototypes. There are a number of reasons why prototypes should also be built for software products (see [Baumgartner90], [Brooks87], and [Weinberg90]):

- The high complexity of typical software products.
- The difficulty of specifying all of the requirements for a product completely and consistently right from the beginning.
- Changes to the requirements, which are typical for software products.
- Often, the inherent complexity of requirements documents, due to their size.

The problems caused by these aspects of software products should be reduced by the development of prototyping-oriented software, and by the construction of executable prototypes in the early phases of the software development process. The general idea is to reduce the effort in later phases of the process, by placing some additional emphasis on the early phases of the software life cycle in order to reduce the overall costs. The key point for understanding why this shift leads to a reduction in the overall costs is the fact that the cost of correcting errors increases dramatically during a project; in other words, the later the errors are found and corrected, the more expensive it becomes.

Nevertheless, it is much more challenging to build software prototypes than to build industrial prototypes (e.g., machines, cars). Industrial prototypes often serve as basis for mass production; therefore, the development costs for an industrial prototype can be distributed over a large number of products, and therefore are of minor importance. In contrast, in many cases software products are individual solutions that are sold to one specific organization. Therefore, the total cost for the product (including the prototyping costs) must be lower than it would have been without the application of prototyping. Successful prototyping (in the sense of achieving the goals sketched out above) is only possible in projects with an established communication culture among the participating partners. Besides general organizational requirements, the availability of appropriate tools is essential to enable the building of working models despite small budgets. Most published reports currently available (e.g., [Bäumer96], [Carey89], and [Gordon91]) concentrate on user interface prototyping, while the approach presented here emphasizes prototypes based on scenarios and contracts, in which user interfaces play a minor role.

After this casual introduction to prototyping, we will provide a more precise definition of the terms "prototype" and "prototyping", with a brief discussion of some related definitions. According to Pomberger [Pomberger96], we can define the term *prototype* as follows:

> A software prototype is an executable model of the proposed software system. It must be producible with significantly less effort than the planned product. It must be readily modifiable and extensible. The prototype need not have all the features of the target system, yet it must enable the user to test all important system features before the actual implementation.

This definition is based on the work of Boar [Boar83] and Connell [Connell89]. Other definitions can be found in Gomaa [Gomaa83], Hollinde and Wagner [Hollinde84], and Jörgensen [Jörgensen84]. The important distinguishing feature for a prototype (according to our definition) is therefore that it must be possible to produce it at low cost—but at the same time the prototype must be executable and must show essential system functionality.

According to Pomberger [Pomberger96], we can define the term *prototyping* as follows:

Prototyping encompasses all activities necessary for the production of such prototypes.

The literature [Bischofberger92, Floyd84, Pomberger96] distinguishes different approaches to prototyping; that is, explorative prototyping, experimental prototyping, and evolutionary prototyping.

Explorative Prototyping: This kind of prototyping is used to find out more about the requirements of the product to be developed. Explorative prototyping is a useful technique when the software engineers involved are not domain experts, or when the customer does not yet know what he or she really wants. The prototype is used as a means of communication, with the aim of obtaining a complete, precise, and unambiguous specification. For explorative prototyping, the common technique is to build a prototype that demonstrates the main functionality by means of prototype user interfaces. Explorative prototyping is typically applied during requirements gathering and analysis, in order to gain a good understanding of the problems to be solved.

Experimental Prototyping: The emphasis of such an approach is to show that the suggested solutions are feasible. The purpose here is to prove experimentally the suitability of subsystem specifications, of architecture models, and of general solution ideas for system components. The general approach is to develop a prototype—that is, an executable model—that implements (simulates) typical application examples to test the interfaces of individual system components. It may also be important here to find out whether the chosen architecture and decomposition is sufficiently flexible with respect to extensibility. The same quality requirements apply as with explorative prototyping; in other words, great functionality, easily modifiability, and (last but not least) rapid development. Experimental prototyping can take place during analysis—but the main emphasis is in the design phase, in order to find out whether the proposed architectures and system decompositions are sufficiently flexible.

Evolutionary Prototyping: Evolutionary prototyping is a kind of incremental software development. The general approach is to start with user interface development and to gather the missing pieces of the requirements during this step. This "first version" of the product is not really usable, but just shows what the system looks like. With each iteration, additional functionality is added to the product—it therefore becomes more and more usable. It must be clear that there is no strict distinction between prototype and product; therefore, it is important to apply higher quality standards to the first prototypes than in explorative or experimental prototyping.

Another important aspect of prototyping-oriented software development is the role of the developed prototypes. Those prototypes may either be thrown away or they can also be reused in the later phases of the software development process. Additionally, the prototype may either be complete or incomplete, depending on the chosen approach.

Independent of the specific support needed, prototyping tools must fulfill a number of general requirements (based on [Keller89] and [Pomberger96]):

- *A simple description at a high level of abstraction:* The approach used to specify a prototype should be adequate; in other words, for a user interface prototype a WYSIWYG editor, or at least a user interface specification language (UISL), is the suitable level of abstraction. For prototypes in the information system area, the declarative language SQL is an appropriate description for dealing with operations on databases. Prototyping tools that support executable scenarios should allow us to describe the behavior of the prototype using an interaction diagram.
- *An executable prototype specification:* On the one hand, the language used for describing a prototype should be simple (see above); on the other hand, it must be semantically exact in order to be executable without time-consuming transformation steps.
- *Short turn-around cycles:* It is important here that changes can be applied easily, and that the time between changes and succeeding testing is hardly noticeable. Some systems even have the facility to change the prototype during execution and to resume its execution immediately; that is, without having to restart the prototype altogether (e.g., the tools developed by us (see later) or the user interface builders contained in Smalltalk environments [IBM03]).
- *Support for evolutionary prototyping:* Regardless of the type of the prototype, it should always be possible to grow it step by step into a final application. If this is not applicable to the entire functionality of the prototype—for example, specialized scripts to simulate the behavior of a user interface prototype—the core capabilities of the prototype must be developable in an evolutionary manner.

Regardless of the approach chosen, it is important to have appropriate tool support in order to be able to develop and change a prototype quickly. We can distinguish various different kinds of tools [Keller89, Pree91]:

- *User interface builders:* User interface builders (UI builders) are especially important for explorative prototyping, in order to capture the requirements based on the graphical user interface. UI builders should support *different user interface paradigms*; that is, depending of the kind of project, they must support the construction of native user interfaces (e.g., for Microsoft Windows), HTML-based user interfaces, WML-based user interfaces, and native user interfaces for PDAs (e.g., Symbian). Another important aspect is the level of abstraction of the prototyping specification. For user interface prototyping tools, a WYSIWYG-style user interface is the state of the art. Nevertheless, a platform-independent user interface specification language (UISL) is desirable for projects that have to deploy different kinds of user interfaces. In such a case, a WYSIWIG editor is still important but, more importantly, the description of the user interface should be platform- independent—it should therefore be possible to have one source for different kinds of user interfaces (e.g., a native MS Windows user interface and a HTML interface). The *flexibility of the specified prototype* is important in order to reduce the prototype development costs. A UI builder is flexible when it is possible to change a prototype (the visual layout as well as the functionality) quickly; that is, without long compile–link–go cycles, but by using an interpreter. An important aspect—especially for the functionality behind the user interface—is the support for evolutionary development. It is important to have scripting support during software development—on the other hand, it must also be easily possible to add and change functionality in the later target system.

- *Fourth-generation systems:* This category of tools is optimized for information systems; that is, for systems in which databases play an important role for the entire project. Fourth-generation tools typically consist of a user interface builder and specialized tools to deal with databases, such as database schema editors, support for database query languages, automatic generation of user interfaces based on database schemas, and report generators. This category of tools can easily be used for exploratory prototyping by means of user interface prototyping, and for explorative prototyping by experimenting with different underlying data models in the database. Typically, fourth-generation systems are used in an incremental style; that is, evolutionary software development is supported.

- *Architecture prototyping tools:* This category of tools is the one that is used least in the industry, as good prototyping support is difficult to achieve. These tools typically support experimental prototyping at the architecture level; that is, they allow us to evaluate different software architecture and system decomposition solutions by means of executable prototypes. Some object-oriented programming languages (e.g., Python [Beazley01], Ruby [Fulton02], and Visual Basic [Microsoft03]) that are interpreted, that lack static typing, and that also comprise component libraries can be used for architecture prototyping, as they fulfill most of the general requirements for prototyping tools (see above). An important requirement for architecture prototyping tools is support for evolutionary prototyping—in most cases this is not supported at the language level, but must be achieved using additional tools. An example of an architecture prototyping tool based on the Modula-2 programming language (the toolset offers a Modula-2 interpreter) is the TOPOS SCT environment [Bischofberger92].

7.2 Contract-Based and Scenario-Based Prototyping

In this section we present our prototyping tools, which allow us to build prototypes based on contracts and interaction diagrams. Figure 44 gives an overview of the tools available. We have developed this toolset in order to show how to support prototyping—tailored for the requirements of prototyping with contracts and scenarios. The tools presented here are prototypes themselves, and can serve as a basis for implementing industrial-strength solutions. The two core prototyping tools *ContractBuilder* and *ScenarioBuilder* rely on a Python infrastructure developed by us. This infrastructure adds contract support to the Python programming language. The contract support is flexible, as changes to contracts during execution are automatically taken into consideration. Along with the interpretative nature of Python, and with the lack of a static type system, this infrastructure is well suited for prototyping tasks.

The *ContractBuilder* allows us to specify contracts; that is, preconditions, postconditions and invariants for classes (new classes, methods, etc. can also be added by means of this tool). The emphasis of *ContractBuilder* is on providing a good overview of the specified contract in order to facilitate the understanding of the system under development. *ContractBuilder* is based on a Python infrastructure and it also allows us to execute Python scripts with contract checking in a debugging environment, in order to understand what happens at run time and to analyze any contract violations. *ContractBuilder* is described in more detail in Sect. 7.2.1, and in Plösch [Plösch97, Plösch98].

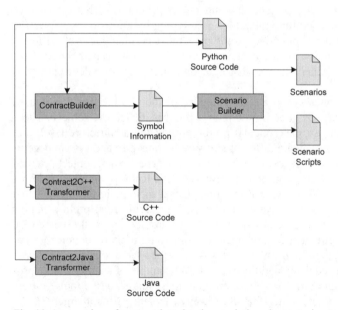

Fig. 44. An overview of contract-based and scenario-based prototyping tools

The *ScenarioBuilder* allows us to specify interaction diagrams based on the symbol information provided by *ContractBuilder*; in other words, only those types and messages can be used that were specified with *ContractBuilder*. Each scenario can be instantiated; that is, several scenario instances can be created by means of a generic object editor. A scenario instance is complete and therefore executable when all types used in the interaction diagram, as well as all parameters for messages, are set. Complete instance scenarios can be executed within *ScenarioBuilder* (with enabled contract checking) or can be stored in (Python) scenario scripts that can be executed separately from *ScenarioBuilder* (also with enabled contract checking). *ScenarioBuilder* is described in more detail in Sect. 7.2.2, and in Plösch and Pomberger [Plösch00].

The *Contract2C++ Transformer* transforms the prototype developed by the *ContractBuilder*—that is, the Python classes and contracts specified—into the C++ programming language. As C++ does not directly support contract checking, we have also developed an infrastructure for C++ to enable contract checking. The Contract2C++ Transformer is described in more detail in Sect. 7.3.3, and in Plösch and Pichler [Plösch99].

The *Contract2Java Transformer* transforms the prototype developed by the *ContractBuilder*—that is, the Python classes and contracts specified—into the Java programming language. As Java technology does not directly support contract checking, we have integrated the existing contract support for the Java programming language. The architecture and design of the tool are sufficiently flexible to allow us to plug in arbitrary components to enable contract support for the Java programming language. Specifically, we have developed and integrated support for the contract-checking environments iContract [Kramer98] and JASS [Bartezko01]. The Contract2Java Transformer is described in more detail in Lettner [Lettner01].

7.2.1   Contract-Based Prototyping

Motivation

The main reason for providing an architecture prototyping tool (*ContractBuilder*) based on contracts was the need for a system that provides support in the analysis and design phase:

- Modeling domain knowledge in an object-oriented fashion.
- Partial specification of the semantics of the domain model by means of formal techniques.
- Experimentation (i.e., prototyping) with the software architecture of the evolving domain model.

We believe that the proposed combination of a contract model and the Python programming language provides a good basis for handling these tasks. Furthermore, in prototyping-oriented development, an interpretable and lean language far outperforms a statically typed programming language such as Eiffel or Java during analysis and the early stages of design. This makes our Python-based approach especially valuable for prototyping-oriented development, no matter whether the contract technique is used during requirements elicitation and specification or in the design phase, where the emphasis is on evaluating different design approaches. Nevertheless, support only at the level of the programming language is insufficient, especially in the first phases of software development. Besides providing the infrastructure, the main emphasis of *ContractBuilder* is to facilitate the understanding of class relations (inheritance and references) and of the behavior of classes (contracts).

Requirements

The requirements for *ContractBuilder* refer not only to the core prototyping tool but also to the infrastructure; that is, to the basic contract support for the execution environment of the prototypes:

- *Compliance with theory:* The semantics of the Python assertion model and thus the semantics as defined by the contract theory must be preserved.
- *Standardization:* The generated Python code must be executable in a standard Python environment; that is, it is not feasible to extend or change the syntax and semantics of standard Python.
- *Readability:* The generated Python code (with the included contracts) must be readable; in particular, this means that the code for assertion checking must be clearly separated from the implementation of a method or class.
- *Configurability:* The configuration process must be configurable; in particular, it must be possible to selectively enable and disable contract checking at the class level.
- *Manipulation of the contract:* It must be easily possible to add and change contracts for classes and methods, as well as to add and change classes by means of specialized editors.
- *Understanding of the contract:* The emphasis of *ContractBuilder* is on facilitating the understanding of the contracts of a set of classes. It is therefore important to incorporate filter mechanisms as well as visualization concepts to facilitate understanding of the developed model.
- *An execution environment with debugging support: ContractBuilder* has to provide an execution environment with contract-checking support according to the theory that supports the prototyping approach—that is, short turnaround circles—and that also provides debugging support in order to better understand state changes of objects and their impact on contracts.

An Overview of ContractBuilder

In this section, we describe the tool support currently available for contract-based prototyping. The description given here is based to a large extent on [Plösch98]. The main emphasis of our DBC support for Python is not related to building bug-free software, but on capturing parts of requirements in the form of assertions. With the particular emphasis on using this technique for requirements elicitation and documentation as well as in the design phase (architecture prototyping), there is a need for interactive tools that allow easy inspection and editing of assertions and inherited assertions.

The general idea was to implement Design by Contract (DBC) for the Python programming language [Lutz01], a dynamically typed, object-oriented, interpreted programming language (for more details, see [Plösch97]). The emphasis of this work was on providing reasonable support throughout prototyping-oriented software development.

We believe that the proposed combination of an object-oriented, dynamically typed, interpreted programming language (which facilitates the construction of prototypes) with a more formal approach such as DBC is a perfect fusion of informality and formalism in the first phases of the software life cycle. Secondly, in prototyping-oriented development, an interpretable and lean language far outperforms a statically typed programming language such as Eiffel during analysis and early design. This makes our DBC–Python approach especially valuable for prototyping-oriented development, no matter whether the DBC technique is used during requirements elicitation and specification or in the design phase, where the emphasis is on evaluating different design approaches. Figure 45 gives an overview of the tools that are currently available.

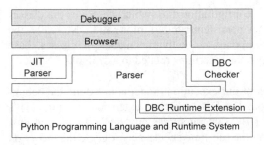

Fig. 45. Tools for contract-based prototyping

The parser, the JIT parser, the DBC checker, and the DBC run-time extension form the infrastructure tools necessary for parsing the assertion statements from the documentation sections of the Python source code and for checking them properly at run time. The tiling structure of Fig. 45 indicates that, for example, the DBC checker is based both on the parser and on the DBC run-time extension. The browser and the debugger, which are suitable during requirements specifications or in the design phase (for architectural prototyping), form the analysis tools and also provide a graphical user interface to make the use of the tools easier. Whereas the browser relies on the information provided by the parser only, the debugger additionally needs the DBC checker in order to check the assertions at run time. In the following sections, we describe the infrastructure tools and provide more details of the analysis tools.

The Parser: We provide support for traditional parsing and for just-in-time (JIT) parsing. Both parsing techniques heavily rely on the reflective capabilities of Python. This means that it is not the source code of files that is parsed, but the meta-information provided by the run-time system. This approach is applicable, as the necessary meta-information (e.g., the class/base class relationships, the methods of a class, and the documentation of a class or method) is available at run time. This availability reduces the parsing effort substantially, as parsing is based on pre-structured symbol information.

In the case of the JIT parser, a class is always parsed in the event of an import. This allows the assertions of a class to be changed and these changes to be applied to a running system. To implement this approach elegantly, interception of the class loading mechanism is necessary, so that the meta-information can be parsed without having to change the code to be parsed. Whether a class has already been parsed, and whether DBC support should be provided by a class, is checked at loading time. A configuration file controls the parsing activities; that is, whether a class has to be parsed. If a class has to be parsed (according to the configuration file), all of its base classes are also parsed. This parsing strategy is important during the prototyping process in order to be able to change contracts at any time (even during prototype execution) and to proceed with the execution of the prototype.

The traditional parser takes a configuration file (which describes the classes to be parsed) as input and generates persistent symbol information. Naturally, the persistent symbol information comprises not only the names of classes, base classes, methods, and so on, but also the assertions related to a symbol.

The DBC Checker: The basic idea of our execution model is to extend the debugger framework provided by Python. The DBC run-time extension (see Fig. 45) is therefore a special debugger for DBC that intercepts any method call, and thus allows the DBC checker to perform the run-time checks according to the theory on the basis of the symbol information provided by the parser.

The process of DBC checking is controlled by an environment variable (to switch checking on and off) and by a configuration file. The configuration file consists of a list of module/class pairs that have to be checked. Thus, by altering the configuration file, DBC checking can be enabled and disabled selectively for certain classes.

The analysis tools provided by our tool environment consist of a contract browser and a contract debugger, and rely upon the infrastructure tools briefly described before. In this description, we want to show that the tools provided are suitable for the intended purpose; that is, for prototyping activities during requirements elicitation and specification and for architectural prototyping. For a more detailed description of the architecture of the analysis tools, and of their integration with the infrastructure tools, see [Plösch98].

The Browser: The browser window depicted in Fig. 46 is divided into three main parts. The upper part (marked *(1)* in Fig. 46) shows all of the classes and methods contained in the project to be analyzed.

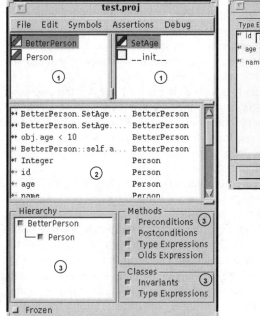

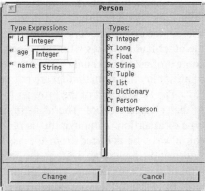

Fig. 46. The DBC browser   Fig. 47. Editing type expressions

The icon in front of the class name or method name gives some basic information about the applicable assertions. The icons in front of the class names show whether any class invariants exist, whereas the icons in front of the method names indicate whether preconditions, postconditions, "old"-expressions, or type expressions for parameters are specified:

- A hollow box indicates that no assertion is specified for the respective symbol, neither in the class itself nor in any subclass or superclass. This information is only related to assertions, not to any inheritance hierarchy in the sense of object-oriented programming.
- A box with a central bar indicates that assertions are specified for the respective symbol, but that there are no assertions specified for any subclasses or superclasses.
- A box with a central bar and gray corners indicates that assertions are specified for the respective symbol and for subclasses and/or superclasses. A filled upper corner of the symbol indicates that assertions apply for superclasses, whereas a filled lower corner of the symbol indicates that assertions apply for subclasses

(it is also the case that both corners may be filled).

We consider this information to be valuable, as it provides a rough overview of the complexity of classes with respect to assertions. Classes with inherited assertions, especially in cases in which many methods of a class inherit assertions, have to be understood and reviewed thoroughly, as they are obviously core components and sources of misunderstandings between the developer and the customers. On the other hand, classes with few assertions or few inheritance relationships (in the context of assertions) indicate either minor importance or white spots; that is, parts of an application domain that are not yet well understood.

The central part of the browser (marked *(2)* in Fig. 46) displays the assertions of the selected symbol. The icons in front of the assertion expression indicate the type of assertion. Although this is redundant information (the type of an assertion can always be deduced from the assertion text), we consider it to be important information for the analyst, as the icons allow quick and easy recognition of the kind of assertions that are most important.

By default, all types of assertions are displayed for a class and all of its superclasses. To facilitate understanding—that is, to reduce the number of assertions displayed simultaneously—filters may be applied. Three different filters (marked *(3)* in Fig. 46) apply to the assertions. First, the analyst may decide whether or not to include the assertions of the base classes. This hierarchy filter always shows the inheritance path of the currently selected class. The analyst may selectively include or exclude the assertions of arbitrary base classes along the inheritance path. Secondly, the analyst may filter the display of assertions related to classes; that is, class invariants and type expressions for instance variables. Thirdly, the analyst may filter the display of assertions related to methods; that is, preconditions, postconditions, "old"-expressions, and type expressions for method parameters. All three groups of filtering conditions are simultaneously applied to the currently displayed assertions. The filter mechanism is useful for selectively browsing the assertions of a class or a family of classes, and thus facilitates understanding of the specified assertions.

Besides merely viewing assertions, the tools allow us to browse the code of arbitrary classes in an associated programming environment. The programming environment is controlled by our browser.

Besides merely browsing assertions, the tools allow us to change existing assertions directly, and to add or delete assertions, as well as adding and changing classes and methods.

The user interface for altering assertions in particular is designed for ease of use. Figure 47 gives an example of a window that allows editing of the type expression of a class.

The currently specified instance variables and their associated types are depicted in the left-hand part of Fig. 47.

The type of an instance variable is easily changed by dragging one of the types shown in the right-hand part of the window across to the respective instance variable in the left-hand part of the window. The types available for dragging are constructed dynamically as, in addition to the built-in types, any class type currently available in the project may be used.

The analyst may export the changes made on demand directly to the Python source code. In addition to the special-purpose editor depicted in Fig. 47, other special-purpose editors are available for other types of assertion.

The Debugger: The DBC debugger is a separate tool, but is tightly integrated with the DBC browser. On selecting the debug mode in the Debug menu of the browser, the browser mutates to the DBC debugger, as depicted in Fig. 48.

The debugger does not restrict the browsing and filtering mechanisms of the DBC browser at all, but extends them for debugging purposes. Specifically, the debugger allows breakpoints to be set arbitrarily; that is, a breakpoint may be set for a class, a method, or an arbitrary assertion.

A breakpoint for a class instructs the run-time system to stop whenever a class invariant is checked; that is, before executing any method of this class. A breakpoint for a method indicates that the run-time system stops before checking the assertions of the particular method. A breakpoint for an assertion instructs the run-time system to stop before checking the marked assertion.

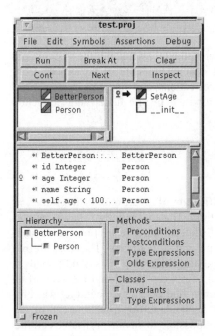

Fig. 48. The DBC debugger

Fig. 49. Inspecting objects

An arrow (see Fig. 48) indicates that a breakpoint has been reached. At this point, the debugger allows inspection of the object in question. For this purpose, we have integrated PTUI [Roadhouse98] into our debugger. The PTUI component is part of the DBC checker. A sample screenshot is given in Fig. 49. The PTUI object browser allows visualization of data members of objects, including inherited members, as well as inspection of class members. As PTUI is completely written in Python, the integration into our DBC checker was painless.

Violations of assertions detected by the DBC checker are displayed in a window. We believe that the debugging support provided, in combination with the analysis support of the browser, contributes to facilitating the understanding of complex contractual relations.

Evaluation

In Section 2.4 we evaluated a number of contract checking systems for programming language that are of industrial importance, i.e., Java, C++ and Eiffel. *ContractBuilder* does not fall into this category of tools, as it's intended purpose is to support prototyping of systems by applying contracts. From this perspective it is also important to evaluate it using the properties defined in Section 2.4.2.

BAS and AAS criteria (OCL)

System	BAS-1	BAS-2	BAS-3	AAS-1	AAS-2	AAS-3
ContractBuilder	ns	3	1	1	1	ns

ContractBuilder allows method calls in assertion expressions, but the system does not ensure that the methods called do not change the state of the object. ContractBuilder supports operations on Python collections, and also provides universal and existential quantification, as this is supported by the underlying collection classes.

SBS and RMA criteria (OCL)

System	SBS-1	SBS-2	SBS-3	RMA-1	RMA-2	RMA-3
ContractBuilder	ns	1	ns	1	3	1

ContractBuilder does not support the specification of assertions for interfaces, as this language feature is not available in Python. The tool strictly follows the correctness rules for contracts as proposed by Eiffel. Stronger restrictions on subcontracts (as demanded by criteria SBS-3 are not supported). The tool throws exceptions in case of contract violations and also writes log files. Additionally it even provides a debugging mode, i.e., breakpoints can be set and the state of an object can be inspected. It is therefore easier to find out, why a contract was broken by the client or by the implementation itself. Assertion checking can be enabled and disabled on the class level. It is not possible to enable or disable contract checking for preconditions, postconditions or invariants selectively. Source code that contains assertions remains fully compatible with the Python programming language, without any performance penalties when no contract checks are used.

Related Tools

Some approaches are available to incorporate contracts into programming languages. The support provided by Eiffel [Meyer92] is the benchmark for other system, as Eiffel realizes the contract theory as described in this book. Some of the approaches for the Java programming language, C++ and Eiffel were presented in Sect. 2.4.3. Other approaches for C++ are the Larch/C++ environment [Leavens99a] or the C- based APP environment, described in Rosenblum [Rosenblum95]. Approaches are also available for Smalltalk [Carillo96] and for other programming languages.

Nevertheless, these approaches are only comparable with the infrastructure provided by our environment. We are not aware of any tool that provides easy-to-use editors, browsers, and execution environments in order to facilitate the editing and understanding of contracts. Furthermore, the approaches for Java technology and C++ have the additional disadvantage that they have to deal with the static type system of the underlying programming language. Furthermore, these approaches typically rely on preprocessing or on native compilation with specialized compilers to incorporate the contract support into the programming language. Thus, these infrastructure tools are not suitable as a basis for developing prototyping tools, as they violate the crucial requirement of quick turnaround cycles for prototyping-oriented development.

7.2.2   Scenario-Based Prototyping

Motivation

In Chap. 4, we discussed the properties of scenarios in general. In Chap. 5, the emphasis was on presenting support for scenarios in the UML, and on developing guidelines for dealing with use cases in general, and with interaction diagrams and use case diagrams in particular. As already stated in Chap. 5, there is some empirical evidence that use case or scenario-based approaches have positive effects on requirements and therefore on the overall product quality.

Our contract-based prototyping approach—that is, specifying classes, methods, and their (contract) interfaces—is independent of specific application examples. In order to get a better feeling about how a class, or a set of classes, is used in an application context, use cases are a good starting point. The idea of our prototyping approach is to refine selected (core) textual use cases into interaction diagrams. These interaction diagrams are executable and therefore provide good feedback on the contract model that has been developed; that is, whether there are any missing or over specified contracts, or contracts that do not capture the requirements properly. Providing the customer with the opportunity to see how a use case works in reality (with simple user interfaces, though), gives him or her a better understanding of the contracts and the domain model developed.

Requirements

The requirements for *ScenarioBuilder* refer not only to the core prototyping tool but also to the infrastructure; that is, to the basic contract support for the execution environment of the prototypes:

- *Compliance with theory:* The semantics of the Python assertion model and thus the semantics as defined by the contract theory must be preserved when executing scenarios.
- *Standardization:* The generated scenario scripts must be executable in a standard Python environment; that is, it is not feasible to extend or change the syntax and semantics of standard Python.
- *Manipulation of scenarios:* It must be easily possible, by means of a graphics editor, to draw scenarios on the basis of the symbol information provided by the *ContractBuilder* tool; that is, only types and messages that were previously specified with *ContractBuilder* are allowed.
- *Instance scenarios: ScenarioBuilder* allows us to specify type scenarios. It must easily be possible to specify an arbitrary number of scenario instances from type scenarios. It must also be possible to store scenario instances. Furthermore, it must be possible to export scenario instances as Python scripts, to enable batch execution outside *ScenarioBuilder*. Obviously, the exported scripts will still need the Python infrastructure for contract checking.
- *The execution environment: ScenarioBuilder* has to provide an integrated execution environment for scenario instances, taking contract checking into consideration; that is, during execution of scenario instances, contract checking must be possible.
- *Understanding the contract: ContractBuilder* has to be integrated into *ScenarioBuilder*; therefore, it must be possible to use *ContractBuilder* from within the *ScenarioBuilder* tool. It should, for example, be possible to view the contract of a selected type in *ScenarioBuilder* or to add new contracts on the fly.

An Overview of ScenarioBuilder

In this section, we describe the tool support that is currently available for scenario-based prototyping. The description given here is based to a large extent on Plösch and Pomberger [Plösch00]. The scenario-based prototyping tool is separate from the contract-based prototyping tool as described in the previous section. Nevertheless, these two tools work together, as the contracts and classes specified with the contract-based prototyping tool are also used by the scenario-based prototyping tool. Additionally, to execute the scenarios (with enabled contract checking) the infrastructure tools as described in the previous section are used. In this section, we give an overview of the architecture of the tools, as well as a functional overview. We concentrate on the scenario editor; the supporting tools (the DBC Editor and the Python Object Editor) are described only in as much detail as is necessary to enable an understanding of the core scenario tool.

Architectural Overview: The architectural overview is necessary in order to understand how the contract-based prototyping tool is integrated with the scenario-based prototyping tool. Figure 50Fig. 50 gives an overview of the architecture of the scenario-based prototyping tool. Roughly, the toolset consists of the contract tools and the scenario tools, which are loosely coupled by means of files. The contract tools allow the enrichment of classes with assertions in the sense of DBC, and also incorporate a run-time environment to check the assertions according to DBC theory. The underlying programming language is Python [Lutz01], an object-oriented, dynamically typed interpreted language. The contract-based prototyping tools were described in the previous section—a more detailed description can be found in Plösch [Plösch98].

The scenario tools (see Fig. 50) rely on the symbol information provided by the contract tools. The symbol files contain information about class names, superclasses, and methods, and the entire set of assertion information (invariants, preconditions, and postconditions). The contract-enriched classes can be used in the scenario editor as entities of a scenario. The scenario editor supports the construction of type scenarios and scenario instances. Instance scenarios are not directly executed by the scenario tool; instead, a Python-based scenario script is generated that uses the DBC run-time support; this ensures that assertion checking takes place while the scenario instance is being executed.

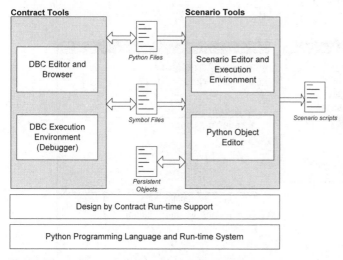

Fig. 50. The architecture of a scenario-based prototyping tool

The execution of scenarios requires the instantiation and editing of Python objects involved in the scenario. This task is supported by the Python Object Editor, which stores the created and edited objects in a persistent manner. The scenario scripts load these persistent Python objects from disk and use them for scenario execution.

Functional Overview: We present the functionality of the toolset by describing a typical usage scenario. This does not imply any methodological issues (i.e., how to best use the tool), but is only used as a mechanism to show the tool's functionality:

- *Step 1—Core classes, and their methods and assertions:* The DBC Editor is used to document core classes, their methods, and the assertions for the classes and methods; that is, the invariants, preconditions, and postconditions. The tool supports the editing of classes and assertions by means of specialized editors, and facilitates understanding as a number of filtering mechanisms may be used to display different types of assertions with respect to inheritance relationships. A more detailed description of the tool can be found in Plösch [Plösch98]. Besides these editing and browsing facilities, the DBC Editor enables exporting of the symbol information of all classes involved in a project. This symbol information comprises not only information about classes (class names, the superclass name, method names, and parameter names) but also the entire set of assertion information; that is, which invariants are associated with a class and which preconditions and postconditions are associated with a method. This symbol information is used by the scenario editor.
- *Step 2—Constructing type scenarios:* The symbol information provided by the DBC Editor (see step 1) can be loaded into the scenario editor and is visualized as depicted in Fig. 51.

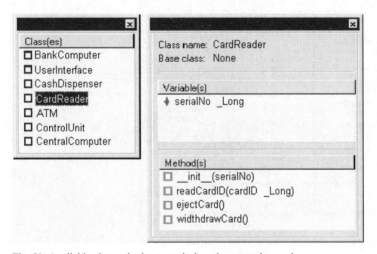

Fig. 51. Available classes in the scenario-based prototyping tool

In our example, modeling parts of an automated teller machine (ATM), the core classes (the left-hand window in Fig. 51) are BankComputer, CardReader, ControlUnit, CentralComputer, CashDispenser, UserInterface, and ATM. For the selected entity (CardReader), all variables and methods are shown (see the right-hand window in Fig. 51). By means of a context-sensitive menu, the invariants of a class, as well as the preconditions and postconditions of each method, may be accessed. The entities of a type scenario are inserted into the drawing area by means of drag and drop; for example, the classes depicted in Fig. 51 can be dragged into the drawing area of Fig. 52.

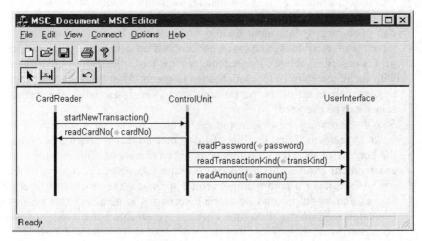

Fig. 52. Constructing a type scenario

The vertical bars denote the types involved in this specific scenario. In Fig. 52, the upper parts of the vertical bars (in gray) indicate that this is a type scenario; that is, a scenario that cannot be executed. Messages are inserted by drawing lines between two arbitrary vertical bars. In our case, no arbitrary messages (free text) may be inserted, but only messages that are associated with the message receiver. In our tool, a dialog pops up that supports the selection of methods understood by the message receiver. The necessary symbol information is provided by the contract tools (see step 1). As depicted in Fig. 52, the parameters of methods are also shown. The dot in front of the parameter name (also in gray) indicates that no object or value is yet associated with the parameter (for more details, see step 3). The chronological order of messages may be changed by means of drag and drop, and messages to the sender (self-reference) are also possible. Conditions or loops cannot be expressed directly in the editor. Nevertheless, it is possible (by double-clicking on a message) to enter program code, in our case Python code. The main advantage is that it is possible to implement important features in a prototyping-oriented manner or to give some implementation hints by means of comments. In the event that the Python source code already contains a method implementation, it is displayed and can be changed in the scenario editor.

- *Step 3—Constructing scenario instances:* Our scenario-based prototyping tool supports a prototyping-oriented approach with executable systems. Hence every type scenario (described in step 2) may be turned into a scenario instance. For this purpose, it is necessary to instantiate every type of the type scenario; that is, CardReader, ControlUnit, and UserInterface in our example (see Fig. 52). Double-clicking on the gray boxes of the vertical bars invokes a generic Python Object Editor, which allows the instance variables of arbitrary Python objects to be set by means of a graphical user interface. After instantiation, the gray boxes turn into green boxes. The same instantiation process must take place for all parameters of methods in the entire scenario. For parameters of an elementary data type, appropriate input dialogs are provided by the scenario editor. Parameters of an arbitrary class type are instantiated using the Python Object Editor (as described above). For parameters that have a value or object associated with them, the color of the dot changes to green. After all of the involved entities, as well as all of the parameters, have been instantiated, the scenario instance can be executed.

- *Step 4—Executing scenario instances:* In order to execute a scenario, a Python script (a scenario script; see Fig. 50) is generated that is afterwards executed in the context of the DBC run-time support environment. This run-time support environment ensures that assertion checking takes place according to the theory. As we favor a prototyping-oriented approach, the process of determining classes and assertions and developing scenarios is iterative. This script-based execution mechanism allows the checking (even in a batch mode) of whether all scenarios work properly; that is, do not lead to violations of assertions. The occurrence of violations of assertions during scenario execution indicates problems with either the class model and its assertions or the scenario. Scenario execution is therefore a valuable mechanism to ensure quality and consistency right from the beginning; that is, in the early phases of the software development process. The main advantage of this script-based approach is that once a scenario has been described and instantiated, it can be replayed easily, and therefore facilitates judging the impact of changes to the involved classes. On the other hand, when new scenarios have to be described or existing scenarios have to be changed (as requirements change), it is also ensured that—at least for the scenarios specified—the assertion model is either correct or it is obvious where any problems occur.

We have sketched the architecture and functionality of our scenario-based prototyping toolset. We have shown that scenarios can be formulated in the context of assertion-enriched classes, with the advantages of enhanced correctness and robustness with respect to changes of the domain model. The prototyping environment presented here relies heavily on the features of the Python programming language, which in many cases is not an appropriate implementation environment.

Related Tools

We are not aware of any tools that allow us to specify executable instance scenarios with contract-checking support. Nevertheless, some systems are available that

support the execution of scenarios in one way or another. In the following paragraphs, we will give a brief description of this related work. For detailed information, follow the references. Besides the tools discussed in this section, a number of
tools exist that allow us to handle the execution of graphical models (e.g., State-
mate [Harel98], Rhapsody [ILogix03], and Rose-RT [Rational03a]). However,
these tools concentrate on dealing with statecharts. As interaction diagrams *per se*
are used to model inter-object communication, we will not discuss statechart-
based approaches..

Live Sequence Charts [Harel01, Harel02a, Harel02b, Harel03]: Live Sequence
Charts (LSCs) are a broad extension of message sequence charts [Z.120 96]. LSCs
are specified using a formal visual language and they support existential charts
(things that may happen) and universal charts (things that must happen). In order
to be able to specify LSCs, a detailed knowledge of their syntax and semantics is
required. In order to facilitate the construction of LSCs, a tool (called a play-
engine) is provided.

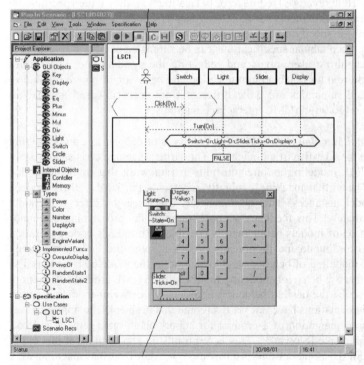

Fig. 53. A screenshot from the play-engine environment

The user who wants to specify an LSC first builds the GUI of the system, with no
behavior built into it. An LSC is constructed by using the GUI and therefore by

specifying which reactions are to be associated with certain events. The specification is done by selecting messages from an object model provided by the tool—this approach is called "play-in". During "play-out", the user can replay the captured scenarios in order to debug the specification. Figure 53 shows a screenshot of a play-engine environment, with a user interface and with the specification of an LSC.

TestConductor [Lettrari01]: This tool is integrated into Rhapsody [ILogix03]. It can be used for monitoring and testing a model using that is specified by a sequence chart specification. The syntax and semantics of the sequence chart are clearly defined and therefore allow the transformation into an automaton that is executed within the Rhapsody environment. The sequence diagrams supported by this tool are a subset of the UML specification—it is, for example, not possible to specify selections of repetitions. The tool is in prototype stage, but integrated into the Rhapsody environment.

The Software Cost Reduction (SCR) Method [Heitmeyer97, Heitmeyer98a, Heitmeyer98b, Heitmeyer00, Heitmeyer02]: This method allows the specification and simulation of requirements for reactive systems. The SCR method provides a tabular notation for specifying the required relation between system and environment variables. Such tabular specifications can be simulated using a graphical user interface for capturing user inputs and reflecting the system state. SCR tables allow us to capture inter-object communication and behavior, although the underlying syntax and semantics are quite different from scenario-based approaches such as MSC [Z.120 96] or UML interaction diagrams.

The UML Virtual Machine [Riehle01]: The emphasis of this work is on describing an architecture for a UML virtual machine. The virtual machine consists of extensions to the UML modeling architecture plus a framework that implements this architecture. The virtual machine explicitly represents the UML, UML models, and UML model instances. This approach lets users see the effects of model changes immediately. This feedback supports rapid model prototyping and innovative exploration of models better than is possible with today's code-generation approaches. According to the proponents of this system, the largest remaining problem is the modeling of behavior and execution of the modeled behavior. The authors claim that the behavior-modeling features of the UML are not sufficient to completely describe the desired behavior; additionally, behavior-modeling extensions and implementations have not yet overcome this problem. The approach was used for the implementation of a product for supply chain management and collaborative e-commerce [Skyva03]. This is a promising approach, as it inherently focuses on rapid development and prototyping—if a UML virtual machine were able to process interaction diagrams (including the evaluation of OCL constraints), this would be quite a perfect solution from a practitioner's point of view.

iUML: [KC03]: The iUML tool suite supports the modeling of an embedded system using the UML with precise action semantics. The toolset also allows the simulation of the modeled system, providing feedback about the system. The precise action semantics used in the iUML tool suite will possibly have an impact on the further development of the UML, as the developers of iUML are part of the consortium working on a submission to the OMG Request for Proposal for precise action semantics for the UML [OMG98].

7.3   From a Prototype to a Target System

7.3.1   Motivation

As presented in the previous sections of this chapter, our prototyping environment relies on a Python infrastructure for contract checking and scenario execution. However, Python cannot be chosen as a target platform, for several reasons. Many organizations and companies have an established development platform—typically with object-oriented programming languages such as C++, Java, or C#—and they don't want to change. Additionally, Python lacks a static type system (a core benefit for prototyping tools), which is often considered as a major drawback for the reliability and stability of the developed software. Furthermore, some projects could not use Python due to efficiency problems associated with the interpretative nature of the language—they have to use compiled languages such as C++.

The general idea here is to provide a tool that allows us to parse contract specifications and to at least check the syntactic correctness. Furthermore, the architecture of the toolset has to be sufficiently flexible to generate the necessary code for classes and methods (based on a specific programming language) and to inject this generated source code with contract support.

In the following sections, we will concentrate on the code-generation mechanism itself, using C++ as the target language. We have chosen C++ here as little related work can be found, while some support is available for the Java programming language.

7.3.2   Requirements

- *Support for iterative development:* The tool for transforming our Python assertions into the target programming language must take our iterative software development approach into account. It must therefore be possible to step back into analysis, to change the analysis model (i.e., our prototype), and to regenerate the target code without any loss. This is the most important requirement.
- *Standardization:* The generated target code must be compilable using a standard compiler of the target programming language; that is, it is not feasible to extend or change the syntax and semantics of the target programming language.
- *Readability:* The generated source code must be readable; in particular, this means that the code for assertion checking must be clearly separated from the implementation of a method or class.
- *Compliance with theory:* The semantics of the Python assertion model, and thus the semantics as defined by Eiffel, must be preserved, as we think that the ex-

perience gained with assertions in the Eiffel context are positive; therefore we do not want to experiment here, but we want to provide this solid kind of support.

- *Configurability:* The configuration process must be configurable; in particular, it must be possible to selectively disable the generation of individual assertions in the source code.
- *Efficiency:* For efficiency reasons, it must be possible to selectively activate and deactivate assertion checking at a class level. No run-time penalties may be associated with deactivated assertion checking.

7.3.3   An Overview of the Contract2C++ Transformer

In this section, we describe the tool support that is currently available for transforming the results from the contract-based prototyping tool into a target system. The description given here is based to a large extent on [Plösch99]. The tool presented here is separate from the contract-based prototyping tool as described in the previous section. Nevertheless, these two tools work together, as the contracts and classes specified using the contract-based prototyping tool are the basis for transforming the classes and contracts specified into a C++ environment.

Architectural Overview: We have developed a transformation tool that relies, as do the prototyping tools, on the symbol information provided by the parsing tool. In this section, we emphasize C++ code generation. Additionally, a configuration tool is provided that allows parameterization of the configuration process; for example, renaming of classes and methods, and exclusion of assertions.

In our system, a C++ class is generated for every Python class. The necessary information (the class name, the superclass, and the method signatures) can be extracted from the symbol files mentioned above. For each generated class, a parallel check class is generated. This generated check class comprises instance variables and methods for assertion checking. Each class inherits from its superclass (provided that it has one) and from the generated check class; thus multiple inheritance is used. Figure 54 shows the principal structure of the generated C++ classes. The name of the check class is equivalent to the name of the core class extended by the string "__dbc". The class Root__dbc is the root class for all check classes and defines the common protocol for all check classes. The code-generation tool allows subsequent regeneration of the code without loss of any C++ implementations made in the meantime.

The generated assertion check code is called via the Require and Return macros, as depicted in Fig. 55. The code-generation tool automatically inserts both macros. The Require macro calls the Person__dbc::Require_SetAge method and passes the parameters to this check method. As Fig. 56 shows, the method Person__dbc::Require_SetAge(int &a) automatically calls the Invariant() method of this check class. This ensures that the invariant checks take place with each method invocation that conforms to the underlying theory. Since a method may be exited from various points during implementation, it is not sufficient to place the code for calling the postcondition check method at the end. To overcome this problem, we have introduced a Return macro. The code generator replaces every return state-ment with our Return macro, and inserts it at the end of a method in case no return statement can be found.

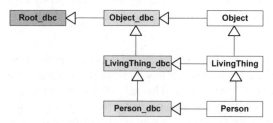

Fig. 54. The structure of the generated code

The assertion code for invariants—that is, the corresponding boolean expression derived from the Python assertion—is generated into a method Invariant() of the check class. The generated code ensures that the Invariant() method of all super-classes is called. Figure 55 shows an example of the generated code. We will discuss the generated code—that is, the transformed Python assertions and the problems associated with this task—in more detail later.

```
void Person::SetAge(int a)
{
    Require(Person, SetAge, (a));
    age= a;
    Return;
}
```

```
bool Person__dbc::Require_SetAge(int &a) {
    if (stack.Top().Switch()) {
        InitRequire();
        stack.Top().AddParam(a);
        this->Invariant();
        stack.Top().Switch(false);
    }
    return LivingThing__dbc::Require_SetAge, (a)
                || Check("self.age > 0", self->age > 0);
}
```

```
bool Person__dbc::Ensure_SetAge(MCI &I) {...}
    bool Person__dbc::Invariant() {
        return Check( ... ) &&
        LivingThing__dbc::Invariant();
    }
```

Fig. 55. The generated code   Fig. 56. The generated check class

For all preconditions of one method, one check method is generated (in Fig. 56, it is the method Person__dbc::Require_SetAge(int a)). Figure 56 shows a typical exam-ple of the generated code. The details will be described later. For all postcondi-tions of one method, one check method is also generated (in Fig. 56, it is the method Person__dbc::Ensure_SetAge(MCI &i)).

To ensure that the check method for postconditions can access the parame-ters of the method, references to the parameters are stored in a vector by the

Require_SetAge(int &a) method (see the call of method AddParam() in the Require_SetAge(int &a) method). Besides other information, the info object passed to Ensure_SetAge(MCI &i) as parameter includes this vector.

Implementation Issues: This section describes a number of implementation details that are necessary in order to understand the problems and our solutions in conjunction with assertions in C++:

- *Supporting preconditions and postconditions:* The call of the check method for the preconditions can be resolved by the Require macro, since the method name and the parameters are passed to the macro. The call of the ensure-check method cannot be resolved directly by the Return macro because neither the method name nor the parameters are passed to the macro. Therefore, at the time of method entry, a pointer to the Person__dbc::Ensure_SetAge()method is initialized (pEnsure) by the Require macro. This pointer is generated as a local variable of the checked method. The corresponding ensure-check method can be called via this pointer. The definition and initialization of the pointer to the Person__dbc::Ensure_SetAge()method of the above example, carried out by the Require macro, looks like this:

```
bool (Person__dbc::*pEnsure)(MCI &i) = &Person__dbc::Ensure_SetAge;
```

The initialization statement requires the class name and the method name, which are both passed as parameters to the Require macro. Since the name of the method pointer as well as the parameters of all ensure-check methods are the same for all ensure methods, the corresponding method call in the Return macro can be resolved without macro parameters to (this->*pEnsure)(info). The parameter info (of type MCI) contains the vector with the references to the parameters of the Person::SetAge(int a) method and thus provides access to them.

For every checked method, the Require macro pushes an MCI object onto the stack; this object is initialized with the class name and method name. The instance variables are added to this info object in the InitRequire() method, a generated method of the check class. The parameters of the checked method are added in the Require_SetAge(int &a) method. Instance variables of the class and parameters of the check method are stored in the MCI object in two ways: one vector contains references to the instance variables and parameters of the method to provide access to these variables for the check methods for postconditions; a second vector contains copies of the instance variables of the class as well as those of the parameters of the checked method. This enables access to the variables in the check method for postconditions with these values at method entry. Since a method may invoke other methods that again are checked for preconditions and postconditions, the MCI objects must be organized in a stack hierarchy similar to the activation records of methods. The MCI object is pushed onto the stack before the check method is invoked for the preconditions. After the return of the check method for the postcondition, the MCI object is popped from the stack. The check method always accesses the top entry on the stack.

- *Handling parameters:* Parameters of methods and instance variables of a class can be of arbitrary types. To hold variables of different types in one vector, every variable is wrapped by a wrapper object that holds a reference to the proper variable. Using the wrapper classes defined in Fig. 57, a vector of type vector<Wrapper*> is able to manage variables of different types:

```
class Wrapper {};                        template<class T>
                                         class PtrVar : public Var<T*> {
template<class T>                          public:
class Var : public Wrapper {                 PtrVar(T *v) { value = new T(*v); } };
  public:                                template<class T>
    Var(T &v) { value = v; }            class Ref : public Wrapper {
    T &var() { return value; }            public:
  protected:                                 Ref(T &r): reference(r) { }
    T value; };                             T &ref() { return reference; }
                                         private:
                                             T &reference; };
```

Fig. 57. Wrapper classes for parameters

- The wrapper Var holds a copy of the variable (the copy is caused by the assignment in the constructor), which is accessible via the var() method of the wrapper.
- For pointer types, the wrapper PtrVar initializes the value with a copy of the object. The statement value = new T(*v) in the constructor of PtrVar creates a copy of the object by calling the copy constructor of the class T.
- The wrapper Ref holds a reference to the variable that was passed to the constructor. The ref() method provides access to the variable held by the wrapper.

The instance variables and parameters can be accessed by a check method via these wrappers. In our above example, the SetAge(int i) method has one parameter of type int. The corresponding wrapper objects stored in the MCI object are therefore Ref<int>(a) and Var<int>(a), respectively. Assuming that the wrapper objects are stored at position 0 in the vectors vars and olds, access to the variable and to the copy of the variable is handled by the following expressions:

```
int a = dynamic_cast<Ref<int>*> (info.vars.at(0));
int copyA = dynamic_cast<Var<int>*>(info.olds.at(0))
```

The index of the particular instance variable or parameter in the vectors vars and olds corresponds to the declaration order of the instance variables of a class and the parameters of a method, where the instance variables are located before the parameters.

- *The invocation sequence order:* For our discussion of the check method invocation sequence of overridden methods, Fig. 58 shows the generated methods of method Base::Set() overridden by method Derived::Set() in a simplified notation. The method invocation anObject->Set(...) on the object anObject of type Derived leads to the following sequence of check method calls. First, the method Derived__dbc::Require_Set() is called (performed by the Require macro). Before the preconditions are checked, the invariants have to be proved by calling the Derived__dbc::Invariant() method (switch was set true in the Require macro), which in turn calls Base_dbc::Invariant(). Therefore, all invariants along the inheritance line to the root class are checked.

Base	Precondition and postcondition	Invariant
Base::**Set (...) {** Require (...); Return; }	**Base__dbc::Require_Set (...){** if (switch) this->Invariant(); switch = false; } **Base_dbc::Ensure_Set (...){** if (switch) this->Invariant(); switch = false; }	**Base__dbc::Invariant(){** ... }
Derived	**Precondition and postcondition**	**Invariant**

Derived::Set (...) {
Require (...);
Return;
}
	Derived__dbc::Require_Set(...){
	if (switch) this->Invariant();
	switch = false;
	Base__dbc:: Require_Set(...); }
	Derived__dbc::Ensure_Set(...){
	if (switch) this->Invariant();
	switch = false;
	Base__dbc::Ensure_Set(...); }
		Derived__dbc::Invariant(){
		Base__dbc::Invariant();
		}

Fig. 58. Check Methods for overridden methods

After all invariants have been proved, switch is set to false. Since the Derived::Set() method overrides Base::Set(), the preconditions of the overridden method have to be proved too (call of Base__dbc::Require_Set()). At this time, no more invariant checks are necessary, because all of the invariants have been proved already. Therefore switch is used to determine the caller of the check method. If the caller was one of the macros Require or Return, the invariants of the class have to be proved; if the caller was a check method, the invariants of the class need not be proved.

- *Recursive invocations of check methods:* The invocation of a method of a class in the invariant expression of the same class would lead to an infinite recursive method call. Consider the invariant expression age() > 0 of a class Person, where age() is a method of the same class. The invocation of the age() method on an object of the class Person forces a check of the invariants. The expression of the invariant calls the age() method again, which in turn forces a check of the invariants of class Person. Since the use of method calls in invariant expressions is possible, the generated check code has to determine such recursive method calls at run time and prevent an infinite loop. A simple approach to overcome this problem is to lock the method that checks the invariants. Before an invariant check method is entered, a lock is set by simply initializing a boolean switch to true. After execution of the invariant checks, the method is unlocked by setting the switch to false. The switch introduced to avoid multiple invariant checks on overridden methods can be used for this task. The switch must be unique for every checked method and thus is included in the MCI object.

- *Handling run-time errors:* In the event that an assertion is violated at run time, corresponding information is stored in a log file. The log file entry describes the class and method, records where the assertion violation occurred, and also indicates which assertion caused the violation. We consider this approach to be sufficient: as demonstrated by the application of our C++ model in the implementation phase, where it suffices to know that an exception occurred that contradicts the developed domain model. From a technical perspective, it would be possible to integrate the handling of assertion violations by means of the exception handling mechanism provided by the C++ programming language.

- *Controlling the code generation process:* There are several reasons why it is desirable to control the assertion-generation process; that is, to selectively enable or disable assertion checking for certain classes or methods:

  - Usually, the specification changes throughout the software production process. These changes may also affect the assertions. Thus it is convenient to disable assertion checking for affected classes as long as the analysis model and thus the assertions are being altered. This change process may take some time, as an impact analysis must be carried out and possible stakeholders must be informed about the changes.
  - It is convenient to disable assertion checking for performance reasons for classes that are implemented and that are thoroughly tested.
  - In the event of major redesigns, it is convenient to disable assertion checking during the redesign process, as assertions might be violated, since the classes that are being redesigned are not yet stable.

  Due to the use of macros and multiple inheritance, it is easy for us to selectively enable or disable assertion checking on a class or method basis. In addition, it would be desirable to see at a glance for which classes or methods assertion checking is currently disabled. This allows specific investigation about the reasons for disabling certain assertions and thus contributes to the overall quality of the software process. A tool with a graphical user interface that provides this overview is currently under construction.

7.3.4   From a Scenario-Based Prototype to Executable Test Cases

The core activity when transforming a prototype into a target system is to transform the entities of the domain model into the respective target language, and to preserve the developed and validated contracts in the target language. This is important in order to ensure that these contracts are not violated during implementation and testing.

Throughout analysis and early design, some of the scenarios specified will be described more formally using visual kinds of notation, such as UML interaction diagrams. Some of these interaction diagrams will be turned into prototypes, as discussed in Sect. 7.2.2. The major idea is to validate the specified contracts in the context of application-specific scenarios.

Our environment for scenario-based prototyping (*ScenarioBuilder*) allows us to export the generated scripts as Python scripts. The generated script sends messages to objects and uses simple control structures such as selections or iterations. It would therefore be easy (although we have not done it yet) to transform these scripts into the target language—that is, Java or C++—and therefore also to have these tests available during design, implementation, and testing.

Our current implementation of *ScenarioBuilder* relies on the serialization mechanism available for Python to store the objects and parameters used for the scenario instances. These objects are needed during execution of the scripts. There are several approaches to making this persistent information available to the target platform:

- *ScenarioBuilder* could be changed to represent Python objects in a platform-independent way; for example, by using an XML-based data format. This XML-based data format could also be made accessible at the target platform—this would be the preferred solution, although it would imply changes to the existing *ScenarioBuilder* implementation.
- The format of the persistent binary objects could also remain, but an additional tool is capable of transforming the binary Python-based representation into the native format of the target platform.
- Finally, each target platform could have the ability to interpret the binary representation of the Python objects and to initialize the "native" objects accordingly.

7.3.5   Related Tools

In Sect. 7.2.1, we presented our approach for prototyping with contracts. No comparable tools exist—most of the available tools can only be compared to our infrastructure. Nevertheless, in Sect. 7.2.1 we referred to the work of Carillo-Castellan [Carillo96]. This work implements contract support for Smalltalk. As Smalltalk is well suited for building prototypes (dynamic typing, an execution environment integrated in the IDE, etc.) this work could serve as a basis for developing a tool that offers more elaborate prototyping support. However, the authors of this work do not propose any special support to enhance the prototyping capabilities; nor do they propose any possibility of switching to a different implementation platform.

In Sect. 7.2.2, we presented our approaches to scenario-based prototyping and we identified a number of related tools:

- *Live Sequence Charts*: The approach relies heavily on a play-engine; that is, a machine that is capable of dealing with LSCs and that is also able to communicate with some kind of user interface. The authors claim [Harel03] that their system could in principle be used throughout the entire life cycle; that is, also for the final system. However, they state that their concepts cannot be applied for systems that are time-critical, or ones that have to be distributed over several machines or processes. There is no support available to transform LSCs to different platforms; for example, C++ or Java technology.
- *TestConductor*: This tool is a prototype, integrated into the Rhapsody environment. The authors give no hints about how the prototype could be used in subsequent phases; nor do they provide any ideas concerning transformation of scenarios to a target platform.
- *The Software Cost Reduction (SCR) method*: Besides the methodological guidance given by this approach, a number of tools—the specification editor, the consistency checker, and the SCR simulator—are part of the system. The emphasis here is to prove that no missing cases or nondeterminisms exist in the specification of the behavior. However, no tool support is available to transform this specification into a Java or C++ environment.
- *The UML virtual machine:* The emphasis of this approach is on building a virtual machine that is capable of executing UML models. This approach explicitly excludes code generation or transformation from its goals. However, with a clearly defined action semantics for the UML it would be possible to build generators that transform an (arbitrary) UML model into source code. It would therefore be a suitable approach to use the UML virtual machine for prototyping tasks; that is, to understand and ameliorate the behavior of the system, by providing class diagrams, interaction diagrams, and so on. The developed model (executable within the UML virtual machine) could also serve as a basis for a code-generation process.
- *iUML*: iUML provides a simulation and execution engine for executable UML; that is, of an extension to the UML that describes the behavior of the UML in more detail. A generator is available that allows us to produce some code; however, the generated code uses the simulator to execute the UML model; that is, there is no real code generation for the underlying models

7.4 Contract-Based and Scenario-Based Prototyping in the Software Development Process

In Chap. 6, we provided an overview of typical software development processes, using the examples of the Rational Unified Process (RUP) and the Scrum approach. We identified a number of tasks that occur in every software development process, and showed how scenario and contract techniques as described in this book can be applied. In this section, we will show how the tools—as presented in this chapter—can be associated with the software development process.

Figure 59 shows the processes that we introduced in Chap. 6 in a combined form for all activities relevant to scenarios and contracts for analysis, design, implementation, and testing. We have marked those activities where tool support is possible and reasonable accordingly. We have also stated which tools could be used in which situation. We give here the names of the tools that we have developed and described in this chapter. However, similar tools could also be used:

- *Analysis of tool support:* During analysis, *ContractBuilder* can be used to capture parts of the analysis model, including associated contracts. *ScenarioBuilder* can be used for selected important scenarios, to capture them in an executable way.
- *Design of tool support:* As far as contracts are concerned, *ContractBuilder* can be used to add new contracts and to adapt existing contracts. In order to ensure conformity with existing scenarios, *ScenarioBuilder* can be used. Therefore, it is possible to execute some scenarios in the prototyping environment and gain additional insights about the behavior of the system.
- *Implementation of tool support:* Depending on the target platform, the analysis model must be transformed into a design model (including contracts). For this purpose, the Contract2Java tool or the Contract2C++ tool can be used. During implementation it will also be possible to add or change contracts—this is best achieved by using *ContractBuilder* in order to ensure that no unwanted side effects occur. For unit testing, an automated test generator (ContractTestGenerator—not described so far), which automatically derives unit tests on the basis of the available contract information, would be of interest (JTest [Parasoft02a, Parasoft02b] is a toolkit that tries to accomplish this).

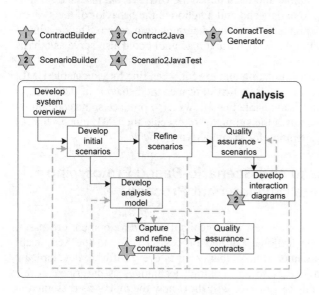

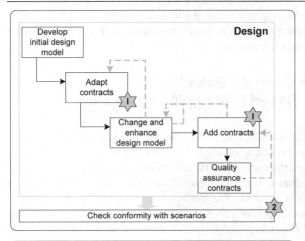
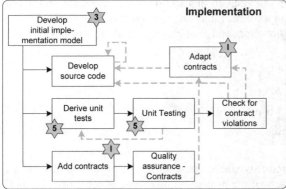
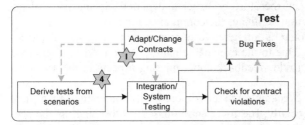

Fig. 59. Prototyping support during software development

- *Testing of tool support:* Contracts can be added and changed by using *ContractBuilder*. *ScenarioBuilder* allows us to execute scenarios in a Python environment. As described in Sect. 7.3.4, it would be interesting to have a tool that allows us to execute the scenarios on a target platform.

Once again, it is important to emphasize that the tools presented here are not mere editing tools but prototyping tools; that is, tools that allow us to experiment with the developed models (contracts and scenarios).

7.5 The Impact of Contract-Based and Scenario-Based Prototyping on Quality

As already mentioned in the introduction to this chapter, the aim of prototyping is to enhance to quality of the products. In Chap. 1 we gave an overview (see Fig. 3) of the positive effects of assertion and scenario techniques on quality.

In Chap. 2 we identified a number of quality criteria that it is important to consider when developing a product. We believe that prototyping has positive effects on a number of these quality criteria. There is some empirical evidence (see [Gomaa86], [Gordon91], and [Sobol89]) that measurable enhancements can be obtained when applying prototypes. In this section, we concentrate on the prototyping capabilities of our approach, rather than on contracts or scenarios—we have dealt with the impact of contract and scenario techniques in earlier chapters:

Ambiguity	Completeness	Understandability	Volatility	Traceability	Architecture	Maintainability	Reusability	Int. Documentation	Ext. Documentation	Resource Usage	Completion Rates	Correctness
+	+	+			+	+	+	+				+

- *Ambiguity:* Prototyping reduces ambiguities, since the prototype can be discussed with the stakeholders of the project—a prototype is not formal but is an executable model and can therefore be better understood. Seeing parts of the prospective model in action facilitates the communication process.
- *Completeness:* Prototyping is an iterative approach that involves all parties working on the project. Due to the executable nature of the models, users tend to be more willing to provide feedback about missing aspects in the scenarios and so on.
- *Understandability:* An executable model is more easily understood than mere paperwork. This is especially true for scenario-based prototyping, as the scenario-based approach itself is better suited to expressing the functionality of a system. Making such models executable allows the developers to gain a better feeling—that is, a better understanding—of the problems to be solved.
- *Architecture:* Contract-based prototyping in particular has a positive effect on architectures, as changes to the architecture are always made from the perspective of contracts; that is, correctness conditions. Hurried changes to the architecture are prevented, as the prototype demonstrates the problems, reveals the errors, and so on.
- *Maintainability:* This quality criterion is enhanced to a large extent, as risk analysis can be performed much better. Changes to the functionality of the

software are either reflected by changes in contracts or by changes in scenarios. In both cases, executable models are available that allow us to find out, by means of experiments, how the changes affect the system.

- *Reusability:* Reusability is enhanced, as possible reusers can use the prototypes to experiment with the system. Accompanied by written documentation, this possibility of experimentation facilitates the understanding of the system (with respect to reusability).
- *Internal documentation:* An executable model complements the written documentation for the software—and surely enhances this internal documentation, as maintenance tasks are facilitated.
- *Correctness:* Scenario-based and contract-based prototyping make a contribution to correctness as, due to the executable nature of prototypes, errors can be detected earlier in the software development process.

8 Contracts and Type Systems

Summary: The general aim of this chapter is to show how assertions are related to ideas from type theory, and especially to algebras and axioms, which are formal mechanisms that are used to specify the behavior of types. We define different views of the term "type" and relate the type concepts of typical programming languages (e.g., Java) to syntactic and existential abstract types; that is, to types that are defined by sets of function signatures. Typical object-oriented programming languages are less flexible, as subclasses must have identical method signatures, although this is not necessary from the point of view of subtyping (contravariant argument types and covariant result types would be possible). At the behavioral level, algebras and axioms are important. They allow us to specify and prove the behavior of a type. We contrast this approach with the assertion approach and show the differences between the two formalisms. We also show that the subtyping rules identified for syntactic subtype relationships are also valid in the semantic case, and we present and discuss the axiom-strengthening rules for subtypes in the context of assertions. Additionally, we present some concepts for formulating contracts that have not yet been discussed, as they are not part of typical contract languages, such as Design by Contract in Eiffel or OCL.

Keywords: Type, Model-based type, Abstract type, Algebraic type, Axiom, Subtyping, Function subtyping, Product subtyping, Record subtyping, Constructors, Transformers, Observers, Syntactic subtyping, Semantic subtyping

8.1 Types

Chapters 2 and 3 present the contract, a mechanism to specify the behavior of classes. The emphasis of Chap. 2 was on the presentation of the general mechanisms and techniques (invariants, preconditions, postconditions, correctness rules, etc.) without considering the theoretic foundations. Chapter 3 focuses on contract specifications in the context of available languages and tools for industry; in other words, the use of OCL, which is part of the Unified Modeling Language (UML).

In this chapter, we give an overview of object-oriented type theory as far as it is necessary to understand the role of assertions in this theoretic framework. Additionally, we present some work that goes beyond the capabilities of contracts as understood in Chaps. 2 and 3, and that is theoretically founded.

In every piece of software, clients have to make certain assumptions about the way in which a software artifact behaves. The artifact can be any reusable piece of software; that is, a subroutine, a procedure, a class, or a component. The supplier of the artifact, on the other hand, wants to build something that meets these expectations. In order to satisfy both clients and suppliers, their views have to be compatible; that is, the expectations of the client must meet the expectations of the supplier. For the sake of simplicity, we will concentrate on classes; therefore, the question can be formulated more precisely: Does the expected behavior of the class (from the client's point of view) match the actual behavior of the class as provided by the supplier?

Traditionally, the notion of type has been used to judge compatibility in software. There are different approaches to the term type:

Bit-Interpretation Schemas: At the level of the machine, a type can be considered as a schema for interpreting bit strings; for example, the bit string 01000001 is "A" when interpreted as a type character, or 65 if interpreted as an integer.

Model-Based Types: A type can also be viewed as being equivalent to a set:

$$x : T \Leftrightarrow x \in T.$$

In this approach, all program operations are modeled as operations on sets.

Syntactic and Existential Abstract Types: This approach thinks of a type as a set of function signatures; therefore, a type is characterized in a more abstract way, by enumerating all possible operations. Using this approach, a type Ordinal would be defined as follows:

Ordinal = $\exists$ ord . { first: $\rightarrow$ ord; succ: ord $\rightarrow$ ord }.

The problem with this approach is that it remains at the abstract level and cannot capture the intended meaning (behavior) of functions. The above definition just states that the Ordinal type provides two operations, first and succ—both operations yield an element of type Ordinal and the function succ has an Ordinal as parameter. As no semantic is defined, faulty expressions such as succ(2) = 2 are possible—this evidently cannot be true for an Ordinal type.

Axioms and Algebraic Types: In this approach, a type is a set of signatures and constraining axioms. Simons [Simons02a] gives an example of an algebraic type Ordinal:

Ordinal = $\exists$ ord . {first: $\rightarrow$ ord; succ; ord $\rightarrow$ ord }
$\forall$x, y : Ordinal . (succ(x) $\neq$ first()) $\wedge$ (succ(x) $\neq$ x $\wedge$ succ(x) = succ(y) $\Leftrightarrow$ x = y

The constraining axioms define that the first() element is distinct from any succ(x), that any element is distinct from its immediate successor succ(x), and that, by induction, all of the elements of the type are eventually distinct.

8.2 Types, Subtyping, and Programming Languages

Typical programming languages such as Java or C++ rely on syntactic and existential abstract types; that is, a type is defined by a set of signatures, without any further specification of the behavior of the functions. An important aspect in modern object-oriented programming languages is the possibility of polymorphic variables, which is best described by the Liskov Substitution Principle [Liskov88]. This substitution property (similarly described in [Cardelli85]) means the following:

> "What is wanted here is something like the following substitution property: if for each object o_1 of type S there is an object o_2 of type T such that, for all programs P defined in terms of T, the behavior of P is unchanged when o_1 is substituted for o_2, then S is a subtype of T."

The subtyping relationship $Y <: X$ ("Y is subtype of X") can be interpreted as the subset relationship $Y \subseteq X$. The subset relationship itself is defined as follows:

$$Y \subseteq X ::= \forall y . y \in Y \Rightarrow y \in X$$

The interesting aspect in object-oriented languages is the possibility of substituting (overriding) a method. In this case, we have to define what it means to say that the behavior remains unchanged. We now view types from a syntactic perspective—in other words, types are compatible if their interfaces are compatible—which reduces to checking the type signatures of related pairs of methods. In order to capture this formally, we will describe a method f of X as $f_x : D_x \rightarrow C_x$. This term indicates that function f accepts an argument of type D and yields a value of type C. This function is substituted into a type Y—that is, $f_y : D_y \rightarrow C_y$—with the intention that Y should behave like X; that is, $Y <: X$. From the syntactic point of view, we have to show under which conditions f_x can safely be replaced by f_y. The function subtyping rule expresses the conditions in which a function type $D_y \rightarrow C_y$ is a subtype of $D_x \rightarrow C_x$:

$$\frac{D_x <: D_y, \; C_y <: C_x}{D_y \rightarrow C_y <: D_x \rightarrow C_x}$$

This means that if the argument type D_y is larger than the argument type D_x, and the result type C_y is smaller than the result type C_x, then the function type $D_y \rightarrow C_y$ is a subtype of the function type $D_x \rightarrow C_x$. We can therefore say that argument types are contravariant (they may be more general), while return values are covariant (they may be more restricted).

The function subtype rule as explained above uses a single argument. Some additional formalisms are necessary (the product subtyping rule) in order to express functions that have more than one parameter:

$$\frac{S_1 <: T_{y1}, \; S_2 <: T_2}{S_1 \times S_2 <: T_1 \times T_2}$$

The product type $S_1 \times S_2$ is a subtype of the product type $T_1 \times T_2$ if the corresponding types in the products are also in subtyping relationships: $S_i <: T_i$.

So far, we have defined a number of rules to define the subtyping relationship and we have considered functions only. Additionally, we also have to consider the instance variables of classes. For example [Simons02d], a Person type with the fields

  Person= {name: String; surname: String; age: Integer; married: Boolean}

might be considered to be a subtype of a DatedThing type that has fewer fields,

  DatedThing= {name: String; age: Integer}

as a Person object can always be coerced into becoming a DatedThing by forgetting the extra fields. Intuitively, this satisfies the Liskov Substitution Principle. This can also be formally captured by use of the record subtyping rule:

$$\frac{a_i : A, S_1 <: T_1, \dots S_k <: T_k}{\{a_1 : S_1, \dots a_n : S_n\} <: \{a_1 : T_1, \dots a_k: T_k\}} \quad \text{for } 1 \le k \le n$$

A longer record type $\{a_1 : S_1,\}$, with n fields, is a subtype of a shorter record type $\{a_1 : T_1,\}$ with only k fields, provided that, in the first k fields that they have in common, every type S_i is a subtype of the corresponding type T_i.

For a more detailed discussion of this rule, and of additional subtleties, see Simons [Simons02d], Cardelli [Cardelli86], and Abadi and Cardelli [Abadi96].

Basically, languages such as Java or C++ are less flexible than the subtyping rules (which we have described here by means of sets of method type signatures) allow, as they do not support contravariant argument types and covariant types of return values, but force identical types in overridden methods.

8.3   Axioms and Assertions

So far, we have provided a short overview of the term "type" and we have shown how a type can be viewed as a set of type signatures. In this context, subtyping rules play an important role. We defined a type as a set of signatures without any further specification of the behavior of the type, and our subtyping rules only relied on contravariance and covariance rules for function arguments and return values.

In Sect. 8.1, we sketched out the idea of an algebraic type. We will discuss this issue and its relation to assertions as understood in this book in depth. In Sect. 8.1, we described a type Ordinal using final algebra semantics. This kind of algebra assumes that all elements of the type are equivalent. In order to be able to deal with objects, we must change our view and use the initial algebra semantics, which implies that all elements of a type are distinct. For this further discussion, we rely on the example of a type Stack, as described in Simons [Simons03a]:

Stack = ∀T. μstk.   {push : T → stk; pop : → stk; top : → T; empty : → Boolean;
                        size: → Natural }; newStack : → Stack;}
∀e : T . ∀s : Stack .
         newStack().empty()   (1)
∧   ¬s.push(e).empty()   (2)
∧   newStack().size() = 0   (3)
∧   s.push(e).size() = 1 + s.size()   (4)
∧   s.push(e).top() = e   (5)
∧   s.push(e).pop() = s   (6)

An interesting question is how we can know when sufficient axioms have been
defined. If too few axioms are provided, the type is under specified while, on the
other hand, redundant axioms make the work harder for the theorem-prover. From
the point of view of the axioms, we can distinguish various different functions of a
type:

- *Constructors:* These are functions that can generate every single instance of the
  type. What we mean here are algebraic constructors, not constructors in the
  sense of programming languages. In our case, the newStack function, as well as
  the push function, are algebraic constructors. The push function (in a pure functional calculus) creates a new Stack object, with the new element added on top
  of the Stack.
- *Transformers:* These are functions that return the type but that can be expressed
  in terms of primitive constructors. The function pop is an example of a transformer function—its result can be defined in terms of other constructors.
- *Observers:* Observers are functions that return something other than the type,
  as they typically inspect part of the type or return a computed value. The functions top, empty, and size are examples of observers.

The above example shows that the use of axioms is quite different from the use of
assertions as described in this book. Axioms are declarative by nature and can be
proved by means of deduction—possibly supported by theorem-provers. There is
no distinction between preconditions, postconditions, and invariants; the entire
behavior of the type is described by means of the axioms. Using OCL, we would
formulate the Stack type example as follows:

```
Stack::Stack()
post: self.empty()

Stack::push(Object o)
post: self@pre.size() + 1 = size()
post: self.top() = o

Stack::pop() : Object
post: self@pre.size() - 1 = size()
post: self@pre.top() = result

Stack::top() : Object
post: self@pre.size() = size()
post: self@pre.pop() = result
```

This example shows that the style in which the behavior is described is quite different from that of the algebraic approach. The above example does not consider empty stacks in the event of pop and top methods. In our opinion, the advantage is that the behavior of a method is defined locally; that is, we need not necessarily understand the behavior of the push method in order to understand the behavior of the pop method. Additionally, the use of normal expressions with a functional style makes it easier to understand the behavior, compared to axiomatic description with its functional calculus. By means of induction, we can derive from axiom (5) that the top function must return the topmost element. We cannot do that at such a general level in our OCL example. The postcondition post: self@pre.pop() = result in the Stack::top() method is only valid when the execution of the pop method does not change the state of our Stack object; that is, the @pre operator is implemented purely functionally and yields a deep copy of the referenced attribute, in our case of the entire object. The @pre operator can only be applied to self, or to attributes of self, which leads to artificial expressions such as post: self@pre.size() = size(); one would expect to write self.size()@pre = size()—that is, to express it in a more functional style. The algebraic specification is more generic, as elements of an arbitrary type can be stored in the Stack. We do not have the concept of a generic type in OCL. Furthermore, our OCL specification is not as precise as our algebraic specification, as we cannot form an expression for the push, pop, and top methods that indicates that the rest of the Stack remains unchanged. In order to achieve this, we would have to change our behavioral specifications as follows:

Stack::Stack()
post: self.empty()

Stack::push(Object o)
post: self@pre.size() + 1 = size()
post: self.top() = o
post: self.content@pre.prepend(o) = self.content

Stack::pop() : Object
post: self@pre.size() - 1 = size()
post: self@pre.top() = result
post: self.content.including(result) = self.content@pre

Stack::top() : Object
post: self@pre.size() = size()
post: self@pre.pop() = result
post: self.content@pre = self.content

```
           Stack
              |
              | -content
            * |
           Object
```

In order to solve the problem, we must rely on the fact that a Stack type manages a Collection (a Sequence) of objects. Using the OCL expressions for Sequence types, we can express the missing behavior. Nevertheless, the style of the specification is quite different from that applied in an algebraic specification.

For a complete algebraic specification one axiom for each constructor paired with every other non-constructor is needed. In our case, a maximum of eight axioms is needed. In the example given above, only six axioms are listed, which means that the type is under specified; that is, in certain situations the behavior is unspecified. In our examples, the missing axioms concern the pop and top functions in the event of empty Stacks. We will come back to this later. A type Queue could be defined similarly to the type Stack, with the difference that the axioms define the FIFO properties of a Queue type (see axioms (5) and (6)):

$$Queue = \forall T. \; \mu que. \quad \{push : T \to que; \; pop : \to que; \; top : \to T; \; empty : \to Boolean;$$
$$size: \to Natural \}; \; newQueue : \to Queue;\}$$

$\forall e : T . \quad \forall q : Queue .$

	newQueue().empty()	(1)
$\wedge$	$\neg$q.push(e).empty()	(2)
$\wedge$	newQueue ().size() = 0	(3)
$\wedge$	q.push(e).size() = 1 + q.size()	(4)
$\wedge$	q.push(e).top() = q.top()	(5)
$\wedge$	q.push(e).pop() = q.pop().push(e)	(6)

Again, the use of OCL might yield the following constraints for the Queue type:

```
Queue::Queue()
post: self.empty()

Queue::push(Object o)
post: self@pre.size() + 1 = size()
post: content.last() = o
post: self.content@pre.append(o) = self.content

Queue::pop() : Object
post: self@pre.size() - 1 = size()
post: self.content.@.first() = result
post: self.content.including(result) = self.contents@pre

Queue::top() : Object
post: self@pre.size() = size()
post: self.content.first() = result
post: self.content@pre = self.content
```

Basically, the Queue specification is similar to the Stack specification. The main differences are the axioms, or postconditions, that ensure the LIFO principle for the Stack type and the FIFO principle for the Queue type.

8.4   Axioms, Assertions, and Subtyping

In the next step, we will derive a type Dispenser, with Stack and Queue as subtypes. On the basis of this example, we will discuss the implications on subtyping rules in the algebraic case, and also in the assertion case. This will give us a better understanding of the rules given by preconditions and postconditions in the event of inheritance (see Sect. 2.2.6):

$$Dispenser = \forall T. \; \mu dsp. \quad \{push : T \to dsp; \; pop : \to dsp; \; top : \to T; \; empty : \to Boolean;$$
$$size: \to Natural \}; \; newDispenser : \to Dispenser;\}$$

$\forall e : T . \quad \forall d : Dispenser .$

	newDispenser().empty()	(1)

$$\land \quad \neg d.push(e).empty() \qquad\qquad (2)$$
$$\land \quad newDispenser ().size() = 0 \qquad\qquad (3)$$
$$\land \quad d.push(e).size() = 1 + d.size() \qquad\qquad (4)$$
$$\land \quad d.push(e).top() = e \text{ if } d.empty() \qquad\qquad (5)$$
$$\land \quad d.push(e).pop() = d \text{ if } d.empty() \qquad\qquad (6)$$

Stack and Queue satisfy this definition, as they have identical signatures and axioms (1)–(4). At the level of the Dispenser type, we cannot say anything about the ordering of the elements. Axioms (5) and (6) state that for the special case of one element in the Dispenser, something can be said about the top and pop functions. Clearly, this has to be refined in the Stack and Queue types. Refining an axiom in a subtype means that the refined axiom must logically entail the original axiom. Keeping this in mind, the Queue type would then be redefined as follows [Simons03a]:

$$Queue = \forall T.\ \mu que.\quad \{push : T \to que;\ pop : \to que;\ top : \to T;\ empty : \to Boolean;$$
$$size: \to Natural \};\ newQueue : \to Queue;\}$$
$$\forall e : T .\ \forall q : Queue .$$
$$newQueue().empty() \qquad\qquad (1)$$
$$\land \quad \neg q.push(e).empty() \qquad\qquad (2)$$
$$\land \quad newQueue ().size() = 0 \qquad\qquad (3)$$
$$\land \quad q.push(e).size() = 1 + q.size() \qquad\qquad (4)$$
$$\land \quad q.push(e).top()\quad = e \text{ if } q.empty() \qquad (5a)$$
$$\qquad\qquad\qquad\quad = q.top() \text{ otherwise} \qquad (5b)$$
$$\land \quad q.push(e).pop()\quad = q \text{ if } q.empty() \qquad (6a)$$
$$\qquad\qquad\qquad\quad = q.pop().push(e) \qquad (6b)$$

We therefore strengthen the axioms in order to cover more cases. Similar changes have to be applied to the Stack type. More formally, we can say that S <: T is true in the semantic case if the following condition holds:

$$S= \{\forall x \in T \mid p(x)\}$$

where $p(x)$ is the extra axiom added in the subtype. Using OCL, we would define the constraints for the Dispenser type as follows:

```
Dispenser::Dispenser()
post: self.empty()

Dispenser::push(Object o)
post: self@pre.size() + 1 = size()
post: self@pre.empty() implies self.content.first() = o

Dispenser::pop() : Object
post: !self.empty() implies self@pre.size() - 1 = size()
post self.empty() implies self@pre.content = self.content && self@pre.size() = self.size()

Dispenser::top() : Object
post: self@pre.size() = size()
post: self.content@pre = self.content
```

Our Stack type would add the following assertions:

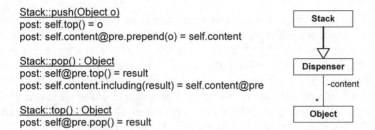

Stack::push(Object o)
post: self.top() = o
post: self.content@pre.prepend(o) = self.content

Stack::pop() : Object
post: self@pre.top() = result
post: self.content.including(result) = self.content@pre

Stack::top() : Object
post: self@pre.pop() = result

In order to ensure that our type Stack is a subtype of Dispenser, we have to obey the function subtyping rule. In the context of assertions, this means the following:

- Postconditions may be strengthened and therefore follow contravariant argument type rules.
- Preconditions may be weakened and therefore follow covariance result type rules.
- Invariants may be strengthened but never weakened, as every invariant must also be true after completion of a method; that is, invariants have to be treated like postconditions (as far as the subtyping rules are concerned).

We have already discussed the concept of strengthening an assertion in Sect. 8.1, but we need to mention it once again here. We consider a type BankAccount and a type SavingsAccount, and assume that SavingsAccount is a subtype of BankAccount at the behavioral level:

BankAccount::deposit(float amount)
pre: amount > 0f

SavingsAccount::deposit(float amount)
pre: amount > 100f

The preconditions specified in SavingsAccount::deposit violate this rule, since the added postcondition does not logically entail the postcondition, as the implication (amount > 0) implies (amount > 100) does not hold. In the general case, it would therefore be necessary to have provers that ensure that the rules for strengthening axioms, as defined above, are applied correctly. Most systems (see Sect. 2.4) perform run-time checks with logical OR-ing of preconditions and logical AND-ing of postconditions. These systems cannot detect faulty assertions as described above. JML [Leavens99b] is an example of a system in which a prover can be used to detect such errors.

8.5   Enhanced Assertion Techniques

In this book so far, we have formed a view on assertions that is driven by the capabilities of popular assertion techniques, such as Design by Contract (DBC), or by the mechanisms provided by OCL. Nevertheless, a number of approaches exist that follow the tradition of specifying the behavior of classes by means of invariants, preconditions, and postconditions, but that provide additional features. Examples of such extensions can be found in Leavens and Baker [Leavens99a], Evans [Evans94], Detlefs et al. [Detlefs98], Leavens et al. [Leavens03], Holland [Holland92], Luckham et al. [Luckham95], Jonkers [Jonkers91], and Han [Han00]. We will discuss some of these properties in the remainder of this section.

The first three techniques were developed by Jonkers [Jonkers91] and also incorporated into the Larch family [Leavens99a]. In order to illustrate the concepts, we will use the syntax proposed by Jonkers and give, as an introductory example, the specification of a Read procedure that returns the next Byte read from a File:

```
PROC   read : File → Byte
IN     f
OUT    b
PRE    offset(f) < length(f)
POST   b= contents(f, offset(f) -1);
       eof(f) <=> offset(f) >= length(f)
```

Framing: As we have already seen in previous examples, specifications of postconditions may become complex in order to ensure that variables remain unchanged. To achieve this in the OCL world, expressions such as length@pre = pre are necessary. A more elegant method is to associate modification rights with procedures [Jonkers91, Leavens99a]. Modification rights indicate which variables may be modified by a function. By definition, all variables not explicitly marked as modifiable remain unchanged. Frame axioms may also contain wild cards and expressions, which allow us to specify modifiable variables more concisely and precisely. If we wanted to express the fact that the file itself remains unchanged during the read operation, we would have to write:

```
PROC   read : File → Byte
IN     f
OUT    b
PRE    offset(f) < length(f)
POST   b= contents(f, offset(f)-1);
       offset(f) = offset'(f) + 1;
       eof(f) <=> offset(f) >= length(f);
       FORALL i : Nat (contents(f,i) == contents'(f,i);
       length(f) == length'(f)
```

The operator ' (e.g., length'(f)) is comparable to the @pre operator known from OCL. Application of the MOD (modifies) construct allows us to rewrite the specification, as it is guaranteed that the variables length(f) and contents(f, i) will remain unchanged:

```
PROC   read : File → Byte
IN     f
OUT    b
MOD    offset(f), eof(f)
PRE    offset(f) < length(f)
POST   b= contents(f, offset(f)-1);
       offset(f) = offset'(f) + 1;
       eof(f) <=> offset(f) >= length(f);
```

Dependent Variables: It often occurs that a variable y is dependent on a variable x (and this can be expressed precisely). This means that for each postcondition where the variable x is changed, we have to assure that the variable y is also changed accordingly. In order to facilitate the specification, variables may be defined explicitly in terms of other variables. The dependent variable varies automatically with the variable on which it depends [Jonkers91, Leavens99a]. All other variables are called independent variables. This approach usually leads to a reduction of constraints in postconditions:

```
PRED   eof : File
IN     f
DEF    offset(f) >= length(f)
```

```
PROC   read : File → Byte
IN     f
OUT    b
PRE    offset(f) < length(f)
POST   b= contents(f, offset(f)-1);
       offset(f) = offset'(f) + 1;
```

Let-Clauses: In order to enhance the readability of preconditions and postconditions, Jonkers [Jonkers91] suggests a mechanism to bind an arbitrary expression to a name. This name can then be used in expressions and is substituted automatically by the associated expression. The latest proposal suggests the incorporation of such a mechanism in OCL (see Sect. 3.2.4):

```
PRED   eof : File
IN     f
DEF    offset(f) >= length(f)
```

```
PROC   read : File → Byte
IN     f
OUT    b
PRE    LET i := eof(f)
       i < length(f)
POST   b= contents(f, i - 1);
       offset(f) = i + 1;
```

9 Summarizing Remarks

In the first sections of this book we presented well known software engineering techniques that can be used to enhance the quality of software.

The idea to enhance the specification of classes, interfaces and methods by adding invariants, preconditions and postconditions is rather old (it dates back to the pioneering days of computer science) and is now ready to be used in modern software development projects, as major ideas of assertions are nowadays part of the Unified Modeling Language (UML)—the major notation to capture analysis and design models. The Object Constraint Language (OCL) is part of the UML and allows to capture constraints at a general level for UML diagrams and is also well suited to capture invariants, preconditions and postconditions. There are some indications that the OCL and therefore assertions in general will be used more often in software development processes—especially in the analysis and design phase:

- *Maturity:* The OCL is a mature language know. From it's first specification in 1997 it was subject to numerous enhancements and changes. The actual version 2.0 overcomes a number of shortcomings of previous specifications and is an essential part of the UML specification.
- *Tool support:* A number of UML tools provide support for formulating contracts. Examples of tools with UML support are Argo/UML [Argo04], Poseidon [Poseidon04] and MagicDraw [MagicDraw04]
- *Enhanced Tool support:* At the date of writing this conclusion (January 2004) a number of tools are available that allow to formulate OCL constraints and that even provide support for syntax checking and for checking of the constraints in the context of the UML models.

  - *Octopus*: Octopus [Octopus04] is an acronym for "OCL Tool for Precise UML Specification". Octopus is able to check the syntax of OCL expressions and fully conforms to version 2.0 of the OCL standard. Additionally Octopus checks the types and the correct use of model elements like association roles and attributes. In further versions of Octopus a complete integration with UML models and validity checks based on this UML model are planned. The integration of UML models will be based on XMI import.
  - *OCLE*: OCLE [OCLE04] is an acronym for "Object Constraint Language Environment". OCLE is a programming environment that allows to edit, check and evaluate OCL constraints based on OCL 2.0 and on UML models

that can be imported in the development environment by means of XMI import.

In our opinion the above mentioned UML centered approach is a good starting point to define an analysis model, to capture constraints, i.e., to formulate invariants, preconditions and postconditions in the early phases of the software development process. Based on an analysis model the derivation of a design model also seems to be possible on the UML level. Some UML protagonists even think that it will be possible to refine a UML model in such a detailed way, that code can be generated automatically. Most of the currently available tools support the generation of source code from the UML model. The MDA (model driven architecture) approach [Frankel03] also heavily relies on code generation mechanisms.

Regardless of these approaches, we think that program code will always play an important role in a software development process, and that it will always be essential to work with the target language (at least) during implementation and testing. Therefore it is important that OCL constraints captured during the analysis and design phase can also be reused for the implementation and test activities of a software development project (regardless of a specific underlying software development process). In Section 2.4 we presented principal strategies for integrating contract support in programming languages that do not have explicit support for contract checking. This section also showed that currently available contract implementations for Java and C++ still lack maturity and especially full support for OCL. In Section 6.3 we also presented which contract-related activities have to be considered during analysis, design, implementation and test.

Successful application of contracts in a software development process only makes sense, when contracts formulated during analysis and design are transferred so that they are available in later phases of the software development process in order to be refined, corrected, extended and enhanced. It is important to know during unit or system testing that an implementation that violates a (correctly specified) postcondition, simply is not correct, i.e., does not satisfy the specification. Having this contract focus in a software project ameliorates the quality of the product, as described throughout this book. On the other hand it does not make much sense to capture contracts during analysis and design and not to reuse this knowledge during implementation and testing activities. In Sect. 3.4 we discussed the positive effects of contracts on quality and discussed which quality factors are positively influenced by this technique (Ambiguity, Understandability, Maintainability, Reusability, Internal Documentation, External Documentation and Correctness).

A second interesting approach we presented in this book is the application of scenarios (use cases) for capturing and specifying requirements for software systems. The major emphasis of a scenario based approach is to concentrate on entire workflows and not on isolated functionality. As scenarios are usually captured during analysis (even before defining an analysis model using an UML class diagram) they are also an important source for capturing constraints that are the basis for deriving contracts later in the process. As described in Chapters 4 and 5 preconditions and postconditions for assertions as well as business rules and (parts of) non-functional requirements are a valuable source for deriving initial contracts for the class model.

One major aim of this book is to show how the contract technique and the scenario techniques can be combined. In Chapter 7 we illustrated for which tasks in a software development process (analysis, design, implementation, testing) contract or scenario related activities should be planned. It is important for us that the activities we defined are independent of any specific software development process, like XP, Scrum or RUP; on the contrary contract and scenario related activities as discussed and suggested in this book can be applied in every software development process. Finally we pointed out (see Chapter 7), that tool support is necessary to facilitate the task of defining and checking the validity of contracts and scenarios. In Sect. 5.5 we discussed the positive effects of contracts on quality and discussed which quality factors are positively influenced by this technique (Completeness, Understandability, Traceability, Maintainability, and Correctness).

Encouraged by current developments on the tool market (Argo/UML, Poseidon, Octopus, OCLE) we plan to provide a set of tools that support our approach for dealing with contracts and scenarios throughout the software development process (see Chapter 7). The prototypes developed and presented in Sections 7.2 and 7.3 will serve as a starting point for this venture.

10 Appendix A:
A Monitoring and Control Case Study—
An Overview of the Deployment Process

In Chaps. 1–4 (and in parts of Chap. 5), we used a number of small and easy to understand examples to show some concepts of assertions in general, of the syntax and semantics of the Object Constraint Language (OCL), and of general aspects of the UML. This was sufficient, as we concentrated on aspects of an assertion or general scenario problem.

This more comprehensive example will serve as a basis to show how to use scenario techniques and contract-based approaches throughout the software development process; we have already made use of it in Chaps. 5, 6, and 7.

We will explain the general requirements, the overall distribution architecture, but we will concentrate on the deployment process for agents in our system (from the conceptual point of view), rather than on design or implementation issues. Readers who are more interested in our system, or in mobile agent systems in general, should refer to Pichler et al. [Pichler02], Plösch and Weinreich [Plösch01], or Weinreich and Plösch [Weinreich01, Weinreich03].

Overview: Our agent system relies on mobile agent technology as the basis for a flexible component system for remote diagnosis and monitoring of hardware and software resources in heterogeneous distributed environments. Currently, the main usage area is monitoring and control of process automation systems, although the system is not limited to this domain. A main characteristic of the system is its highly dynamic structure. Diagnosis and monitoring components may move within the network to their intended place of action, which is the hardware or software resource to be monitored or analyzed. This requires support for code mobility. Other features that are needed and supported by our system are dynamic service discovery, dynamic services, native-code management, multi-protocol remote access of various types of components, robustness, and security. A more detailed description of these features can be found in Plösch and Weinreich [Plösch01] and Weinreich and Plösch [Weinreich01, Weinreich03].

Besides remote configuration and management of installed components (agents) over Internet connections, the seamless deployment of agents over the Internet is a crucial aspect.

Distribution Architecture: The two main parts of the structure of a system supported by our environment are depicted in Fig. 60. The left-hand part of the figure shows the elements of the system for remote administration and configuration. The right-hand part depicts the target environment for supervision and retrieval components. Both are connected via the Internet. An administration server hosts component repositories. Each repository contains various kinds of components for supervision, information retrieval, and other tasks to be performed in a specific target environment (the repository contains Java code packages as well as native libraries).

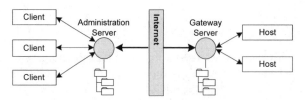

Fig. 60. The Insight agent system—the system structure

Administration tasks are carried out by thin clients. This means that tools need not be pre-installed at administration hosts. Instead, they are loaded dynamically from the administration server.

The target environment (or unit) for components is a heterogeneous distributed system, which consists of an arbitrary number of hosts, typically within a local area network. The hosts may have different operating systems, but each host has to provide an agent server, which acts as the run-time environment for agents. A distinguished host, the gateway server, is used as the entry point for accessing the unit from the Internet. The gateway server manages a repository of components (both Java code packages and native libraries) installed in this target system.

An Overview of the Deployment Process: Deployment is the process of installing and customizing applications in an operational environment [Kassem00]. A more general description of deployment activities can be found in Hall et al. [Hall99]. The units of deployment in our environments are mainly software components for supervision and data retrieval in the target system. These components are implemented as mobile agents, mainly in the Java programming language. In our example, we deal with one activity in the deployment process; that is, the initial installation of a component in a target system. The main activities are to create deployable packages, to make these packages available to deployment tools, and to deploy these packages to the target system.

In our environment, a deployable component may consist of either one or several packages (see Fig. 61).

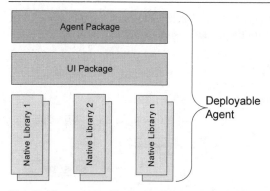

Fig. 61. The structure of a deployable component

The Agent Package consists of all of the Java classes that implement the agent's behavior and structure. The UI Package contains Java classes and sometimes HTML pages for configuring an agent during installation and operation. This package is not part of the Agent Package, since the user interface code and resources are not needed during normal operation. The user interface is only needed by the configuration and installation tools. However, it is deployed to the target environment to allow configuration via arbitrary administration servers and to provide support for multiple versions of the same type of agent (with possibly different UI packages).

Interaction with legacy systems and access to native operating system services are important requirements for components in our environment. The API provided by the Java 2 platform is often not sufficient to access such systems and services. Thus, each agent may have a number of associated platform-specific (or native code) libraries (see Fig. 61), which have to be deployed with the Agent Package and the optional UI Package. The symbols for platform-specific packages or libraries are stacked in Fig. 61, which shows that mobile agents might need to have different native libraries for the same purpose on different operating systems.

All of the packages are made available for deployment by putting them into a code repository at the administration server. The repository supports multiple categories for different kinds of agents. The repository contains not only packages but also deployment descriptors for each domain component, specifying the packages that have to be deployed in order to successfully deploy the whole component. More specifically, the deployment descriptor contains a reference to the Agent Package, to an optional user interface package, and to optional platform-specific libraries that are needed by the component in the target environment.

The Structure of a Deployable Agent: In the previous paragraphs, we have provided an overview of the deployment process. In order to better understand which artifacts are part of the deployment process, we will describe the structure of an agent (with an emphasis on the deployment process) in more detail. Figure 62 shows a UML class diagram for the artifacts that have to be deployed when installing an agent. The description given here describes the conceptual model, but does not necessarily correspond with the actual design or implementation.

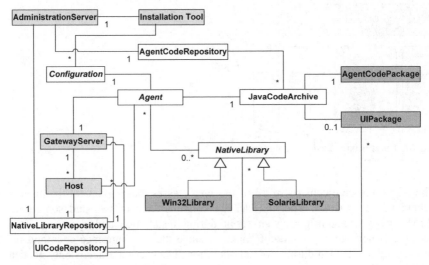

Fig. 62. The deployable artifacts of a mobile agent

The central component depicted in Fig. 62 is the Agent, which has a reference to a JavaCodeArchive and may also have a number of NativeLibraries. NativeLibraries are optional for an agent. As already mentioned in the introduction, an agent may need native libraries in order to access resources that have to be monitored or controlled by the mobile agent—for example, no native (platform-specific) implementation is necessary to monitor the size of a file, since this information can be obtained via a Java interface. For each agent, one Configuration exists that represents the agent's configurable properties. The default values for a Configuration are initialized out of configuration files. The Installation Tool is used to change a Configuration—that is, the properties of an agent—via a graphical user interface. During the installation process (see later), this configuration information is transferred from the client—that is, from the Installation Tool—to the Host, where the agent has to be installed.

Due to the heterogeneity of the typical environment in which mobile agents operate, it is not sufficient to provide the agent with one platform-specific implementation (e.g., a Win32 library) of the interface to the resources to be monitored and controlled, but it is necessary to provide it with all implementations that the agent may possibly need during its lifetime. In Fig. 62, a Win32Library as well as a SolarisLibrary are depicted—of course additional implementations (depending on the platform requirements) can be added.

A JavaCodeArchive must contain the code of the agent itself (AgentCodePackage), and it optionally contains the UIPackage; that is, a set of classes necessary for the graphical configuration of an agent. This package is optional because agents need not have a graphical user interface. The Win32Library, SolarisLibrary, AgentCodePackage, and UIPackage (all in dark gray) are the artifacts that have to be deployed from the administration server to the target environment.

The classes InstallationTool, AdministrationServer, GatewayServer, and Host (all in light gray) reflect the system structure as depicted in Fig. 60. Each of these classes is active—that is, has its own flow of control—and resides in a different location in the system.

The InstallationTool is responsible for deploying and configuring individual agents. The InstallationTool runs in a client node (see Fig. 60) and has access to an AdministrationServer. All deployment and configuration activities are carried out via this AdministrationServer.

The AdministrationServer resides on the administration server (see Fig. 60) and manages a native code repository (NativeLibraryRepository) as well as an agent code repository (AgentCodeRepository). Basically, the AdministrationServer manages all code (Java libraries as well as native libraries) of all agents that can be deployed and therefore installed via the administration server. During the deployment process, the AdministrationServer checks whether the Java libraries and native libraries needed for an agent are already available in the target system. Missing libraries are transferred to the target system and managed there in the code repositories of the GatewayServer.

The GatewayServer resides on the gateway server (see Fig. 60) and manages a native library repository (NativeLibraryRepository) as well as code for the graphical configuration of properties of individual agents (UIPackage). The repositories of the GatewayServer contain the libraries (native libraries and Java libraries) of all agents that have been deployed to this target. The Java libraries for the agent itself (AgentCodePackage) are not explicitly managed by the GatewayServer, but this management task is carried out by the underlying agent system—in our case, Aglets SDK [Lange98] or Grasshopper [IKV01]. Each GatewayServer manages a number of hosts; that is, computational nodes to which mobile agents can be deployed.

A Host represents a computational unit and contains an agent platform that is capable of hosting an arbitrary number of agents. Each Host manages its own NativeLibraryRepository. The main difference compared to the repository at the administration server and at the gateway server is that, at the host, only the native libraries that can be executed in the host's operating system are stored. The NativeLibraryRepository at the Host is used as a cache—it would of course also be possible to load the required native libraries directly on demand from the GatewayServer.

Figure 63 illustrates the deployment process for native libraries (which is the more complex case, compared to the deployment of the Java code archive). In order to facilitate the understanding of the deployment process, we have omitted the fact that the native libraries of an agent are stored at the administration server, but we have assumed that they are somehow accessible for the installation tool.

The agent to be deployed needs three native libraries to fulfill its task in the target system. These libraries are available for two platforms—we will assume that the Arabic numbers denote Win32 libraries, while the roman numbers denote Solaris libraries. The target system consists of one gateway server (GS) and two

Hosts (Host1 and Host2). The gateway server manages a repository that currently contains three libraries—library I (Solaris version), library 2 (Win32 version), and library III (Solaris version). Host1 is based on the Win32 platform and currently only manages library 2 (Win32 version) in its native library repository. Host2 is based on the Solaris platform and currently only manages library III (Solaris version).

Before deploying the agent to the target host (which we assume to be Host1), the installation tools checks whether all libraries potentially needed by the agent in the target system are available at the gateway server. Although the agent will be deployed to Host1 (which needs Win32 libraries only), the available Solaris libraries are also deployed to the native library repository of the gateway server. This action anticipates that the installed agent will possibly travel to other hosts (e.g., Host2) during its lifetime, where the Solaris libraries will be needed. As we have assumed in our system that any client is disconnected from the target system after performing arbitrary operations, we cannot guarantee that the agent will be able to fetch the required libraries on demand—the respective administration server might not be reachable. This is why we have to assure, during the installation process, that all libraries that are potentially required are stored in the native library repository of the gateway server—regardless of whether all of the versions stored will ever be used by this agent later on.

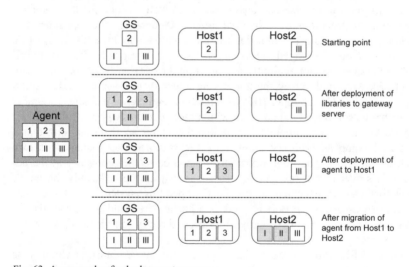

Fig. 63. An example of a deployment process

Installation of the agent at Host1 is realized by first requesting the gateway server to create the required agent and to configure it using the configuration information provided by the installation tool. Afterwards the agent migrates to Host1, where it initially checks whether all required libraries are available at this host. In our example (see Fig. 63), libraries 1 and 3 (for the Win32 platform) are not available at

Host1, and therefore are fetched from the gateway server and stored locally in the native library repository of Host1.

During the agent's lifetime it migrates (in our example) to Host2, which is based on the Solaris platform and lacks libraries I and II (Solaris versions). Upon arrival of the agent at Host2, the missing libraries are fetched from the gateway server. As all of the libraries were installed when the agent was initially deployed, we can guarantee the availability of the missing libraries. The agent performs its monitoring and control tasks after proper installation of the missing libraries.

A Description of the Deployment Process: After reading the previous sections, you should have gained a basic understanding of the architecture of our system and of the artifacts to be deployed when installing an agent. Additionally, you should have an overview of the deployment process. The overall deployment process can be captured as a use case diagram. This diagram (see Fig. 64) captures the core actors (Agent Administrator, Administration Server, Gateway Server, and Host) and use cases (Install Agent, Deploy Agent Libraries, Deploy Native Libraries, Set Up Agent Configuration, Migrate Agent, and Deploy Native Libraries to Local Host), as well as the relationships between the use cases.

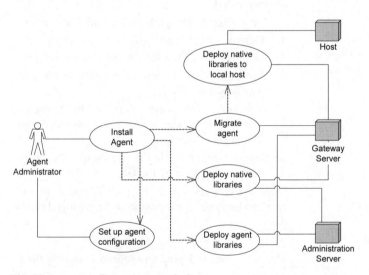

Fig. 64. A use case diagram—agent deployment

The installation of an agent (the Install Agent use case) is a central use case in our system (as far as installation is concerned), since it includes several other use cases (Migrate Agent, Deploy Native Libraries, Deploy Agent Libraries, and Set Up Agent Configuration). The Migrate Agent use case includes the Deploy Native Libraries to Local Host use case. The Agent Administrator is the only physical person involved in these use cases. The actors Host, Gateway Server, and Administration Server represent systems that are involved in the fulfillment of these use cases. The use case diagram (see Fig. 64) gives a rough overview. We will now describe the identified scenarios using a tabular representation (for a detailed description of the individual entries in this table, see Sect. 4.4). Some entries that are described in Sect. 4.4 (Iteration, Author, and Date) are intentionally omitted in this description, to tighten up the scenario descriptions. Furthermore, the emphasis here is on understanding the behavior of the deployment process—nevertheless, the omitted entries are important in a project setting.

Scenario Name:	Install Agent
Overview:	Installs an agent along with its initial configuration at a specified host, and insures that all agent and native libraries necessary for execution at the target system are transferred to the gateway server.
Basic Course of Events:	1. The agent administrator (AA) retrieves a list of deployable agents from the administration server (AS). 2. The AA selects one agent to configure and deploys it. 3. Set up agent configuration (included use case). 4. Deploy agent libraries (included use case). 5. Deploy native libraries (included use case). 6. Send the configuration information to the gateway server (GS). 7. The GS creates a new agent of the requested type and initializes it using the provided configuration information. 8. Migrate agent (included use case)—the operation is performed by the GS.
Alternative Paths:	Steps 4–8 only take place when a valid configuration data can be found for the agent to be deployed on the AS.
Exception Paths:	None.
Trigger:	The AA wants to deploy an agent to a target system.
Assumptions:	All libraries (native or Java) are available in the AS repositories, and the GS is properly initialized and running.
Preconditions:	Configuration information for this agent must be available at the AS.
Postconditions:	None.
Related Business Rules:	None.

Scenario Name:	Deploy Agent Libraries
Overview:	Deploys the agent code library and optionally the user interface library for the agent in the Java code repository (JCR) at the administration server (AS) to the JCR at the gateway server if it is not yet available there.
Basic Course of Events:	1. The AS retrieves the agent code library from the local JCR and transfers the library to the GS. 2. The GS stores the library in the local JCR at the GS and acknowledges proper receipt of the library to the AS. 3. If the agent needs a user interface library for configuration purposes, the AS retrieves this library from the local JCR and transfers it to the GS. 4. The GS stores the library in the local JCR at the GS and acknowledges proper receipt of the library to the AS.
Alternative Paths:	The transfer of libraries (see steps 1 and 3): if the library is not yet available in the JCR at the GS; that is, in an optimal case, no library has to be transferred at all.
Exception Paths:	Throughout the scenario, any errors are logged and the system tries to carry on with the installation process. If any missing library cannot be installed properly, the GS signals an error to AS.
Trigger:	The AS receives the request to deploy the Java code libraries of a specific agent to a specified target system.
Assumptions:	» The GS is up and running. » No version conflicts can occur, as the name of each library is unique.
Preconditions:	» The agent code library must be available in the JCR at the AS.
Postconditions:	» Each library whose proper deployment was acknowledged by the GS is guaranteed to be available in the JCR of the GS.
Related Business Rules:	» Naming convention for agent code libraries: Name (type) of the agent + "_ac_" + a version tag (max. two digits) + extension (".jar"). » Naming convention for user interface packages: Name (type) of the agent + "_ui_" + a version tag (max. two digits) + extension (".jar").

Scenario Name:	Deploy Native Libraries
Overview:	Deploys all required native libraries available for the agent in the native code repository at the administration server (AS) to the native library repository (NLR) at the gateway server (GS).
Basic Course of Events:	1. The AS retrieves descriptions of all available native libraries for the agent to be installed from its own NLR. 2. The AS sends a description of each native library to the GS. 3. The GS returns a list of libraries that are missing in the NLR of the gateway server. 4. For each missing library (see the previous step), the AS retrieves the native library from the NLR at the AS (on the basis of the description) and transfers it to the GS. 5. The GS stores each received native library in its local NLR and acknowledges proper receipt of the library to the AS.
Alternative Paths:	None.
Exception Paths:	Throughout the scenario, any errors are logged and the system tries to carry on with the installation process. If any missing library cannot be installed properly, the GS signals an error to AS.
Trigger:	The AS receives the request to deploy native libraries of a specific agent to a specified target system.
Assumptions:	» The GS is up and running. » No version conflicts can occur, as the version information for a native library is coded into the library name.
Preconditions:	» All native libraries required by an agent are at least available for one platform (e.g., the Win32 platform).
Postconditions:	» Each library whose proper deployment was acknowledged by the GS is guaranteed to be available in the NLR of the GS.
Related Business Rules:	» Naming conventions for native libraries: Each native library name consists of the name of the library plus a version number. The version number is obligatory and consists of one or two digits. The first digit represents the major release number, and the second digit the minor release number. The library extension terminates the name of the library. The library extension

	has two to four letters and is separated from the rest of the name by a dot (e.g., "dll" is a valid extension for a Win32 library).
	» Compatibility of native libraries: Each native library is backward compatible with any library with a lower minor version digit. Native libraries with different major version digits are incompatible.

Scenario Name:	Set Up Agent Configuration
Overview:	Initializes the default configuration of the agent from a default configuration file and allows the agent administrator (AA) to alter this configuration by means of a configuration editor (CE).
Basic Course of Events:	1. The AA requests a CE for a specific agent from the administration server (AS). 2. The AS locates the proper UI package from its own Java library repository (JLR) and returns the CE to the AA's host as an applet. 3. The CE requests initial (default) configuration data from the AS. 4. The AS locates the property file for this type of agent, initializes the configuration data, and returns it to the CE. 5. The AA may change the configuration using the CE. 6. If the AA saves the configuration data, it is transferred to the AS; otherwise, the configuration data is lost.
Alternative Paths:	In step 2: When no agent-specific CE can be found for an agent, a generic (not so convenient) configuration editor has to be loaded. In step 6: If the configuration data cannot be stored at the AS, the AA has to be notified with an operator message.
Exception Paths:	If no property file can be found for this type of agent, empty configuration data is returned to the agent.
Trigger:	The AA wants to provide an initial configuration for an agent to be installed.
Assumptions:	» The CE can itself provide valid configuration data; that is, the CE must not assume that the AS can provide valid configuration data for an agent.

Preconditions:	The browser used by the AA for configuration tasks can deal with Java 2 (Swing) applets.
Postconditions:	None.
Related Business Rules:	» Unique agent identifier: Each agent (to be installed) is identified uniquely at the AS by category name + agent name. » Unique property file naming: Name (Type) of agent + ".props".

Scenario Name:	Migrate Agent
Overview:	Migrates an agent to another host in the target system, insuring that the state of the agent is maintained and that possibly missing native libraries are deployed to the target host (TH).
Basic Course of Events:	1. The agent waits until the active measurement is finished. 2. The state of the agent is serialized and transferred together with the agent code to the TH. 3. Native libraries are deployed to local host (included use-case). 4. The agent starts execution of its monitoring or control tasks.
Alternative Paths:	Step 1 can be omitted if the agent is not yet working. This is especially true during the first installation of an agent at a TH, as the agent is created at the gateway server (GS) and then migrated to the TH (see use case Install Agent).
Exception Paths:	If any missing library cannot be deployed properly (see step 3), the TH discontinues the agent and protocols this error.
Trigger:	An agent is requested to migrate to a host at the target system or migrates itself due to some computational logic.
Assumptions:	None.
Preconditions:	» The state of an agent is serializable.
Postconditions:	» After migration and before the start of the execution of the monitoring task (see step 7), the state of the agent is equivalent to the state before migration.
Related Business Rules:	None.

Scenario Name:	Deploy Native Libraries to Local Host
Overview:	Deploys all native libraries required by an agent at a target host from the native library repository (NLR) at the gateway server (GS) to the NLR at the target host (TH).
Basic Course of Events:	1. The agent passes a description of all libraries needed by itself to the TH. 2. The TH determines which native libraries are not yet available in its repository. 3. For each missing library (see the previous step), the TH retrieves the native library from the NLR at the GS (on the basis of the description) and transfers it to the TH. The TH only retrieves those libraries that are executable at the TH. 4. The TH stores each received native library in its local NLR and acknowledges proper receipt of the library to the AS.
Alternative Paths:	None.
Exception Paths:	Throughout the scenario, any errors are logged and the system tries to carry on with the installation process. If any missing library cannot be installed properly, the TH signals an error to the agent.
Trigger:	The TS receives a request from an agent to install missing native libraries in its local NLR.
Assumptions:	» The GS is up and running.
Preconditions:	None.
Postconditions:	» Each library whose proper deployment was acknowledged by the TH is guaranteed to be available in the NLR of the TH.
Related Business Rules:	» Native library platform compatibility: A native library is assumed to be executable at a target host if the description of the expected platform (a string) matches with the platform description of the native library, and if the library extension (e.g., "dll") conforms to the expected extension of this platform.

11 Appendix B:
Grammar of SCL (Simple Contract Language)

This appendix describes the grammar for specifying contracts as used in this book. The grammar was developed using the Java Compiler generator. The description uses an EBNF Syntax, where "|" means selection, "?" denotes optional statements, "*" denotes zero to infinite repetitions, and "+" denotes one to infinite repetitions:

start	:=	(constraint)*
constraint	:=	("pre" | "post" | "inv") [name] ":" expression
expression	:=	relational (logicalOperator relational) *
relational	:=	sum (relationalOperator sum) ?
sum	:=	term (addOperator term) *
term	:=	unary (multiplyOperator unary) *
unary	:=	(unaryOperator postfix)	postfix
postfix	:=	primary (("." properties)	("->" collectionFeatureCall)) *
properties	:=	("oclIsTypeOf" "(" pathName ")"
			"oclIsKindOf" "(" pathName ")"
			featureCall)
primary	:=	literal
			featureCall
			"super"
			"self"
			"result"
			"(" expression ")"
featureCallParameters	:=	"(" [declarator] [actualParameterList] ")"
simpleTypeSpecifier	:=	pathName
featureCall	:=	pathName
		(timeExpression | featureCallParameters) ?
collectionFeatureCall	:=	("forAll" featureCallParameters)
			("exists" featureCallParameters)
			featureCall
declarator	:=	name ("," name) * ":" simpleTypeSpecifier "|"
pathName	:=	name ("::" name) *
actualParameterList	:=	expression ("," expression) *
literal	:=	number	string
logicalOperator	:=	"and"	"or"	"xor"	"implies"
relationalOperator	:=	"="	"<"	">"	"<>"	">="	"<="
addOperator	:=	"+"	"-"
multiplyOperator	:=	"*"	"/"

unaryOperator	:=	"+"	"-"	"not"
timeExpression	:=	"@pre"
number	:=	["0" - "9"] (["0" - "9"]) *
name	:=	(["a" - "z", "A" - "Z"])
		(["a" - "z", "A" - "Z"]	["0" - "9"]) *
string	:=	""

```
((~["''","\\","\n","\r"])
|    ("\\"
        ( ["n","t","b","r","f","\\","''","\'"]
          | ["0"-"7"] ( ["0"-"7"] )?
          | ["0"-"3"] ["0"-"7"] ["0"-"7"]
        )
    )
)*
""
```

Bibliography

[Abadi96]   Abadi M., Cardelli M.: *A Theory of Objects*, Monographs in Computer Science (Springer-Verlag, Berlin Heidelberg New York 1996)

[Abrahamsson02]   Abrahamsson P., Salo O., Ronkainen J., Warsta J.: Agile software development methods—review and analysis. In: *Espoo 2002, VTT Technical Research Centre of Finland*, VTT Technical Report 478 (2002)

[Achour99]   Achour C.B., Rolland C., Maiden N.A.M., Souveyet C.: Guiding use case authoring: results of an empirical study. In: *Proceedings of the Fourth IEEE International Symposium on Requirements Engineering (RE'99)*, June 7–11, 1999 (University of Limerick, Ireland 1999)

[Ada95]   *Ada 95 Reference Manual*, International Standard ANSI/ISO/IEC-8652 (1995)

[Adolph02]   Adolph S., Bramble P., Cockburn A.: *Patterns for Effective Use Cases* (Addison-Wesley, Reading, MA 2002)

[AgileManifesto02]   Agile Manifesto, available via http://agilemanifesto.org/ (last visited April 2003)

[Ambler02]   Ambler S.W.: *The Elements of UML Style* (Cambridge University Press, Cambridge 2002)

[America91]   America P.: Designing an object-oriented programming language with behavioral subtyping. In: *Proceedings of Foundations of Object-Oriented Languages*, Lecture Notes in Computer Science, vol 489 (Springer-Verlag, Berlin Heidelberg New York 1991)

[Anda02]   Anda B., Sjoberg D.I.K.: Towards an inspection technique for use case models. In: *Fourteenth IEEE Conference on Software Engineering and Knowledge Engineering (SEKE'02)*, July 15–19, 2002, Ischia, Italy, pp 127–134

[Andersson95]   Andersson M., Bergstrand J.: Formalizing use cases with message sequence charts. Master thesis, Department of Communication Systems, Lund Institute of Technology, Sweden (1995)

[Argo04]   Argo/UML: Website about the Argo/UML tool – see http://argouml.tigris.org/ (last visisted January 2004)

[Armour01]   Armour F., Miller G.: *Advanced Use Case Modelling* (Addison-Wesley, Reading, MA 2001)

[Bäumer96]   Bäumer D., Bischofberger W.R., Lichter H., Züllighoven H.: User interface prototyping—concepts, tools, and experience. In: *Proceedings of the 18th International Conference on Software Engineering (ICSE)*, Berlin, Germany, March 1996, (IEEE Computer Society Press, Los Alamitos CA 1996, pp 532–541)

[Bartezko01]   Bartezko D., Fischer C., Möller M., Wehrheim H.: Jass—Java with assertions. In: *Electronic Notes in Theoretical Computer Science, Proceedings of RV 01*, Paris, France, vol 55, issue 2 (July 2001)

[Baumgartner90]   Baumgartner R.: *Objektorientierte Vorgehensmodelle: Anforderunen und potentielle Möglichkeiten für das Software Engineering* (in German) (ADV, Vienna, March 1990)

[Beazley01l]   Beazley D.M.: *Python Essential Reference* , 2nd Edition (New Riders Publishing, Indianapolis, Indiana USA, 2001)

[Beck99a]   Beck K.: Embracing change with extreme programming. IEEE Computer **32**(10), (1999), pp 70-77

[Beck99b]   Beck K.: *Extreme Programming Explained: Embrace Change* (Addison-Wesley, Reading, MA 1999)

[Behringer97]   Behringer D.: Modelling global behaviour with scenarios in object-oriented analysis. Ph.D. thesis no. 1655(1997), Ecole Polytechnique Federale de Lausanne (1997)

[Beugnard99]   Beugnard A., Jézéquel J.M., Plouzeau N., Watkins D.: Making components contract aware. IEEE Computer (July 1999), pp 38-45

[Bischofberger92]   Bischofberger W., Pomberger G.: *Prototyping-Oriented Software Development* (Springer-Verlag, Berlin Heidelberg New York 1992)

[Bittner02]   Bittner K., Spence I.: *Use Case Modeling* (Addison-Wesley, Reading, MA 2002)

[Boar83]   Boar B.H.: *Application Prototyping—A Requirements Definition Strategy for the 80s* (John Wiley, New York / Chichester / Brisbane / Toronto / Singapore 1984)

[Boehm76]   Boehm B.: Software Engineering. IEEE Transactions on Computers **25**(12), (1976), pp 1226-1241

[Boehm78]   Boehm B., Brown J.R., Kaspar H., Lipow M., MacLeod G.J., Merrit M.J.: "Characteristics of Software Quality", 1978

[Boehm88]   Boehm B.: The spiral model of software development and enhancement. IEEE Computer **21**(5), (1988), pp 61-72

[Boldsoft02]   Boldsoft et al.: Response to the UML 2.0 OCL RfP (ad/2000-09-03), Revised Submission Version 1.3 (March 2002)

[Booch99]   Booch G., Rumbaugh J., Jacobson I.: *The Unified Modeling Language User Guide*, Object Technology Series (Addison-Wesley, Reading, MA 1999)

[Broh82]   Broh R.A.: *Managing Quality for Higher Profits* (McGraw-Hill, 1982)

[Brooks87]   Brooks F.P.: No silver bullet: essence and accidents of software engineering. IEEE Computer **20**(4), (1987)

[Cardelli85]   Cardelli L., Wegner P.: On understanding types, data abstraction and polymorphism. ACM Computing Surveys **17**(4), (1985), pp 471-522

[Cardelli86]   Cardelli L.: *Amber–Combinators and Functional Programming Languages*, Lecture Notes in Computer Science (LNCS) vol 242 (Springer-Verlag, Berlin Heidelberg New York 1986)

[Carey89]   Carey J.M., Currey J.D.: The prototyping conundrum. Datamation, June 1, 1989, 29–33

[Carillo96]   Carillo-Castellon M., Garcia-Molina J., Pimentel E., Repiso I.: Design by Contract in Smalltalk. Journal of Object-Oriented Programming, **9**(7), (1996), pp 23–28

[Chandy88]   Chandy K.M., Misra J.: *Parallel Program Design* (Addison-Wesley, Reading, MA 1988)

[Cicalese99]   Cicalese C.T.T., Rotenstreich S.: Behavioral specificaton of distributed software component interfaces. IEEE Computer, **32**(7), (1999), pp 46-53

[Cockburn00]   Cockburn A.: *Writing Effective Use Cases* (Addison-Wesley, Reading, MA 2000)

[Cockburn02]   Cockburn A.: *Agile Software Development* (Addison-Wesley, Reading, MA 2002)

[Coleman94]   Coleman D., Arnold P., Bodoff S., Dollin C., Gilchrist H., Hayes F., Jeremaes P.: *Object-Oriented Development—The Fusion Method*, Object-Oriented Series (Prentice Hall, Hemel Hempstead 1994)

[Connell89]   Connell J.L, Shafer L.B.: *Structured Rapid Prototyping*, Computing Series, (Prentice Hall/Yourdon Press, Upper Saddle River, NJ 1989)

[Constantine99]   Constantine L.L., Lockwood L.A.D.: *Software for Use: A Practical Guide to the Models and Methods of Usage-Centered Design* (Addison-Wesley Professional, Reading, MA 1999)

[Cook94]   Cook S., Daniels J.: *Designing Object Systems—Object Oriented Modeling with Syntropy* (Prentice Hall, Upper Saddle River NJ 1994)

[Councill01]   Councill B., Heineman G.T.: Definition of a software component and its elements. In: *Component-Based Software Engineering—Putting the Pieces Together*, ed by G.T. Heineman and W.T. Councill (Addison-Wesley, Reading, MA 2001)

[Cox00]   Cox K., Phalp K.: Use case authoring: replicating the CREWS guidelines experiment. Empirical Software Engineering Journal **5**(3), 245–268 (2000)

[Cox01]   Cox K., Phalp K., Shepperd M.: Comparing use case writing guidelines. In: *Proceedings of REFSQ'2001—Seventh International Workshop on Requirements Engineering: Foundation for Software Quality*, Interlaken, Switzerland, 2001

[Dahl68]   Dahl O.J., Myrhaug B., Nygaard K.: *Simula 67—Common Base Language* (Norway Computing Center 1968)

[Davis93]   Davis A.: *Software Requirements—Objects, Functions and State* (Prentice Hall, Upper Saddle River, NJ 1993)

[Detlefs98]   Detlefs D.L., Leino K.R.M., Nelson G., Saxe J.B.: Extended static checking. SRC research report no. 159, Compaq Systems Research Center (1998)

[Dijkstra75]   Dijkstra E.W.: Guarded commands, nondeterminacy, and formal derivation of programs. Communications of the ACM, **18**(8), (1975), pp 453-457

[DIN91]   DIN ISO 9126: *Informationstechnik—Beurteilen von Softwareprodukten, Qualitätsmerkmale und Leitfaden zu deren Verwendung* (in German) (September 1991)

[D'Souza99]   D'Souza D.F., Wills A.C: *Objects, Components, and Frameworks with UML: The Catalysis Approach* (Addison Wesley, Reading, MA 1999)

[Duncan98]   Duncan A., Hölzle U.: Adding contracts to Java with handshake. Technical report TRCS98-32, University of California at Santa Barbara (December 1998)

[Ellis96]   Ellis M.A., Stroustrup B : *The Annotated C++ Reference Manual* (Addison-Wesley, Reading, MA 1996)

[Enseling01]   Enseling O.: iContract: Design by Contract in Java. JavaWorld, November 2001, see http://www.javaworld.com/javaworld/jw-02-2001/jw-0216-cooltools_p.html (last visited March 2002)

[Evans94]   Evans D.: Using specifications to check source code, TR MIT-LCS-TR-628, Massachusetts Institute of Technology (1994)

[Findler01]   Findler R.B., Felleisen M.: Contract soundness for object-oriented languages. In: *Proceedings of OOPSLA 2001,* Tampa Bay, FL, October 2001 (ACM Press, NY 2001), pp 1-15

[Finney96a]   Finney K.: Mathematical notation in formal specification: too difficult for the masses. IEEE Transactions on Software Engineering **22**(2), (1996), pp 158-159

[Finney96b]   Finney K., Fedorec A.: An empirical study of specification readability. In: *Educational Issues of Formal Methods*, ed. by M. Hinchey and N. Dean (Academic Press, 1996)

[Firesmith95]   Firesmith D.: Use cases: the pros and cons., SIGS Publications, ROAD (July–August 1995), pp 2-6

[Firesmith99]   Firesmith D.G.: Use case modeling guidelines. In: *Proceedings of TOOLS U.S.A. 1999* (IEEE Computer Society Press, Los Alamitos, CA 1999)

[Floyd67]   Floyd R.W.: Assigning meaning to programs. In: *Mathematical Aspects of Computer Science*, ed. by J.T. Schwartz, Proceedings of Symposium in Applied Mathematics, vol 19 (American Mathematical Society, Providence, RI 1967)

[Floyd84]   Floyd C.: A Systematic Look at Prototyping, In: *Approaches to Prototyping* ed. by R. Budde et al, (Springer-Verlag, Berlin Heidelberg New York 1984)

[Floyd89]   Floyd C., Reisin F.-M., Schmidt. G.: STEPS to software development with users. In: *Proceedings of ESEC 89 Conference*, Lecture Notes in Computer Science No. 387 (Springer-Verlag, Berlin Heidelberg New York 1989)

[Fowler99]   Fowler M., Scott K., Booch G.: *UML Distilled*, 2nd edn (Addison-Wesley, Reading, MA 1999)

[Fulton02]   Fulton H.: *The Ruby Way* (Sams Publishing, Indianapolis, Indiana 2001)

[Frankel03]   Frankl D.S.: *Model Driven Architecture*, (John Wiley New York / Chichester / Brisbane / Toronto / Singapore 2003)

[Gamma95]   Gamma E., Helm R., Johnson R., Vlissides J.: *Design Patterns: Elements of Reusable Object-Oriented Software* (Addison-Wesley, Reading, MA 1995)

[Garvin84]   Garvin D.A.: What does product quality really mean? Sloan Management Review, (1984), pp 25-43

[Gilmore74]   Gilmore H.L.: Product conformance cost. Quality Progress (June 1974)

[Glass01]   Glass R.L.: Agile versus traditional: make love, not war! Cutter IT Journal **14**(12), (2001), pp 12-18

[Gomaa83]   Gomaa H.: The impact of rapid prototyping on specifying user requirements. ACM Software Engineering Notes **8**(2), (April 1983)

[Gomaa86]   Gomaa H.: Prototypes—keep them or throw them away. In: *Prototyping—State of the Art Report*, ed. by M.E. Lipp (Pergamon Infotech Ltd, Maidenhead 1986), pp 41–54

[Gomes96]   Gomes B., Stoutamire D., Vayssman B., Klawitter H.: *A Language Manual for Sather 1.1* (August 1996)

[Gordon91]   Gordon S., Bieman J.: Rapid prototyping and software quality: lessons from industry. Technical report CS-91-113, Department of Computer Science, Colorado State University (1991)

[Gosling96]   Gosling J., Joy B., Steel G.: *The Java Language Specification* (Addison-Wesley, Reading, MA 1996)

[Grady87]   Grady R.B., Caswell D.L.: *Software Metrics: Establishing a Company-Wide Program* (Prentice Hall, Upper Saddle River, NJ 1987)

[Graham94a]   Graham I.: *Object-Oriented Methods*, 2nd edn (Addison-Wesley, Reading, MA 1994)

[Graham94b]   Graham I.: Beyond the use case: combining task analysis and scripts in object-oriented requirements capture and business process re-engineering. In: *Proceedings of TOOLS Europe' 94*, Versailles, 1994, (Prentice Hall, Hemel Hempstead, 1994), pp 203-216

[Graham96]   Graham I.: Task scripts, use cases and scenarios in object oriented analysis. Object Oriented Systems **3**(3), (September 1996), pp 132-142

[Hall99]   Hall R.S., Heimbigner D., Wolf A.L.: A cooperative approach to support software deployment using the software dock. In: *Proceedings of the International Conference on Software Engineering 1999 (ISCE '99)*, Los Angeles, California, 1999, (IEEE Computer Society Press, Los Alamitos, CA 1999), pp 174-183

[Han00]   Han J.: Temporal logic based specification of component interaction protocols. In: *Proceedings of WOI'00 2nd ECOOP Workshop on Object Interoperability, In Association with 14th European Conference on Object-Oriented Programming*, Sophia Antipolis—France, June 12, 2000   (available   via http://webepcc.unex.es/juan/woi00/papers/position_papers.html)

[Harel87]   Harel D.: Statecharts: a visual formalism for complex systems. Science of Computer Programming **8**, 231–274 (1987)

[Harel98]   Harel D., Politi M.: *Modeling Reactive Systems with Statecharts: The SATEMATE Approach* (McGraw-Hill, 1998)

[Harel01]   Harel D.: From play-in scenarios to code: an achievable dream. IEEE Computer **34**(1), 53–60 (January 2001)

[Harel02a]   Harel D., Kugler H.: Synthesizing state-based object systems from LSC specifications. International Journal of Foundations of Computer Science (IJFCS) **13**(1), 5–51 (February 2002)

[Harel02b]   Harel D., Kugler H., Marelly R., Pnueli A.: Smart play-out of behavioral requirements. In: *Proceedings of 4th International Conference on Formal Methods in Computer-Aided Design (FMCAD'02)*, Portland, Oregon, 2002, (Lecture Notes in Computer Science, Volume 2517, 2002), pp 378-398

[Harel03]   Harel D., Marelly R.: Specifying and executing behavioral requirements: the play in/play-out approach. Journal of Software and System Modeling (SoSyM), **2003**(2), pp 82-107

[Heineman01]   Heineman G.T., Councill W.T.: *Component-Based Software Engineering—Putting the Pieces Together* (Addison-Wesley, Reading, MA 2001)

[Heitmeyer97]   Heitmeyer, C.L., Kirby J., Labaw B.. Tools for formal specification, verification, and validation of requirements. In: *Proceedings of 12th Annual Conference on Computer Assurance (COMPASS '97)*, June 16–19, 1997, Gaithersburg, MD, 1997

[Heitmeyer98a]   Heitmeyer C., Kirby J., Labaw B., Bharadwaj R.: SCR*: a toolset for specifiying and analyzing software requirements. In: *Proceedings of International Conference on Computer Aided Verification (CAV'98)*, Lecture Notes in Computer Science, vol 1427 (Springer-Verlag, Berlin Heidelberg New York 1998), pp 5–51

[Heitmeyer98b]   Heitmeyer C.: Using the SCR* toolset to specify software requirements. In: *Proceedings, Second IEEE Workshop on Industrial Strength Formal Specification Techniques (WIFT'98)*, Boca Raton, 1998, (IEEE Computer Society Press, Los Alamitos, CA 1998), pp 12-16

[Heitmeyer00]   Heitmeyer C., Bharadwaj R.: Applying the SCR requirements method to the light control case study. Journal of Universal Computer Science (JUCS), **6** (7), (August 2000), pp 650-678

[Heitmeyer02]   Heitmeyer C.: Software cost reduction. In: *Encyclopedia of Software Engineering*, ed. by J.J. Marciniak (Wiley-Interscience, New York / Chichester / Brisbane / Toronto / Singapore 2002)

[Hitz02]   Hitz M., Kappel G.: *UML at Work—Von der Analyse zur Realisierung* (in German) (dpunkt Verlag, Heidelberg, 2002)

[Hoare69]   Hoare C.A.R.: An axiomatic basis for computer programming. Communications of the ACM, **12**(10), (1969), pp 576-580

[Hoare72]   Hoare C.A.R.: Proof of correctness of data representations. Acta Informatica **1**, 271–281 (1972)

[Hoffman01]   Hoffman D.M., Weiss D.M. (eds): *Software Fundamentals—Collected Papers by David L. Parnas* (Addison-Wesley, Reading, MA 2001)

[Holbrock90]   Holbrock H.: A scenario-based methodology to conducting requirements elicitation. ACM SIGSOFT **15**(1), (1990), pp 95-104

[Holland92]   Holland I.M.: Specifying resuable components using contracts. In: *Proceedings of ECOOP 92 Conference*, Lecture Notes in Computer Science, vol 615 (Springer-Verlag, Berlin Heidelberg New York 1992)

[Hollinde84]   Hollinde I., Wagner K.H.: "Experience of Prototyping in Command and Control Systems", In: *Approaches to Prototyping* ed. by R. Budde et al, (Springer-Verlag, Berlin Heidelberg New York 1984)

[Hsia94]   Hsia P. et al.: Formal approach to scenario analysis. IEEE Software, **11**(2), (March 1994), pp 33-41

[Hyatt96]   Hyatt L., Rosenberg L.: A software quality model and metrics for identifying project risks and assessing software quality. In: *Proceedings of 8th Annual Software Technology Conference*, Utah, April 1996

[IBM03]   IBM: VisualAge Smalltalk, available via http://www-3.ibm.com/software/awdtools/smalltalk/ (last visited April 2003)

[IEEE89]   IEEE Std 610.3-1989, *IEEE Standard Glossary of Modeling and Simulation Terminology* (IEEE, New York 1989)

[IEEE98]   IEEE Std 830-1998, *IEEE Recommended Practice for Software Requirements Specifications* (IEEE, New York 1998)

[IKV01]   IKV++: *Grasshopper Programmer's Guide*, Release 2.2 (March 2002), available via http://www.grasshopper.de (last visited January 2003)

[ILogix03]   Rhapsody product information, available via http://www.ilogix.com/products/rhapsody/ (last visited April 2003)

[ITU99]   ITU-T: *Series Z: Languages and General Software Aspects for Telecommunication Systems, Formal description techniques (FDT)— Specification and Description Language (SDL)* (ITU-T 1999)

[Jacobson92]   Jacobson I., Christerson M., Jonsson P., Overgaard G.: *Object-Oriented Software Engineering—A Use Case Driven Approach* (Addison-Wesley, Reading, MA 1992)

[Jacobson99]   Jacobson I., Booch G., Rumbaugh J.: *The Unified Software Development Process* (Addison-Wesley, Reading, MA 1999)

[JavaCC03]   JavaCC: Java Compiler Compiler Product information, available via
                  http://www.webgain.com/products/java_cc/ (last visited April 2003)

[Jézéquel00]   Jézéquel J.-M., Train M., Mingins C.: *Design Patterns and Contracts*
                  (Addison-Wesley, Reading, MA 2000)

[Jonathan99]   Jonathan L., Nien-Lin X.: Analyzing user requirements by use cases: a
                  goal-driven approach. IEEE Software, **16**(4), (July/August 1999), pp
                  92-101

[Jonkers91]   Jonkers H.B.M.: Upgrading the pre- and postcondition technique. In:
                  *Proceedings of VDM '91—Formal Software Development, 4th
                  International Symposium of VDM Europe*, Noordwijkerhout, The
                  Netherlands, October 21–25, 1991, vol 1: *Conference Contributions*,
                  Lecture Notes in Computer Science 551 (Springer-Verlag, Berlin
                  Heidelberg New York 1991)

[Jörgensen84]   Jörgensen A.H.: "On the Psychology of Prototyping", In: *Approaches to
                  Prototyping* ed. by R. Budde et al, (Springer-Verlag, Berlin Heidelberg
                  New York 1984)

[Karaorman96]   Karaorman M., Hölzle U, Bruno J.: jContractor: a reflective Java library
                  to support design by contract. In: *Proceedings of Meta-Level
                  Architectures and Reflection*, Lecture Notes in Computer Science
                  (LNCS), vol 1616 (Springer-Verlag, Berlin Heidelberg New York
                  1996)

[Kassem00]   N. Kassem (ed.): *Designing Enterprise Applications with the Java 9 2
                  Platform*, Enterprise edn (Addison-Wesley, Reading, MA 2000)

[KC03]   Kennedy Carter: Product information on iUML toolset, available via
                  http://www.kc.com (last visited April 2003)

[Keller89]   Keller R.M.: *Prototypingorientierte Systemspezifikation—Konzepte,
                  Methoden, Werkzeuge und Konsequenzen* (in German) (Verlag Dr.
                  Kovac, Hamburg 1989)

[Kizub98]   Kizub   M.:   Kiev   language   specification,   see
                  http://www.forestro.com/kiev, 1998

[Kölling97]   Kölling M., Rosenberg J.: *Blue: Language Specification Version 0.94*
                  (1997)

[Kotonya97]   Kontonya G., Sommervill I.: *Requirements Engineering* (John Wiley,
                  New York / Chichester / Brisbane / Toronto / Singapore 1997)

[Kramer98]   Kramer R.: iContract—the Java Design by Contract tool. In:
                  Proceedings of TOOLS U.S.A. '98 Conference (IEEE Computer Society
                  Press, Los Alamitos, CA 1998)

[Kruchten00]   Kruchten P.: *The Rational Unified Process—An Introduction*, 2nd edn
                  (Addison-Wesley, Reading, MA 2000)

[Kulak00]   Kulak D., Guiney E.: *Use Cases—Requirements in Context* (Addison-
                  Wesley, Reading, MA 2000)

[Lange98]   Lange D., Oshima M.: *Programming and Deploying Java Mobile
                  Agents with Aglets* (Addison-Wesley, Reading, MA 1998)

[Leavens99a]   Leavens G.T., Baker A.L.: Enhancing the pre- and postcondition
                  technique for more expressive specifications. In: *FM'99: World
                  Congress on Formal Methods in Development of Computer Systems,
                  Toulouse, France, September 1999*, ed. by J. Wing and J. Woodcock,
                  Lecture Notes in Computer Science, vol 1709 (Springer-Verlag, Berlin
                  Heidelberg New York 1999), pp 1087–1106

[Leavens99b]   Leavens G.T., Baker A.L., Ruby C.: JML: a notation for detailed design. In: *Behavioral Specifications of Businesses and Systems*, ed. by H. Kilov, B. Rumpe, and I. Simmonds (Kluwer, Dordrecht 1999), chap. 12, pp 175–188

[Leavens03]   Leavens G.T., Baker A.L., Ruby C.: Preliminary design of JML: a behavioral interface specification language for Java, Department of Computer Science, Iowa State University (2003)

[Leffler82]   Leffler K.B.: Ambiguous changes in product quality. American Economic Review, **72**(5), (December 1982), pp 956-967

[Lettner01]   Lettner C.: "Integration von OCL und Design by Contract—Konzepte und Werkzeugunterstützung" (in German). Master thesis, Johannes Kepler University, Linz, Austria (2001)

[Lettrari01]   Lettrari M., Klose J.: Scenario-based monitoring and testing of real-time UML models. In: *4th International Conference on the Unified Modeling Language*, Toronto, October 2001, (Lecture Notes in Computer Science, Volume 2185, Springer-Verlag Heidelberg), pp 317-328

[Lilly99]   Lilly S.: Use case pitfalls: top 10 problems from real projects using use cases. In: *Proceedings of TOOLS U.S.A. 1999 Conference* (IEEE Computer Society Press, Los Alamitos, CA 1999)

[Liskov74]   Liskov B., Zilles S.: Programming with abstract data types. Computation Structures Group, Memo No. 99, MIT Project MAC, Cambridge, MA (1974) [see also SIGPLAN Notices **9**(4), 50–59 (April 1974)]

[Liskov76]   Liskov B.: Introduction to CLU. In: *New Directions in Algorithmic Languages 1975*, ed. by S.A. Schuman (INRIA, 1976)

[Liskov88]   Liskov B.: Data abstraction and hierarchy. ACM Sigplan Notices **23**(5), (1988), pp 17-34

[Liskov94]   Liskov B.H., Wing J.M.: A behavioral notion of subtyping. ACM Transactions on Programming Languages and Systems, **16**(6), (November 1994), pp 1811-1841

[Liskov99]   Liskov B.H., Wing J.M.: Behavioral subtyping using invariants and constraints. Technical report CMU CS-99-156, School of Computer Science, Carnegie Mellon University (July 1999)

[Luckham95]   Luckham D.C. Kenney J.J., Augustin L.M., Vera J., Bryan D., Mann W.: Specification and analysis of system architecture using Rapide. IEEE Transactions on Software Engineering **21**(4), 336–355 (April 1995)

[Lutz01]   Lutz M.: *Programming Python*, 2nd edn (O'Reilly & Associates, Sebastopol 2001)

[MagicDraw04]   MagicDraw: UML toolset by Interactive Objects; information about this project can be found at http://www.magicdraw.com

[Mannion98]   Mannion M., Phillips R.: Prevention is better than a cure. Java Report (September 1998)

[McCall77]   McCall J.A., Richards P.K., Walters G.F.: *Factors in Software Quality* (Rome Air Development Center 1977)

[McCauley01]   McCauley R.: Agile development methods poised to upset status quo. ACM SIGCSE Bulletin **33**(4), (2001), pp 14-15

[Meyer92]   Meyer B.: *Eiffel—The Language*, Object-Oriented Series (Prentice Hall, Hemel Hempstead 1992)

[Meyer96]   Meyer B.: Building bug-free O-O software: an introduction to Design by Contract. Object Currents, SIGS Publication **1**(3), (March 1996)

[Meyer97a]   Meyer B.: *Object-Oriented Software Construction*, 2nd edn (Prentice Hall, Upper Saddle River, NJ 1997)

[Meyer97b]   Meyer B., Jézéquel J.M. Design by Contract—the lessons of Ariane. IEEE Computer **30**(2), (January 1997), pp 129-130

[Microsoft03]   Microsoft: Visual   Basic,   available   via http://msdn.microsoft.com/vbasic/ (last visited April 2003)

[Mitchell85]   Mitchell J.C., Plotkin G.D.: Abstract Types Have Existential Type, In: Proceedings of Twelfth Annual ACM Symposium on Principles of Programming Languages, New Orleans, Louisiana, January 1985. POPL 1985, pp 37-51

[Mitchell97]   Mitchell R., Howse J., Hamie A.: Contract-oriented specifications. In: *Proceedings of Tools U.S.A. 24* (IEEE Computer Society Press, Los Alamitos, CA 1997)

[Mitchell99]   Mitchell R., McKim J.: Extending a method of devising software contracts. In: *Proceedings of Tools U.S.A. 32* (IEEE Computer Society Press, Los Alamitos, CA 1999)

[Mitchell01]   Mitchell R., McKim J.: *Design by Contract—by Example* (Addison-Wesley, Reading, MA 2001)

[MMS00]   Man Machine Systems: "Design by contract for Java using jmsassert", see http://www.mmsindia.com/DBCForJava.html, 2000

[Naur63]   Naur P.: Revised report on the algorithmic language Algol 60. Communications of the ACM **6**(1), (1963), pp 1-17

[Octopus04]   Octopus: "OCL Tool for Precese UML Specification", Klasse Objecten for Quality in Object and Component Technology; information about this project can be found at http://www.klasse.nl/ocl/octopus-intro.html

[OCL97]   *Object Constraint Language Specification, Version 1.1*, OMG document ad970808 (1997)

[OCLE04]   OCLE: "Object Contraint Language Environment", toolset for specifiying constraints on UML models; Computer Science Research Laboratory at the Bolyai University of Cluj-Napoca, Romania; see http://lci.cs.ubbcluj.ro/ocle/index.htm (last visited January 2004)

[Odell93]   Odell J.: Using business rules with diagrams. Journal of Object-Oriented Programming **6**(4), (July–August 1993)

[OMG97]   Object Management Group/IBM: *Object Constraint Language Specification, Version 1.1* (September 1997); the specification can be found at http://www.omg.org/uml

[OMG98]   Object Management Group: Action Semantics for the UML RFP. OMG document 98-11-01 (1998); available from http://www.omg.org

[OMG99]   Object Management Group: *The Common Object Request Broker: Architecture and Specification, Version 2.3.1* (October 1999)

[OMG00]   Object Management Group: UML 2.0 OCL RfP. Document id: ad/2000-09-03 (September 2000)

[OMG01]   Object Management Group: *OMG Unified Modeling Language Specification Version 1.4* (September 2001); available from http://cgi.omg.org/docs/formal/01-09-67.pdf

[Palmer02]   Palmer S.R., Felsin J.M.: *A Practical Guide to Feature-Driven Development* (Prentice Hall, Upper Saddle River 2003)

[Palph02]   Palph K., Cox K.: Supporting communicability with use case guidelines: an empirical study. In: *Proceedings of EASE 2002—6th International Conference on Empirical Assessment and Evaluation in Software Engineering*, Keele University, Staffordshire, UK, 2002

[Parasoft02a]   Parasoft: Using Design by Contract to automate software and component testing; available from http://www.parasoft.com/jsp/products/tech_papers.jsp?product=Jcontra ct (last visited July 2002)

[Parasoft02b]   Parasoft: Automatic Java software and component testing: using Jtest to automate unit testing and coding standard enforcement; available from http://www.parasoft.com/jsp/products/article.jsp?articleId=839&produc t=Jtest (last visited July 2002)

[Parnas72a]   Parnas D.L.: A technique for software module specification with examples. Communications of the ACM **15**(5), 330–336 (May 1972)

[Parnas72b]   Parnas D.L.: On the criteria to be used in decomposing systems into modules. Communications of the ACM **15**(12), 1053–1058 (December 1972)

[Parnas85]   Parnas D.I., Clements P.A.: A rational design-process. How and why to fake it. In: *Proceedings of TAPSOFT 85* (Springer-Verlag, Berlin Heidelberg New York 1985)

[Payne98]   Payne J.E., Schatz M.A., Schmid M.N.: Implementing assertions for Java. Dr. Dobb's Journal **23**(1), (January 1998), pp 40-46

[Pichler02]   Pichler J., Plösch R., Weinreich R.: MASIF und FIPA: Standards für Agenten Übersicht und Anwendung. Informatik Spektrum **25**(2), (April 2002), pp 91-100

[Pirsig74]   Pirsig R.M.: *Zen and the Art of Motorcycle Maintenance* (William Morrow, New York 1974)

[Plösch93]   Plösch R., Rumerstorfer H., Weinreich R.: TOPOS: a prototyping-oriented open CASE system. In: *Proceedings of the International Conference on Requirements Engineering 1993*, Bonn, Germany, April 25–27, 1993 (B.G. Teubner, Stuttgart 1993)

[Plösch94]   Plösch R.: Prototyping verteilter objektorientierter Prozeßsteuerungssysteme. Doctoral dissertation (in German) (Trauner Verlag, Linz 1994)

[Plösch95]   Plösch R.: A process model and an associated tool for prototyping of distributed process control systems. In: *Proceedings of the 3rd International Symposium on Applied Corporate Computing (ITESM)*, Monterrey, Mexico, October 25–27, 1995, pp 95–104

[Plösch97]   Plösch R.: Design by Contract for Python. In: *Proceedings of Joint APSEC'97, ICSC'97 Conference*, December 2–5, 1997, Hong Kong, (IEEE Computer Society Press, Los Alamitos, CA 1997), pp 213–219

[Plösch98]   Plösch R.: Tools support for Design by Contract. In: *Proceedings of the TOOLS-26 Conference*, August 1998, Santa Barbara, U.S.A. (IEEE Computer Society Press, Los Alamitos, CA 1998) pp 282–294

[Plösch99]   Plösch R., Pichler J.: Contracts: from analysis to C++ implementation. In: Proceedings of the TOOLS-30 conference, Santa Barbara, U.S.A., August 1–5, 1999 (IEEE Computer Society Press, Los Alamitos, CA 1999)

[Plösch00]   Plösch R., Pomberger G.: Tool support for contract enhanced scenarios. In: *Proceedings of the TOOLS Eastern Europe Conference*, Sofia,

October 2000 (Kluwer International Series in Engineering and Computer Science, Secs 732, March 2003), pp 220-231

[Plösch01]   Plösch R., Weinreich R.: Ein agentenbasierter Ansatz zur Ferndiagnose und -überwachung von Automatisierungssystemen (in German). Wirtschaftsinformatik, special issue on Agent Technology **2/2001**, (2001), pp 167-173

[Pomberger96]   Pomberger G., Blaschek G.: *Object-Orientation and Prototyping in Software Engineering*, Object-Oriented Series (Prentice Hall, Hemel Hempstead 1996)

[Porat95]   Porat S., Fertig S.: Class assertions in C++. Journal of Object- Oriented Programming **8**(2), (May 1995), pp 30-37

[Poseidon04]   Poseidon: UML toolset by Gentleware Inc.; information about this project can be found at http://www.gentleware.com/products/

[Powell01]   Powell B., Weeks R.: *C# and the .net Framework* (Sams Publishing, Indianapolis, Indiana 2001)

[Pree91]   Pree W.: Object-oriented versus conventional construction of user interface prototyping tools. Doctoral dissertation, Johannes Kepler University, Linz (1991)

[Rational03a]   Rational Real-Time product information, available via http://www.rational.com/products/rosert/ (last visited April 2003)

[Rational03b]   Rational Unified Process product information, available via http://www.rational.com/products/rup (last visited April 2003)

[Regnell95]   Regnell B., Kimbler K., Wesslén A.: Improving the use case driven approach to requirements engineering. In: *Proceedings of the 2nd International Symposium on Requirements Engineering*, York (IEEE Computer Society Press, Los Alamitos, CA 1995)

[Regnell99]   Regnell B.: Requirements engineering with use cases—a basis for software development. Ph.D. thesis, Lund University, Department of Communication Systems, Lund Institute of Technology, KF Sigma (1999)

[Riehle01]   Riehle D., Fraleigh S., Bucka-Lassen D., Omorogbe N.: The architecture of a UML virtual machine. In: *Proceedings of the 2001 Conference on Object-Oriented Programming Systems, Languages, and Applications (OOPSLA'01)* (ACM Press, NY 2001)

[Roadhouse98]   Roadhouse Z.: see http://starship.skyport.net/crew/zack/ptui for more details

[Robertson99]   Robertson S., Robertson J.: *Mastering the Requirements Process* (Addison-Wesley, Reading, MA 1999)

[Rogers01a]   Rogers P.: J2SE 1.4 premieres Java's assertion capability—Part 1. JavaWorld, November 2001; available from http://www.javaworld.com/javaworld/jw-11-2001/jw-1109-assert_p.html (last visited March 2002)

[Rogers01b]   Rogers P.: J2SE 1.4 premieres Java's assertion capability—Part 2. JavaWorld, November 2001; available from http://www.javaworld.com/javaworld/jw-12-2001/jw-1214-assert_p.html (last visited March 2002)

[Rolland98]   Rolland C., Ben Achour C.: Guiding the construction of textual use case specifications. Data and Knowledge Engineering Journal **25**(1–2), 125–160 (1998)

[Rosenberg01]   Rosenberg D., Kendall S.: *Applying Use Case Driven Object Modeling with UML: An Annotated e-Commerce Example* (Addison-Wesley, Reading, MA 2001)

[Rosenblum95]   Rosenblum D.S.: A practical approach to programming with assertions. IEEE Transactions on Software Engineering **21**(1), (January 1995), pp 19-31

[Rubin92]   Rubin K.S., A. Goldberg A.: Object behavior analysis. Communications of the ACM, **35**(9), (September 1992), pp 48-62

[Sametinger97]   Sametinger J.: *Software Engineering with Resusable Components* (Springer-Verlag, Berlin Heidelberg New York 1997)

[Schneider97]   Schneider G., Winters J.P.: *Applying Use Cases—A Practical Guide* (Addison-Wesley, Reading, MA 1997)

[Schwaber02]   Schwaber K., Beedle M.: *Agile Software Development with Scrum* (Prentice Hall, Upper Saddle River, NJ 2002)

[Simons99]   Simons A.J.H.: Use cases considered harmful. In: *Proceedings of TOOLS Europe 1999* (IEEE Computer Society Press, Los Alamitos, CA 1999)

[Simons02a]   Simons A.J.H.: The theory of classification, part 1: perspectives on type compatibility. Journal of Object Technology **1**(1), May–June 2002, https://www.jot.fm/issue_2002_05/column5

[Simons02b]   Simons A.J.H.: The theory of classification, part 2: the scratch-built typechecker. Journal of Object Technology **1**(2), July–August 2002, https://www.jot.fm/issue_2002_07/column4

[Simons02c]   Simons A.J.H.: The theory of classification, part 3: object encodings and recursion. Journal of Object Technology **1**(4), September–October 2002, https://www.jot.fm/issue_2002_09/column4

[Simons02d]   Simons A.J.H.: The theory of classification, part 4: object types and subtyping. Journal of Object Technology **1**(5), November–December 2002, https://www.jot.fm/issue_2002_11/column4

[Simons03a]   Simons A.J.H.: The theory of classification, part 5: axioms, assertions and subtyping. Journal of Object Technology **2**(1), January–February 2003, https://www.jot.fm/issue_2003_01/column2

[Simons03b]   Simons A.J.H.: The theory of classification, part 6: the subtyping inquisition. Journal of Object Technology **2**(2), March–April 2003, https://www.jot.fm/issue_2003_03/column2

[Skyva03]   Skyva, Inc.: Product information for *n*-tier supply chain management, available via http://www.skyva.com/art.asp?ID=305 (last visited April 2003)

[Sobol89]   Sobol M. G., Kagan A.: Which systems analysts are more likely to prototype? Journal of Information System Management , 36–43 (Summer 1989)

[Sommerville97]   Sommerville I., Sawyer P.: *Requirements Engineering—A Good Practice Guide* (John Wiley, New York / Chichester / Brisbane / Toronto / Singapore 1997)

[Spivey92]   Spivey J.M.: *The Z Notation: A Reference Manual*, International Series in Computer Science (Prentice Hall, New York 1992)

[Stapleton97]   Stapleton J.: *Dynamic Systems Development Method—The Method in Practice* (Addison-Wesley, Reading, MA 1997)

[Sun02a]   Sun   Microsystems: Java   Assertion   Facility—
                http://java.sun.com/j2se/1.4/docs/guide/lang/assert.html (last visited
                March 2002)

[Sun02b]   Sun Microsystems: Sun ONE Message Queue Developer Guide—
                http://docs.sun.com/source/816-5923-10/index.html (last visited
                October 2002)

[Szyperski02]   Szperski   C.:   Component   Software—Beyond   Object-Oriented
                Programming, 2nd edn (Addison-Wesley, Reading, MA 2002)

[Templ94]   Templ J.: Metaprogramming in Oberon. ETH dissertation no. 10655,
                Zurich (1994)

[UML97]   UML 1.1 Specification, OMG documents ad970802-ad0809 (1997)

[VModel03]   V-Modell 1997—resources available via http://www.v-modell.iabg.de/
                (mostly in German; last visited April 2003)

[Waldén95]   Waldén K., Nerson J.-M.: Seamless Object-Oriented Software
                Architectures—Analysis and Design of Reliable Systems, Object-
                Oriented Series (Prentice Hall, Hemel Hempstead 1995)

[Warmer99]   Warmer J., Kleppe A.: The Object Constraint Language—Precise
                Modeling with UML (Addison-Wesley, Reading, MA 1999)

[Weinberg90]   Weinberg R., Guimaraes T., Heath R.: Object-oriented systems
                development. Journal of Information System Management 7(4), (1990)

[Weinreich01]   Weinreich R., Plösch R.: An agent-based component platform for
                dynamically adaptable distributed environments. Informatica Journal,
                Special Issue on Component Based Software Development 25(4),
                (November 2001), pp 483-491

[Weinreich03]   Weinreich R., Plösch R.: Issues in remote configuration of adaptable
                component-based and agent-based systems. Journal of Object
                Technology, accepted for publication in the Journal of Object
                Technology, November 2003

[Wilkinson95]   Wilkinson N.M.: Using CRC Cards: An Informal Approach to Object-
                Oriented Development (Prentice Hall, Upper Saddle River, NJ 1990)

[Wirfs-Brock02a] Wirfs-Brock R.J., Schwartz J.A.: The art of writing use cases. Tutorial
                presented at OOPSLA 2002: The ACM SIGPLAN Conference on
                Object-Oriented Programming, Systems, Languages and Applications

[Wirfs-Brock02b] Wirfs-Brock R.J., McKean A.: Object Design: Roles, Responsibilities,
                and Collaborations (Addison-Wesley Professional, Reading, MA 2002)

[Wirth71]   Wirth N.: The programming language Pascal. Acta Informatica 1,
                (1971), pp 35-63

[Wirth83]   Wirth N.: Programming in Modula-2, 2nd edn (Prentice Hall, Upper
                Saddle River, NJ 1983)

[XPScrum03]   XP@Scrum, information about integration of XP and Scrum, available
                via http://www.controlchaos.com/ (last visited April 2003)

[Z.120 96]   Z.120 ITU-TS Recommendation Z.120: Message Sequence Chart
                (MSC), ITU-TS, Geneva (1996)

Index

Printing: Strauss GmbH, Mörlenbach
Binding: Schäffer, Grünstadt